Verner C. Bickley, after Cardiff University and service in the Royal Navy in India and Ceylon (Sri Lanka), joined the British Colonial Service and served as an Education Officer in Singapore before joining the British Council in Burma, Indonesia and Japan. He later returned to the Overseas Service as Director of the Hong Kong Government's Institute of Language in Education. He is an Honorary Research Fellow at the University of Hong Kong and Chairman of the English-Speaking Union, Hong Kong.

FOOTFALLS ECHO IN THE MEMORY

A Life with the Colonial Education Service and the British Council in Asia

Verner C. Bickley

The Radcliffe Press
LONDON • NEW YORK

To Gillian for her patience and love

Supported by

香港藝術發展局
Hong Kong Arts Development Council

Hong Kong Arts Development Council fully
supports freedom of artistic expression. The
views and opinions expressed in this project
do not represent the stand of the Council.

Published in 2010 by Radcliffe Press
An Imprint of I.B.Tauris & Co. Ltd
6 Salem Road, London W2 4BU
175 Fifth Avenue, New York NY 10010
www.ibtauris.com

Distributed in the United States and Canada Exclusively by Palgrave Macmillan,
175 Fifth Avenue, New York NY 10010

ISBN   978 1 84885 085 9

A full CIP record for this book is available from the British Library
A full CIP record for this book is available from the Library of Congress
Library of Congress catalog card: available

FSC
Mixed Sources
Product group from well-managed
forests and other controlled sources
Cert no. SGS-COC-2953
www.fsc.org
© 1996 Forest Stewardship Council

Typeset in Minion by
Dexter Haven Associates Ltd, London
Printed and bound in Great Britain by
CPI Antony Rowe, Chippenham

CONTENTS

LIST OF ILLUSTRATIONS

ACKNOWLEDGEMENTS

I wish to thank the following publishers for their permission to include the following material in this book: The Penguin Group (UK) for an extract (as an epigraph) from *The Go-Between* by L.P. Hartley; The Scout Association for the lyrics to, 'We're Riding Along on the Crest of a Wave', by Ralph Reader; David Higham Associates for the poem, 'For Johnny', by John Pudney; Warner/Chappell Music for the lyrics of the song, 'If a Grey-Haired Lady', by Ted Waite; seven lines from the song, 'The Teddy Bears' Picnic', words and music by John W. Bratton and Jimmy Kennedy © 1907, reproduced by permission of B. Feldman & Co Ltd, London, W8 5SW; Faber and Faber Limited for permission to quote three lines as an epigraph and one line as part of the title from T.S. Eliot's poem, 'Burnt Norton'. An excerpt from 'Burnt Norton' in *Four Quartets* by T.S. Eliot, copyright 1936 by Harcourt, Inc. and renewed 1964 by T.S. Eliot, reprinted by permission of Houghton Mifflin Harcourt Publishing Company.

I wish to thank Dr Lester Crook of The Radcliffe Press and Liz Friend-Smith for their encouragement, thoughtful help and suggestions.

I am most grateful to the Headmaster of The Grammar School, Altrincham, for permission to include photographs of the School and of the Scout Hut.

Last, but certainly not least, I would like to express my gratitude to my wife, Gillian for her forebearance, her practical help and her moral support over a long period. It would not have been possible without her.

FOREWORD

Rt Hon the Lord Hunt of Wirral, MBE

Although he was born in the Northwest of England and educated there and in Wales and London, Verner Bickley has lived in Asian and Pacific countries for over fifty years. In these engrossing memoirs he retraces his steps from childhood and early schooling through his involvement as a nineteen-year-old naval officer in pre-independent Sri Lanka and India.

After demobilisation, early in the bitter winter of 1947, we find him completing his university education and then serving in the Colonial Education Service in Singapore and, later, as a British Council officer in post-independent Burma, Indonesia and Japan. We learn what Verner's life was like as he took each adventurous step as teacher, broadcaster and cultural diplomat in a life often enlivened by music and song, dance and entertainment.

In this informed personal narrative, he shows empathy, sympathy and concern for those he has met, irrespective of their place in the world, using his own passage through time and terrain to illustrate and bring alive what the world has been like for many persuasions and personalities of people.

In spite of parenting that bordered on benign neglect, or perhaps because of it, the author had an innocent childhood and youth. In the Navy from the age of eighteen, the round edges began to be hardened just a little and he learned quite young that he had to find his own way in the open spaces of the world.

Refusing to retire, Verner now lives in Hong Kong where he writes and publishes on a variety of topics (most recently on the 2008 Olympic Games) and devotes himself to the English-Speaking Union (Hong Kong) as Chairman of its Executive Committee, providing invaluable service to an organisation that is very close to my heart. I commend this book to you.

FOREWORD

Valerie Mitchell, OBE
Director-General, the English-Speaking
Union of the Commonwealth

In 1945 at the age of nineteen, Verner Bickley left Britain for the first time. As a young naval officer he found himself in Sri Lanka (then Ceylon) and India. Both countries were then still part of the British Empire, although there were anti-colonial rumblings in both countries. In India, he was present at a mutiny staged by the then Royal Indian Navy and in Ceylon (Sri Lanka) he sat patient – but wondering – in a train that was deserted without warning by its Sinhalese, anti-colonial crew. These early experiences introduced him to cultures and communities in countries other than his own. They were to be reinforced over a long career spent in the Colonial Education Service and the British Council and strengthened in recent years by his membership of the English-Speaking Union, most recently as Chairman in Hong Kong which has grown and developed under his strong leadership.

These memoirs give a well-rounded impression of a person who wanted to see the world, and has indeed seen a great deal. Clearly he has never lost his own identity nor abandoned his own background and point of view but he did 'fall in fascination' with the Asia of his own experiences. Major political figures as well as political events are mentioned, described or discussed. Surprising viewpoints emerge about some well-publicised persons, today greatly praised and admired. At another end of his spectrum, the reader is reminded of both the popular and the high cultures of the various countries where the writer has lived. He has met jazz musicians, impresarios, publishers, authors, linguists and educationists. He tells us of strikes and insurgents, demagogues and prime ministers, princes and emperors, businessmen, watermen and geisha girls.

The narrative is lively and well told with humour, variety of style and a large frame of reference.

Footfalls Echo in the Memory is a lively and unsentimental remembrance of times past, untinged by nostalgia or regret. The world should still be as it was and the writer refuses to accept that some of its innocent gaiety and golden virtues are really beyond recall.

PREFACE

Footfalls echo in the memory
Down the passage which we did not take
Towards the door we never opened

– T.S. Eliot. 'Burnt Norton'

There were alternatives but I did not take advantage of them. There were doors that remained shut. But I have no regrets. When I began to write this book, I believed that my self-imposed task was simply to tell the story of some part of my life (to age forty-five or thereabouts). It would be an honest, although incomplete, record that might be of interest to family and friends and (I hoped) many strangers. Yet there was also the tiny thought that it could be intriguing to follow in the autobiographical shoes of successful politicians such as Lee Kuan Yew (*The Singapore Story*),[1] or gifted Asian novelists such as R.K. Narayan (*My Days*)[2] or Michael Ondaatje (*Running in the Family*).[3] After all I, too, had spent a large portion of my life in Asia and the Pacific, although in much humbler roles.

In his fourth-century autobiography, *The Confessions*, Saint Augustine referred guiltily to such misdemeanours as stealing pears from an orchard and harbouring carnal thoughts. Saint Augustine was strongly motivated to atone in some way for his self-perceived weaknesses and to confess what he clearly believed to be heinous sins.

In this 'Life' I have not felt the need to confess anything in particular since my sins have been so mundane that recounting them would bore the reader as well as myself. I began to write this as a means of passing time when employed for two years by a Middle Eastern airline and given very light duties in a managerial position. It was not until I began to shape the first chapter that I thought seriously about my purpose and began to gather together letters, diaries and thoughts to enable me to bring elements of the past into the present. The result is something of a mixture. It is not an *apology* (a defence or vindication) or a *confession*. It is a *memoir* in that it records moments in certain periods of my life and does not purport to be a full history. It is an *autobiography* in that it touches on social, cultural and historical issues as well as on personal matters. It is certainly not that 'most chilling of literary forms: the celebrity life story',[4] yet 'celebrities' appear, if only fleetingly, in places as far apart as Singapore, Burma, Indonesia and Japan.

When questioned about their motives, some mountaineers claim that they climb mountains 'because they are there'. I am able to write this first volume of a 'Life' because it has passed by.

Verner Bickley
Hong Kong

INTRODUCTION

I am conscious that some readers may not wish to follow all the Steps of this 'Life', in particular, those that refer to personal and family matters. I have therefore tried to make each Step self-sufficient.

The mutiny of the Royal Indian Navy against the British in February 1946 is long forgotten. I was there. You can join me if you wish. Please see the Third Step.

In 1947, I enjoyed a holiday in Paris with three friends. One of them, Peter Marychurch, was later knighted and became Head of the intelligence agency 'GCHQ' in Cheltenham, England. Sir Peter Marychurch is referred to in laudatory terms in Peter Wright's notorious exposé, *Spy Catcher*. The Fourth Step.

C. Northcote Parkinson ('Parky' to his friends) worked in Singapore and wrote 'Parkinson's Law' there, originally for the entertainment of his university colleagues. I chatted to him once on a friendly roof and he told me that he *never* read the newspapers. The Fifth Step.

I failed to meet Anthony Burgess, when he was attached to a teachers' training college in Malaya. But I performed in some of the children's programmes that he wrote for Radio Malaya under his real name, John Burgess Wilson. The Fifth Step.

Remember the anti-British riots in Singapore in 1956? You probably don't. You may read my account in the Fifth Step.

Graham Greene's play, *The Living Room*, had its first overseas premiere in Singapore in 1954. Greene missed that performance but, fresh from a clandestine visit to Vietnam, he came backstage to congratulate the actors who performed in my production of Sir John Vanbrugh's play, *The Relapse, or Virtue in Danger*. His kind remarks were encouraging. The Fifth Step.

If you are attracted to Burma as it was at the beginning of the 1960s, please consult Chapter Eighteen. Was the late General Aung San really the hero that he has been made out to be? The Sixth Step.

If Indonesia intrigues (and it does!), you may wish to turn to Chapter Twenty-One. In 1963 it was disturbing to watch the (new) British Embassy building burn after a mob set it on fire. The Seventh Step.

At lunch in May 1975 with Princess Chumbhot, the Crown Princess of Thailand, I listened as her other guests suggested that North Vietnam's victory over American and American-backed forces might persuade the Communist forces to turn their attention to Thailand. Would there be a 'domino' effect? The Eighth Step.

Are you interested in the late Princess Margaret's behaviour when she visited Japan? She and her then husband, Anthony Armstrong Jones (Lord Snowdon), worked hard but were reluctant to leave a good party. The Eighth Step.

Tokyo was chosen for the twenty-two-year-old Prince Charles's first official visit. We worked him remorselessly. How many visits has he made since and to where? The Eighth Step.

But you can make your own list, too!

V.B.

THE FIRST STEP

THE FIRST SHIP

– 1 –

Beginnings

'The past is a foreign country: they do things differently there.' – L.P. Hartley[1]

The Aymara people of the Andes are said to gesture behind them when referring to the future. Mentioning the past, they gesture in front.[2]

On 16 March 1926 at Auburn in Massachusetts, Dr Robert H. Goddard's liquid fuel rocket travelled 184 feet in 2.5 seconds and in Britain on 3 May a general strike was declared in support of one million locked-out miners.

My mother Lillian was not on strike on 28 April; for I was born on that day, although not at the speed of Goddard's experimental rocket. Contrary to the modern practice in many countries, the birth took place at 'Denehurst', a small house in Rosslyn Drive in the village of Moreton. Moreton is in the Wirral Peninsula, Northwest England.

The village has a long history. Known originally as Moreton-cum-Lingham, the name Moreton stems from an Anglo-Saxon word, 'More', meaning 'Lake' and 'Ton', meaning Town. Many Roman coins have been found in the area and artifacts have been discovered from even earlier times. By 1900, the village had grown in reputation and was considered a place for a healthy holiday on the Wirral coast. One of my earliest memories is the salty perfume of the sea and the tickling of the coarse grass as I ran barefoot among the sand-hills.

Today, the village has changed both in appearance and governance. The pretty village that I remember has given way to ugly urban sprawl, traffic jams and industry, for example, a Cadbury's chocolate factory. The population of approximately three thousand in 1926, the year of my birth, has grown to over 25,000 and it is still growing. In 1928 the city of

Wallasey absorbed Moreton, with powers obtained by means of an Act of Parliament. More recently (1974), Moreton became part of the county of Merseyside:

> In the past quarter-century, few places in Wirral have altered more than Moreton. Since the district was incorporated in the Borough of Wallasey in the year 1928, the green meadows which surrounded and isolated the village have been carved up into dozens of roads serving a vast housing scheme of several hundred houses… However, it serves no purpose now to theorise about Moreton, the houses are built… Moreton is so obviously brand-new that we will not stop here longer than we must; not even to look at the ultra-modern chocolate factory or the gargantuan 'pub' of such imposing presence that it is known far and wide as 'Moreton Cathedral.'[3]

I was named Verner Courtenay, after my father, Stephen Verner, and his younger brother, Herbert Courtenay. Although an only child all my life, I was my parents' second child. My sister was born 'above the shop' in my father's pharmacy on 23 May 1924 and christened Jacqueline Irene. Jacqueline died of enteritis six months after her birth. She is buried in the churchyard of Moreton Parish Church. Her burial fees amounted to three pounds and eleven shillings, 'for a new grave and etc'.

Although I had been christened Verner Courtenay, I was soon given an 'in house' name that, at least in family circles, stuck until my early twenties. After demanding an explanation for my nickname, 'Bunty', I was told by my parents that, as a baby, and as a very small boy, I used to play with pieces of string, looping, winding, sucking and stretching them. This curious habit reminded my parents of the title of a popular play, *Bunty Pulls the Strings*, first produced at the Haymarket Theatre in London in 1911. Written by Graham Moffat, the play was a great success. Since the opening night in 1911 at London's Haymarket Theatre, it has been performed by many different professional and amateur groups.[4]

I am quite certain that I acquired my nickname as a result of one or other of my parents enjoying a performance of Moffat's play. I am also certain of the origin of my first given name, Verner, my father's second given name. Why did Grandfather Stephen and Grandmother Mary choose that name for their first son? I found the answer when I came across the Victorian novel, *Verner's Pride*, written by Mrs Henry Wood:

> 'Steevy,' said old Mr Verner to his younger son, after giving a passing lament to Sir Lionel. 'I shall leave Verner's Pride [the house] to you.'
>
> 'Ought it not to go to the lad at Eton, father?' was the reply of Stephen Verner…[5]

Stephen Verner! These were my father's names. It is clear where the name 'Verner' came from. My father was born in 1888. Mrs Wood's book was published in 1863.

My father told me once that, as a youth, he had the ambition to become an engineer, but instead he was apprenticed to a chemist in Birkenhead, Cheshire, where his parents had moved from Chester. This apprenticeship began when he was seventeen in 1905.

After completing his apprenticeship, and after a spell as a veterinarian's assistant, Stephen Verner joined John Thompson and Company, a firm of wholesale druggists in Liverpool. By the outbreak of the First World War, when he was twenty-six, he had become a skilled pill-maker. This was done by hand, perhaps making use of a pill machine such as that invented in Germany in the eighteenth century. This machine

> was a piece of hardwood inset into the centre of which was a grooved brass cutting plate, a two-handled flat wooden cutter about three inches wide, the underside of which had a similar grooved cutting plate, a tray to hold the cut portions, and one of two boxwood 'rounders,' disks, with two recessed surfaces.[6]

Such machines are now to be found occasionally on antique stalls, since far more advanced methods of making pills have now been introduced.

The writer's parents, Stephen Verner and Lillian Bickley.

Because of this skill, my father was listed in a 'reserved occupation' and was not recruited into the Armed Forces.

By 1918, the last year of the War, Father had saved enough for marriage and had accumulated sixty pounds in capital with which to open a pharmacy at The Cross, 14 Main Road, Moreton.

'The Pharmacy' did well at first and, in the small country village of Moreton, my father was much in demand as chemist and druggist and also as a surrogate doctor and veterinarian. The shop was small but well stocked with both pharmaceutical and veterinary supplies. There were living quarters above the shop, later used as stockrooms; an additional stockroom at the back of the shop and a yard with a sink in which bottles were washed and where steel vats were kept in which small, sick animals could be 'put down'.

The working hours were very long (9am to 9pm) but the work must have been satisfying and I am sure that both my parents felt that they were providing a public service.

I have a few more scattered memories of my early childhood, such as learning to tie knots by using my pyjama cord (and some of that string?); bathing in an enamel bath by the kitchen fire and learning to read without much instruction. My only venture into the murky world of politics was when I was allowed to drive through Moreton village in a toy motor-car with a sign hanging around my neck, 'Vote for Grace' (a candidate for membership of the local Council).

I have sharper memories of experiences at the age of four-and-a-half, particularly at a kindergarten owned by two maiden ladies, the Misses Lunt. The two Lunts were the only members of the kindergarten staff. No other help was required, since the number of pupils was never more than ten. One of the two ladies would meet us at the front door every morning. She would make sure that we undid our gaiters, took off our outdoor coats and shoes and replaced the shoes with slippers. She also watched us put on our aprons, proof – it was thought – against ink, paint and dirty plasticine. I cannot recall that we were encouraged to be very active. We all sat round a long table, recited the English alphabet and tried to understand the whole words in the simple readers that were provided. Perhaps bored by these proceedings, one of my four-year-old companions caused a sensation at the end of one lesson. He tore out some of the pages of a large Bible that lay on the table. We were all made to feel very guilty, although I am sure that the villain meant no harm. Tearing paper can be quite satisfying.

I do not remember feeling particularly guilty at home on the day that I was sent to bed without supper for some childish offence. The live-out maid, Mona, smuggled up a tray of lamb, potatoes, vegetables, gravy and mint sauce. She came from a gypsy family and took me once to her horse-drawn caravan in the nearby village of Leasowe. Her bearded and somewhat saturnine father gave me a piece of Cornish pasty to eat. Heaven! It oozed with gravy and had a fine, rich, peppery taste.

The 1920s roared, even in Moreton. Returning from parties in overcrowded cars, 'Bright Young Things' clung precariously to 'dicky' seats and running boards. They argued about the relative merits and private affairs of actors and actresses, such as Sonny Hale and Evelyn Laye. They discussed the latest Aldwych theatre farces, starring the (apparently) silly asses, Tom Walls and Ralph Lynn, and the grotesque Robertson Hare. They talked about the new invention of radio and the 'cat's whiskers' which helped it to work. Many of the men played golf with 'drivers', 'niblicks', 'spoons' and 'mashies', resplendent in their 'fair isle' pullovers and 'plus fours'. There was the ever-present smell of 'scent' and cigarettes. I was taken sometimes to fancy dress balls in my father's 'Charron-Laycock'[7] car, dressed once as a jockey, and once as a question mark. The costumes were made by a local dressmaker who fitted them in our living room. Sometimes, the dressmaker was followed into the house by the 'Spirella' representative, bearing corsets of different sizes.

*****

My father founded his business in 1918, as I have said. It did well in the 1920s but, in 1925, lack of capital made it necessary for him to take in a partner, William Leonce Male. The business then took the name, 'Bickley and Male, Dispensing Chemists'. This arrangement may also have become necessary for legal reasons. It had become a requirement for such businesses to have a qualified 'Pharmacist Director' and my father was qualified only by virtue of his apprenticeship and long experience. William Male had passed the Minor examination and registered as a Chemist and Druggist ten years previously on 10 July 1915.

The two partners opened a branch in Birkenhead and, on the expectation of a real estate development, they opened an additional small shop in the village of Leasowe. Unfortunately, when the electoral districts were re-ordered, control passed from the hands of the Borough of Birkenhead to the Borough of Wallasey and the development scheme was abandoned. No development meant that there were no customers for the small pharmacy and it became a drain on the other two shops.

At the beginning of the 1930s, the main pharmacy at The Cross in Moreton was in trouble. The world was then experiencing the worst effects of the Depression which had followed the effervescent 1920s and the Great Crash of 1929. My mother told me once that one of my father's mistakes was to supply customers with too many medicines on credit and then fail to press them for payment. That may have been the case. Whatever the reason for the decline in business, the pharmacy was forced into voluntary liquidation in 1933.

It seems that, in addition to his share of the business in Moreton, William Male had been running his own pharmacy at 'The Mount', in Heswall, Cheshire. He also lost this business in the liquidation proceedings. In 1933, his registered address is recorded as 92 Bildeston Avenue, Birkenhead. His address changed frequently after that.

The pharmacy at The Cross continued under the ownership of J.L. and O. Jones (Moreton) Ltd and the pharmacy at The Mount began to function with a new owner, a Mr C.H. Maitland.

I believe that my father was defeated by several factors. He was grossly undercapitalised and had no reserves to fall back on when business declined and the Depression reached its climax. He was thoroughly familiar with the professional side of the business and was an amiable salesman. It appears, however, that he was not ruthless enough with customers who assured him that they would pay later, but not now. The business expanded too rapidly and the lack of firm capitalisation argued for caution, although it is true that the decision to open two more shops was made when the economy was booming in the 1920s.

In 1933, my father was forty-five years old. He had no business, no money, no house. (He had sold our home to pay his creditors.) Neither did he have any diplomas, beyond a matriculation certificate. After he acquired his own business, he became too caught up with everyday affairs and long working hours to consider acquiring the additional 'pieces of paper'. These were necessary to enable him to become a licensed pharmacist, able to dispense medicines without supervision. Ironically, he may have been better qualified by experience than many of those who had studied for and had been awarded their diplomas.

My father was a sweet man, once described as 'one of Nature's gentlemen'. He never became angry; never blasphemed and, if surprised or disturbed, relied on two expressions, 'stone the crows' and 'sink the boat'. Unfortunately, his own boat sank, after he lost the business into which he had put so much effort.

Aged seventy-two years, Stephen Verner died on 28 May 1960 of left ventricular failure, arteriosclerosis and chronic bronchitis. My mother survived him by sixteen years. She died aged eighty-four, on 30 March 1976 of renal failure, ischaemic heart disease, diabetes mellitus and a duodenal ulcer, at least that is what is recorded in the death certificate. Really, she died because she was worn out and lonely.

– 2 –

Fun and Games

As a little boy in Moreton I played frequently with Ann and Nancy, the girls next door. I must have been a convenient living toy for they were two or three years older than me. What did we play? 'House' of course (copying the activities of the older people) and 'pretend' ironing, washing and cooking. Later, 'Shop' (buying and selling to imaginary customers) and sometimes 'Dip' (a counting rhyme used to select a person for an activity):

> One Potato, Two Potatoes, Three Potatoes, Four.
> Five Potatoes, Six Potatoes, Seven Potatoes, More!

Sometimes, as an echo of the politics of the time, we might shout:

> *Ha! Ha! Ha! Hee! Hee! Hee!*
> *Ghandi on the lavatree…*

We knew nothing then of Gandhi's regime of self-denial (*brahmacharya*) and his reputed fondness for daily enemas.

As I grew older, fed by 'twopenny bloods'[1] and films, my imagination flowered. A tree in the woods became a jungle hideout; a packing case became a 'safe house' where 'drops' of secret information could be made; a fishing rod became a lance to be hurled across the lawn in the manner of the heroes of the popular films, *Lives of the Bengal Lancers*, *The Four Feathers*, *Kim* and *The Drum*. A cap pistol served several purposes, sometimes to be used for practising a quick draw in imitation of characters in the 'Western' novels of Zane Grey or Clarence Mulford. On other occasions, nestling in a shoulder holster, it would be of comfort to the budding secret agent…

Saturday matinees were held countrywide in local cinemas. The prices of admission in the Cheshire town of Sale (we moved there in 1934) were twopence, threepence and fourpence. Twopence bought a seat in the front, downstairs. Threepence secured a place at the back, downstairs, and fourpence was for the patricians who preferred the balcony. I usually found myself to be in the 'threepennies'. A fourpenny seat would have been an extravagance.

The noise created at these matinees was appalling since we all participated actively in the films, supplementing the actions of those on the screen. We cheered heroes such as Flash Gordon, Buster Crabbe and Hopalong Cassidy. The villains were howled down. Any 'love scenes' were booed loudly. It was too early in the game for most of us.

Some activities were seasonal. Some followed the fashions of the moment. In the autumn and winter 'conkers' (horse chestnuts) were popular. I would drill a hole in a nut and thread a piece of string through it. The game was to pit my oven-baked shiny conker against another boy's conker by hitting it with mine. Then it was his turn. I won if my opponent's conker was smashed to pieces. He won if mine disintegrated.

Marbles appeared at springtime. Some were known as 'alleys' made of glass, coloured inside. The owner of a particular 'alley' would prop it against a wall and the first boy to hit it, won it. A variation was to dig a small hole in grass or gravel and try to roll the 'alley' into the hole.

We treasured cigarette cards for their images of footballers, cricketers, motorcars and (best of all for some) film stars such as Alan Ladd, Clark Gable, Myrna Loy, William Powell and many others. But the cards were not valued simply for their images. They were essential tools in an interesting game. The idea was to prop one card against a wall and then take turns to flick other cards at the upright card, hoping to knock it down. Those who were successful at this were allowed to pick up all the cards that lay on the ground. Boys who collected cards in sets and were wise enough to keep them until adulthood are now in possession of valuable artifacts; for 'cartophily', as it is now called, is a well-developed hobby for some and a business for others. Sets of cigarette cards in good condition can fetch high prices in the appropriate market-place.

There were games and activities during holidays and on occasions such as All Hallows Eve ('Halloween'), the evening before All Saints' Day. Apples were hung on strings from a convenient shelf and the game was to try to eat the apples without handling them. Sometimes the apples were placed in a tin bath full of water. The victim had to lift the apples out with his or her teeth. This version of the game was called 'Apple Bobbing'. It seems to be a modern version of a custom observed by the Romans who, at this time of year, recognised *Pomona*, goddess of fruit and trees whose symbol was an apple ('Pomme' to the French).

Shrove Tuesday was a favourite day. We could look forward to a dessert of delicious pancakes, coated with glistening sugar and spiced with lemon. At Urban Road Primary School in Sale, a teacher would bring a container of cooked pancakes into the playground and toss them high into the air. The game was to try to catch the pancakes before they fell to the ground. Hardly hygienic but fun (at least for the children!).

On the Fifth of November – 'Guy Fawkes' Day' – we collected branches, built bonfires and made effigies of Guy Fawkes, dancing round the flames in the foggy autumn evenings as we munched 'parkin' (ginger cake) and treacle toffee.

Remember, Remember, the Fifth of November
Gunpowder, Treason and Plot.

Around and around the fires we would prance as the rockets soared, the 'cartwheels' fizzed and the 'rip-raps' ('jumping jacks') exploded.

It is difficult to believe that now, in Britain's increasingly litigious society, fears over legal claims from parents have persuaded many schools that snowballs, conkers and marbles should be banned. It seems that successful claims involving playground incidents are lodged each school day against local Councils.

*****

In the 1930s and 1940s, I used to look forward to Christmases. We spent most of these festivals enjoying the hospitality of my aunts and uncles in Liverpool, a once great city, sadly affected by shifting trading patterns and wars. One day, in the mid-1930s, the novelist J.B. Priestley was so desolated by Liverpool's problems that he took refuge in the dining room of the Adelphi Hotel and wrote, 'Miserably I decided that somebody else must give a plain, fair account of this great city.'[2]

I have not forgotten an experience at the beginning of 1944 when I sat at the open top of a green-coloured tram (a 'Green Goddess'), heading in the general direction of the famous Royal Liver Building, headquarters of the Royal Liver Insurance Company. We passed a row of once proud houses. Men in dirty singlets, slatternly peroxided women and snotty-nosed children sprawled on nearly every porch. It was deeply depressing.

Today it seems that there has been something of a transformation. European Union funding has helped to promote Merseyside as a tourist and investment location. Liverpool was the European Capital of Culture in 2008. Substantial redevelopment of the docks area is taking place. A Housing Market Renewal Initiative is underway and there is to be a new football stadium for the Liverpool Football Club. The World Museum flourishes. New businesses have started up and optimism is in the air.

At the better end of the city, my relatives lived in a house that was large enough to cater for a crowd. At 86 Allerton Road, Christmas Eve began with a large 'high tea' and continued with carvings from a fresh ham, supplemented by bread, butter and homemade jam, fruit cake, 'maids-of-honour', 'parkin' (left over from Guy Fawkes' Day), apple tart, scones and lots of tea, served with milk and sugar. After tea, we would all go upstairs to the lounge. There would be Uncle George and Auntie Edie (Edith), Uncle Jim and Auntie Flo (Florence), Uncle Reg (Reginald) and Auntie Min (Evelyn), my father and mother, my older cousins, Alma and Eric, and assorted friends.

The radio would be turned on but the programmes would be drowned by the buzz of gossip. Sometimes, the gramophone would be played – Bing Crosby perhaps, or George Formby, or Gracie Fields. Invariably, a decanter of port would circulate, as would Reg's homemade wine. Then there

86 Allerton Road, Liverpool.

would be indoor games such as 'Musical Chairs', 'Blindman's Buff' and 'Murder'. After the games, card tables would be set up and 'hands' dealt. Very early on, I was introduced to 'Strip Jack Naked', Whist and Rummy. For two or three Christmases, 'Monopoly' was the game to play and, subsequently, 'Canasta'.

I would go to bed after midnight, an adventure in itself, and was often given a double bed in a large bedroom at the top of the house. I would wake up on Christmas Day to see an apple and a banana and perhaps a tangerine on a plate at the bedside table. There would be a heavy weight on my feet – a pillowcase filled with gifts from Father Christmas – books, 'Dinky' toys and a box of Meccano perhaps. These would keep me busy until the adults stirred and the first cups of tea were distributed around the bedrooms. After a light breakfast, the morning might be spent (at least by me) in reading comics, some featuring 'Little Orphan Annie', 'Dick Tracy' and 'Life with Father'.

Christmas 'Dinner' was always served at midday. There would be turkey, stuffing, cranberry sauce, Brussels sprouts, potatoes and rich, dark gravy followed by Christmas pudding, brandy butter and mince pies. It was strange that I always found a sixpence, or a shilling, or a threepenny 'joey'[3] in my helping of pudding. No one else did.

Boxing Day was recuperation day. Cold turkey and salad for lunch. Salmon sandwiches and fruit cake for tea. The men, wrapped in overcoats, scarves and gloves, would go off to watch a football match in the afternoon. How I envied them!

On 27 December, the Bickleys would prepare to return to their home in Sale, hoping fervently that the outside water pipes had not frozen. Before departure, I would be expected to shake hands with all the uncles. The coins that were usually transferred from their hands to mine would keep me going until Easter. They have all gone now, as have the aunts and cousins.

*****

In 1934, after first arriving in Sale, I was given a temporary place in a primary school (Saint Alban's) run by the Anglican Church. The summer of that year was unusually hot and dry and so much dust arose from the dirt playground that my heavily starched white shirts and shorts quickly became grubby.

Before I left Saint Alban's, I had developed asthma. Playground dust may have been the prime cause but 'passive smoking' may also have been a contributory factor. Both my parents smoked and so did most of their friends. Whatever the cause, the consequence was a long trail through doctors' surgeries. I have forgotten most of the earlier doctors' names but young Gibson and older Robson come to mind. The treatments were amazingly varied and none were particularly successful. Allergy tests, exercises, Friar's Balsam inhaled from a kettle, Vick's Vapour Rub, Scott's Emulsion, various cough mixtures, a course of injections.

My tonsils and adenoids were removed and for this event I was incarcerated for a few days in a Cottage Hospital. I was given castor oil to clean out my bowels before the surgery took place. 'There's some lemonade at the bottom of the glass,' said a nurse. Perhaps there was but I could not find it.

Some doctors prescribed tiny tablets of the drug, *ephedrine hydrochloride*. It causes constriction of the blood vessels and an accompanying widening of the bronchial passages. It is also a stimulant, generating (at least in me) a more rapid heartbeat. For a severe attack of asthma, however, I found it to be a godsend.

Ephedrine is now strictly regulated, having been abused by people seeking a 'high'. Athletes found to have taken ephedrine in the Olympic Games held in 1972 and 1984 were disciplined severely. At the 1992 Olympics, a Bulgarian athlete was discovered to have used *norephedrine* and in the Sydney Games of 2000 a Romanian gymnast was banned for taking *pseudoephedrine*. Ephedrine is found in some ephedras, an ephedra being an evergreen shrub with trailing stems and scale-like leaves.

None of the remedies prescribed for my asthmatic condition worked particularly well although I am sure that the physicians did their best, given their relatively limited knowledge and the absence of effective drugs. Fortunately (for some) a number of breakthroughs in treatment were made in the late 1970s and life for many (but not all) chronic asthmatics has become easier. I am among the lucky ones.

Frequent bouts of asthma affected my attendance at school and I needed constantly to 'catch up' at my primary school in Sale. This was a custom-built school, with pleasant facilities and attractive, well-equipped classrooms. Miss Pendleton, the headmistress, was a plump authoritarian lady who occasionally felt it necessary to cane her pupils on the hands. I think that any pain caused came more from anticipation than from the strength of her right arm.

I enjoyed my time at the school despite frequent absences. I benefited from having well-developed vocal folds (i.e. 'a loud voice') and a certain aggressiveness instilled into me by my mother. In jest, she would warn adults who engaged in a mock boxing contest with me to 'watch that left' (I am left-handed). If I complained about being struck by another child, my mother would say, 'I hope you gave as good as you got.'

Over the years, my mother also gave me less challenging but nevertheless useful advice:

> A gentleman always shines the back of his shoes.
> Don't smoke, eat or drink in the street. (Not many people seem to know that one today.)
> Don't hang around street corners.
> Don't speak with your mouth full.
> Always stand up in the presence of a lady.
> (On public transport) Give up your seat to a lady, or an older person.
> On the pavement, walk on the outside of a lady (to protect her from the splashes of passing traffic, if any).
> Raise your hat to a lady.
> Always dry between your toes.

I was the 'boss' and the 'ideas man' of a small gang at my school in Sale. My ideas were derived largely from comics and from *Nelson Keys*, a 'mystery magazine'. I have a copy in front of me now as I press the computer keys. Published on 27 November 1926, it featured a complete 'powerful yarn of schoolboy life' entitled, *Caught in the Meshes*, and the first episode of a new serial, *Sons of the Men of Mons*, 'a story of schoolboys in England caught up in a war of revenge declared by Germany'. My issue of *Nelson Keys* sold for twopence, and this included a 'free stand-up figure of the comedian, Charlie Chaplin'. The magazine also printed other tempting offers which included:

> The Bully Boy 2-shot Rapid Repeater Action Pea Pistol.
> A Bing Stationery Engine, 'built to scale by expert engineers'.
> A solid silver English hall-marked lever watch, priced at sixpence.
> A parcel of magic tricks, priced at two shillings and sixpence.
> A complete course to increase a person's height. Price five shillings.

In addition to *Nelson Keys*, I took ideas from two other (now defunct) magazines, *Chums* and *The Boys' Own Paper*. My trusty lieutenants in the gang were Jimmy Hope, whose father owned a garage, and Fred Spence whose father was a stonemason. I had more contact with Fred than with Jimmy. Fred's father's stonemason's yard was in Sale and he would allow us to practice chiselling our names on rejected gravestones. Fred's elder brother was a soldier who distinguished himself on the Northwest Frontier by allowing himself to be shot in the foot.

– 3 –

A Good Environment

Famous for its rugby teams, Sale provided a good environment for a boy despite the fact that it was damp. Nearby Manchester and other surrounding towns in Lancashire were once centres of the cotton industry, chosen because of their humidity. Cotton became more pliable and did not break as easily in such an atmosphere.

Named after Sir Hugh De Trafford, Manchester's Trafford Park belied its name. Hardly a green oasis, it was a thriving centre of polluting heavy industry, playing host to such companies as the Dunlop Rubber Company, Metropolitian-Vickers, Carborundum and others.

Scarred by years of industrial growth, Manchester had no claim to being an elegant city. But appearance was not all. It was a place of dignity; proud of Carl Halle's famous orchestra, its well-stocked Central Library, its Opera House, its highly respected Grammar School and its University where the scientists Rutherford, Chadwick, Cockcroft and others contributed hugely to atomic research. Today it seems that parts of the city are plagued by illiterate, melancholy gangs with their knives, guns and stupid oaths. Some newspapers have even dubbed this fine place, 'Gunchester'.

Sale became part of the Metropolitan Borough of Trafford, Greater Manchester, in 1974. When I lived there, it was still known as a town in the county of Cheshire. Although only seven miles or so from Manchester city, it was a world apart from the machines and the accompanying grime. We felt ourselves to be nearly, although not quite, in the countryside. Farmer Wilkinson owned the field at the bottom of our garden. It was mainly kept fallow but in some years Wilkinson would cultivate crops of rhubarb and turnips, and sometimes potatoes. He was primarily a dairy farmer who provided his clientele in Chestnut Drive with milk, cream and eggs. He would deliver these in his horse-drawn 'float'.

Wilkinson was but one of a number of tradesman who catered efficiently for our needs, even during wartime. We were always pleased to welcome the coalmen; sturdy, wrinkled men carrying sacks of (rationed) 'black diamonds' on leather back-protectors. Sometimes we could find objects to give to the rag and bottle collectors and receive in exchange a piece of 'donkey-stone', useful for cleaning the front and back door steps. 'Rags! Bottles! Bones!' they cried.

Our quite small house boasted a dining room, a sitting room and three bedrooms. There was a kitchen, a wash-house and a 'coal-place'. The wash-house was equipped with a sink and a copper 'boiler', essential equipment for the Monday morning wash. My mother's housework was done according to a strict timetable. Monday was wash day. Tuesday was for ironing and for cleaning the bedrooms. Wednesday was dedicated to the living room and so on. The furniture was polished regularly and the dusters and dishcloths were changed every day. The dirty clothes were scrubbed and boiled in the wash-house, squeezed semi-dry in a 'mangle' and then dried on a 'maiden' (or 'clothes-horse') in front of the coal-fed dining-room fire. It was hard work. It is easier today with the introduction of central heating, detergents, washing machines, spin dryers and refrigerators.

Chestnut Drive was not a bad place for a boy. Mr Wilkinson's field lay beyond the hedge at the bottom of the garden, providing grazing for a friendly horse that my father used to feed whenever he had the opportunity. A brook ran slowly at one end of the field, enriched by tiddlers and algae. Just beyond Chestnut Drive there were woods, with trees to climb and a pond that sported a raft made of logs, as if made by Jack and Ernest in *The Swiss Family Robinson*.

I left Urban Road Primary School at the age of eleven, a few months before we moved into our house in Sale. I still maintained my friendships with Jimmy Hope and Fred Spence but also found something in common with Willy Hammond who lived in a house opposite to ours. Willy and I used to exchange boys' magazines, the so-called 'twopenny bloods'.

One of these – *Gem* – featured the adventures of a group of schoolboys, led by a certain Tom Merry. In its sister magazine – *Magnet* – the boys at Greyfriars School were commanded by Harry Wharton. His band of brothers included an Indian boy, Ram Jamset Singh, as well as the famous fat boy, Billy Bunter. Bunter appeared first in the introductory issue of the Magnet Library in February 1908.

As is now well known, all the stories appearing in *Gem* and *Magnet* were written by the same man, Charles Edward St John Hamilton, better known by one of his twenty-eight pseudonyms, Frank Richards. His lifetime output was about 100,000,000 words. I read quite a number of them.

My first real book was a Victorian edition of the above-mentioned, *The Swiss Family Robinson*, which oddly did not include the name of the author. No writer would tolerate that today.

As I grew older, I began to haunt our local public library, beginning first with the children's corner and then turning to the well-stocked adult shelves with their eclectic variety of novels. Eventually, I joined the experienced readers who stood ready to pounce when the librarian's assistant wheeled a trolley of books round the room. Were other people's choices better than one's own?

The Altrincham Public Library was built of faded, weathered brick. Inside, it favoured dark-brown, scuffed woodwork, green-painted pillars and tiled floors covered with 'linoleum'. It housed an adult library from which up to four books could be borrowed at one time, plus a childrens' library, and a reference room supplied with dictionaries, encyclopedias, trade directories and newspapers, invariably open at the 'Situations Vacant' pages.

Soon I was borrowing four books a week, working my way steadily through a mixture of 'school stories', including such favourites as *Tom Brown's Schooldays* and *The Fifth Form at St Dominics*. Later, as a change from the lives of fictitious schoolboys, I took to swashbuckling novels, detective stories and espionage.

*****

In certain American Colleges and Universities, it is possible to take courses in Popular Culture. I think that I might have done well on one of these courses if they had been available for children and adolescents in England in the late 1930s and early 1940s. Like many others, I was exposed on most nights to music and chitchat on the radio. Perhaps I should have been banished more often to another room, the better to struggle with Clement Durell's *General Arithmetic*,[1] and to attempt to unravel the intricacies of German modal verbs. But 'stocks and shares' and the conjugating of *wollen*, *mögen* and *sollen* sometimes took second place to shows such as, 'Music Hall' and 'Bandwagon'.

'Music Hall' was a slicker version of the music hall performances of the late nineteenth and early twentieth centuries that were blessed with entertainers such as Gus Elen, Marie Lloyd, Florrie Ford, Little Tich and others. On the radio, the then modern version consisted of a series of acts, each lasting three or four minutes except in the case of the 'star turn' who might be allocated up to ten minutes. We could hear the mass tapping of 'The Dancing Daughters' but, of course, we could not see the chorus line. Comedians such as George Robey, Billy Bennett and Max Miller and the impressionists, Florence Desmond and Beryl Ord were among the popular and regular acts.

The producers of 'Bandwagon' devised a successful format that was used, not only in their own show, but in others which followed it in the 1940s and 1950s. First, a signature song. Then a sketch, always involving the same characters. Halfway through the programme there would be a 'band number', followed by a second sketch and sometimes a third. 'Bandwagon' starred a Liverpool-born, stand-up comedian named Arthur Askey, supported by his straight man, urbane Richard ('Dicky') Murdoch.

By the end of the 1930s, 'catch-phrases' had become immensely popular, derived from the commonplace exchanges of everyday life. Arthur Askey's mantra was, 'I thank you,' pronounced 'I thangyeow.' This was, of course, the bus conductor's pat expression as he walked up and down the length of his bus collecting fares. It was not at all funny in itself but perhaps it reminded people of the ups and downs of life, the bus queues, the ever-increasing fares, dripping raincoats and umbrellas, the struggles with shopping bags. All these were made tolerable by the rough humour of the conductors and the 'clippies' and the linguistic formulas used in daily social interactions such as 'You're welcome,' 'Thanks very much,' 'Nice day again, isn't it?' 'That's all right, love,' 'Mornin' my handsome,' and others. Whatever the reason for its popularity, Askey's use of the familiar words in his weekly programme invariably brought a laugh and thousands of people must have repeated them to each other every day, for several years.

Catch-phrases were used regularly in 'ITMA' ('It's That Man Again'), a significant propaganda weapon made use of by the British during the Second World War. The show included many references to rationing, politicians, Lord Haw-Haw (William Joyce, the American-born traitor who broadcast nightly for the Germans) and various Nazi leaders. The title of the show was often used to refer to Hitler, the Nazi dictator. For example, during a bombing attack, someone might remark 'It's that Man Again,' meaning Hitler. The prime mover in the show, Tommy Handley (another Liverpudlian), died shortly after the War when still only in his fifties. He was a great loss.

Some radio programmes were intended to generate more than laughter. There were also shows to inform and to test the wits. In a programme, named 'The Brains Trust', questions contributed by listeners were discussed. 'Why did brontosaurs disappear from the earth and yet cockroaches are still with us?' Such a question would be given first to a selected member of the 'Trust' and then opened up for general discussion. The regular members were Commander Campbell, a retired Naval Paymaster and a bluff type who had an anecdote for every port: 'Now, when I was in Patagonia…'

Campbell was joined by Julian Huxley, the biologist and brother of the novelist, Aldous, both being sons of the Victorian scientist and educationalist, Thomas F. Huxley. The third member of the team was C.E.M. Joad, a Professor of Philosophy at the University of London, apparently irascible, pedantic and a precise semanticist: 'Of course – erm – it depends what you mean by…'

Joad disgraced himself in April 1948 by attempting to travel on a Waterloo to Exeter train without paying for a ticket. He was caught, brought into court, fined two pounds and banned for life from the BBC. This episode was said to have had a severe effect on his health. Thrombosis and cancer followed later.

Religious broadcasts were given reasonable prominence. Services were broadcast from churches around the country and, at other times, talks on differing aspects of faith were given by both clerics and laypersons. Such presentations were appropriately reverent and relatively unchallenging.

Alistair Cooke's weekly 'Letter From America' was very popular, as were the novelist, J.B. Priestley's, 'Fireside Chats'. News bulletins were read straight, with little emotion, by newsreaders who – before the Second World War – were anonymous voices which could be distinguished only by timbre. An exception to the 'no name rule' was made during the War for security reasons (an interloper might deliver a propaganda message and spread misinformation) and the newsreaders were told to reveal their names. There was, perhaps, more bad news than good news for a long time, and yet the voices were somehow reassuring:

'This is the BBC Home Service.
Here is the News, read by Alvar Liddell.'

'This is the BBC Home Service.
Here is the News read by Stewart Hibberd.'

'This is the BBC Home Service.
Here is the News read by Bruce Belfrage.'

The last-named, Bruce Belfrage, distinguished himself on 8 December 1940 when a 500lb bomb fell on the BBC's headquarters at Broadcasting House in London's Portland Place. Halfway through his reading of the 9 o'clock news there was a loud crash. Belfrage wavered only for an instant and then said, 'I beg your pardon,' and continued with the reading.

I did not imagine, as I listened to those men, that in the mid-1950s I would be sitting in front of a microphone in a dusty studio in Singapore, announcing:

'This is the BBC Far Eastern Station
We are broadcasting on 9.69 megacycles…'

*****

I first became conscious of music when we were living at 'Denehurst' in Moreton. With the help of my Uncle Reginald, my father built a 'crystal set'. It was housed in a small mahogany box that I was later able to use as a receptacle in which to store keepsakes. By then it lacked its 'cat's whisker' and other essential parts. When it functioned as a radio, it brought us the station '2LO' from London (the first station, 2MT, broadcast from Writtle in Essex). After a while the crystal set was replaced by a battery set with power supplied by an 'accumulator', a device that was about the size of today's car battery and which needed to be charged regularly.

What came out of this machine? News items and entertainment were broadcast by the National Programme and the Regional Programme, in our case the North Regional Programme. For children, 'Auntie Muriel' (Muriel Levy) and 'Uncle Mac' (Derek McCullough) presented 'Children's Hour', a programme that featured short plays and stories, games and competitions. Proud parents would write to the station to give advance information about their children's birthdays. These would be acknowledged by Auntie Muriel: 'Hello, Mary! Hello, John! Hello, Diane! Hello, Twins!'

Music to suit all tastes was presented on the North Regional Programme. This included symphonies, chamber music, different forms of jazz and music for dancing. Henry Hall's BBC Dance Orchestra was particularly popular. Tall, lean and pomaded, Hall was invariably photographed, at least for publicity purposes, in a morning suit. He would announce his own programmes with a slight stutter: 'Good evening everyone. This is Hen – Hen – Henry Hall and His Orchestra.'

Novelty tunes were included in each of Hall's programmes. These included, quite often, 'The Teddy Bears' Picnic'.

> If you go out in the woods today
> You're sure of a big surprise.
> If you go out in the woods today
> You'd better go in disguise.
> For every bear that ever there was
> Will gather there for certain, because
> Today's the day the teddy bears have their picnic.

In addition to Henry Hall's band, many other bands competed for radio slots and for work in hotels, clubs and ballrooms. Jazz enthusiasts (as I am) considered the band that was managed and led by Benjamin Baruch Ambrose (professional name 'Bert Ambrose') to be a cut above the rest. Perhaps the best remembered of Ambrose's female vocalists are Evelyn Dall and Vera Lynn. Dall was a vivacious, former American cabaret singer whose style seemed to be modelled on Peggy Lee, then a great success in the United States. Vera, later Dame Vera, Lynn became a favourite of the 'Forces' during the War. Perhaps it was her very *ordinariness* that attracted; her resemblance to 'the girl next door'. Today, Bert Ambrose is remembered on a plaque affixed to a building in London's Mayfair. In the past, such plaques were reserved normally for soldiers, politicians, writers and artists.

Although London suffered very badly during the German bombing campaign that began in 1940, ballrooms and night-clubs continued to offer their services whenever this was possible. At the Café de Paris night-club in London, Ken 'Snakehips' Johnson led a civilian band of great potential. One day, my copy of the *Melody Maker* newspaper reported that Johnson had been killed by a bomb dropped on the Club during the 'blitz'. Mr Poulson, the manager, Al Bowlly, the vocalist and Tom Bromley, the talented bassist, died in the same incident.

A few days before the Café de Paris incident, the Right Honorable Malcolm Macdonald visited the Club with a party of friends. They were there to celebrate his appointment as High Commissioner to Canada. Some nights later, all members of a party who dined at the same 'gallery table' was killed when the bomb landed.

THE SECOND STEP

SCHOOL DAYS
AND CONFLICT

– 4 –

The Grammar School

In early 1937 when I was eleven years old, my primary school (and my parents) arranged for me to take a County Minor scholarship examination. This examination consisted of papers in English and Arithmetic, plus an 'IQ' (Intelligence Quotient) test. The examination was used for the purpose of grammar school selection and was the precursor of a later examination that became known as the '11 Plus', intended to determine which level of education was most appropriate for a child in relation to his or her age, ability and aptitude. The split into three kinds of secondary school – grammar, secondary modern and secondary technical – was introduced after the 'Butler' Education Act was passed in 1944.

I was lucky. My examination results were satisfactory and I was given a scholarship, the only boy at Urban Road Primary School to be granted one in that year. One girl, Christina Oribin, was also successful. The scholarship gave me a 'special place' at Altrincham (pronounced Altringham) Grammar School and I began to attend the school in September 1937, two years before the outbreak of the Second World War.

My ideas about Altrincham Grammar School were certainly influenced by *Gem* and *Magnet*. It must be understood that the fictitious schools that these magazines described were boarding schools, so-called 'public schools'. The illustrations usually depicted boys wearing cut-away dark jackets, striped dark trousers and high white 'Eton' Collars. They lived in 'Houses' under the supervision of Housemasters who invariably wore gowns and mortarboards. There were 'raggings', teas taken in front of study fires and dormitory feasts. In the school corridors, Billy Bunter, 'the Fat Owl of the Remove', was always said to be 'rolling along'. A favourite

29

expression used by all the boys was 'Oh, I say!' Laughter (and there was a good deal of it because of the many 'japes') was characterised by 'Ha! Ha! Ha!' Punishments included 'detention' and writing out 'lines'. Boys leaving the school grounds had to apply for 'exeats'. Looking back, what is extraordinary is that in all likelihood most of the readers of these magazines were boys who would never attend or have any contact with the schools or the milieu that they described.

Altrincham Grammar School (AGS) was established in 1912 following the Balfour Education Act of 1902 which aimed to create a national system of, partly fee-paying, secondary education. The school opened with fifty-seven pupils and three staff. In 1974, it was passed to the newly formed Trafford Metropolitan Borough until 1996 when it became Grant Maintained. In September 1999 it was transformed into a Foundation School and in 2003 it was given the status of a specialist language college. The Ofsted[1] Report of 21 and 22 November 2007 rated it as 'Outstanding'.

Although it was a day school, AGS was organised to some extent along public school lines. For this reason, Latin had an honoured place in the curriculum and the school was divided into 'Houses' named after local dignitaries. My House was named after John Dalton, the chemist and inventor who lived in Sale, Altrincham's neighbouring borough. Born in Eaglesfield, Cumberland, Dalton worked for many years in Manchester where he developed the atomic theory of matter and the law of partial pressures. He also wrote what may have been the first scientific paper describing colour blindness, from which he suffered. The condition later became known as 'Daltonism'.

Today, the new status of Altrincham Grammar School as a Foundation School provides (to some extent) protection against government intervention of the kind sponsored in the 1960s by the Labour Minister of Education, Anthony Crosland. His second wife, Susan, reported in a biography of her husband that he was determined (as he malignantly put it), to 'f–' the grammar schools. Clearly he could wield a big (and nasty) stick and he was successful in many cases. Over 90 per cent of secondary schools in England, Wales and Northern Ireland are now 'comprehensives'. AGS survived the purge and has done well so far in the government's annual league tables published in British newspapers.

Life at AGS was not all work and no play. There were spacious playing-fields, a well-equipped gymnasium and good changing-room facilities. I played both soccer and cricket but really preferred the latter. That being so, it would have been interesting for me to have attended the school in the early 1970s, when Paul Allot was a pupil. After Allot left the school, he played county cricket for Lancashire and also made thirteen appearances for England's Test team as a medium fast bowler.

In 1938 – one year after I first attended AGS – England won an 'Ashes' Cricket Test series against Australia. In those days Tests were timeless, played until both sides had completed two innings. The tactic for each team therefore was to occupy the crease for as long as possible. Len Hutton of Yorkshire accumulated 364 runs in one innings of the series and another young player, eighteen-year-old Denis Compton of Middlesex, acquitted himself well after a poor start. Both Hutton and Compton were *players*, paid for their efforts. The 'Gentlemen' were not. Each year, the 'Gentlemen' and the 'Players' competed against each other in a festive three-day match. This annual event continued to be played until after the Second World War when cricket was finally democratised.

1938 was also the year for another – rather more flamboyant – game. At Spithead in England, the Royal Navy mounted a Grand Review of the then large and powerful British Fleet. There were battleships, battle cruisers, destroyers, frigates, sloops, minelayers, minesweepers, aircraft carriers, motor torpedo boats, motor launches, submarines, tenders and

Staff of Altrincham Grammar School, Cheshire, 1942. Middle row, far R: Sergeant Hammond, Physical Training Master. Front row: 2nd L, 'Bus' Thompson, Latin Master; 3rd L, 'Archie' Hill, French Master; Centre, W. Hamblin, Headmaster; 4th from R, 'Joe Egg', English Master; 2nd from R, 'Pug' Page, German Master.

sundry other vessels. The Review was 'covered' by a BBC wireless commentary, given by a certain Tom Woodruff. Formerly a Lieutenant Commander in the Navy, Tom was invited to drinks by former shipmates. This became obvious as he began to speak since his voice was distinctly slurred. His downfall came when, as dusk fell, all the ships in the decorative parade turned on their review lights. 'They're lit up,' said Tom, with drunken glee, '... the whole bloody Fleet's lit up.' Harman Grisewood, the announcer on duty, was taken aback and faded Tom out after five minutes. Poor Tom was dismissed from the BBC on the next day for using improper language. Such a reaction by officialdom can scarcely be imagined today after 'F–' was uttered by the late critic, Kenneth Tynan, on television. Of course, Tynan was not a member of the regular staff.

*****

In 1938 I joined the 3rd Altrincham (Grammar School) Scout Troop. The Troop was founded in 1912 very shortly after the Scout Movement itself was created, following the first experimental camp established on Brownsea Island by the Founder of the Movement, Lord Baden-Powell, the hero – at least for some (and certainly for me) – of the siege of Mafeking in the Boer War.

The 3rd Altrincham Troop was very well organised and equipped. After the First World War, a group of AGS Old Boys clubbed together to build a hut on the school grounds. The building boasted a large assembly room, a utility room, a kitchen, a lavatory, a small library and two large lofts designed for the storage of tents, bridge-building materials and cooking utensils.

When I first joined 3rd Altrincham, I was given the customary title of 'Tenderfoot'. After a few weeks I was allowed to give a 'Promise' and following that became a fully-fledged Scout attached to a six-member patrol, 'The Swifts'. The Promise has now been changed but when I gave it, it ran like this:

> I promise on my honour
> To do my best
> To do my duty
> To God and the King
> To help other people at all times
> And to obey the Scout Law.

The 3rd Altrincham Troop was particularly well-blessed, having been in existence long enough to develop its own way of doing things. For example, it had established a tradition of recognising merit and progress by awarding 'Woodcraft' names and 'Impeesa' medals. It organised camps at Easter for 'Patrol Leaders' and 'Seconds' and joint New Year Training Camps for Patrol Leaders from the Scout Troop and members of the Rover Crew (Senior Scouts).

I enjoyed my Scouting years. There was the companionship at regular meetings in Altrincham, cemented at training camps held every Easter at Delamere Forest in Cheshire. At these camps boys were accommodated in 'Niger' tents, each holding eight persons. Patrol Leaders might be provided with 'Good Companion' hike tents, accommodating two persons. Camp 'officers' might find themselves quartered in a wooden camp hut.

In the winter, tents were exchanged for Youth Hostel accommodation in the Lake District at the foot of the mountain known as 'The Old Man of Coniston'. We were told that the name had nothing to do with an old man but that 'maen' was Welsh for 'stone' and 'old' was derived from the old Welsh word meaning, 'cliff'.

In addition to the camping and the climbing, there was the excitement and pleasure of being awarded a 'Woodcraft Name'. At one Easter Training Camp I was dubbed 'Mohawk'. Later, before joining the Rover Crew, I became a 'King's Scout' and was awarded a 'Bushman's Thong', something

The Scout Hut at Altrincham Grammar School, Cheshire, 1935, 'After the First World War, a group of Old Boys of the school clubbed together to build a hut in the school grounds.'

to do with gaining a number of badges in a particular group. But the honour that gave me the most pleasure was the award of the 'Impeesa' medal, given at a Summer Training Camp held under canvas at Ullswater, in the Lake District. 'Impeesa' means 'The Wolf Who Never Sleeps'.

In 1943, I joined the Altrincham Grammar School Air Cadet Corps. I learned marching and weapons drill and discovered the art of projecting my voice. I had never taken the opportunity to do this at the Grammar School in any of its annual theatrical productions. In those days they were usually versions of Gilbert and Sullivan comic operas.

There was, however, an exception. At Christmas 1942, the usual Gilbert and Sullivan production failed to materialise and the Scouts were asked to present a 'Gang Show', fashioned along the lines of the popular shows written and directed by the stage director and performer, Ralph Reader.[2] The formula was simple; a series of sketches with musical interludes and breezy, cheerful songs performed by a chorus of men and boys. The chorus of Reader's signature tune, 'We're riding along on the crest of a wave', was often performed with actions:

> (*Verse*)
> All Hands aboard boys, all Hands aboard boys
> The ship is calling for more.
> We're getting ready, now for the steady
> Pull away from the home shore.
> We're off to find adventure anyhow,
> Because we know that now…
> (*Chorus*)
> We're riding along on a crest of a wave
> And the sun is in the sky
> All our eyes on the distant horizon
> Look out for passers-by.
> We'll do the hailing
> When all the ships are round us sailing.
> We're riding along on the crest of a wave
> And the world is ours.

The 3rd Altrincham Gang Show was directed by a sixth form boy named I.G. Lowndes who revelled in the nickname, 'Igle'. I was given a small part in this extravaganza, in a very short sketch:

One bucolic character encounters another bucolic character, centre stage:

A. Mornin.
B. Mornin.

(Both go off stage and then come on again)
A. Mornin.
B. Mornin.
A. What did oo give yor cow when ee were sick?
B. Turpentine.
(They go off and come on again)
A. Mornin.
B. Mornin.
A. What did oo say oo gave yor cow when ee were sick?
B. Turpentine.
A. Arr.
(They both go off and then come on again)
A. Mornin.
B. Mornin.
A. When oi gave my cow turpentine, ee died!
B. Aye, and so did mine!
(Curtain)

Despite this sketch, the show was a great success.

The Grammar School was well-equipped for theatrical productions. It had a large, modern auditorium that could seat the entire school, plus green rooms and a well-equipped stage, with good lighting.

Aside from the Gilbert and Sullivan presentations, I can remember one other show, *Gallows Glorious*, a play about the slavery abolitionist, John Brown, written by Ronald Gow, an Old Boy of the School and author of another well-received play, *Love on the Dole*. Gow married a rising young actress, Wendy Hiller, chosen by George Bernard Shaw to play the part of Eliza in *Pygmalion*. She later played the same role in a film version that also starred the actor Leslie Howard as Professor Higgins. Ronald Gow died aged 96 in April 1993.

*****

I think that it was in 1943 that I began to attend dancing lessons. I enrolled because others had enrolled and – besides – there were *girls*. The classes were conducted by Mr Frank Burroughs and his wife, both of them former dance champions. Frank possessed a Bachelor of Science degree in addition to his dance diplomas and, due to wartime exigencies, he was taken on as a temporary member of the Grammar School staff. His main interest, however, was his dancing school, The Frank Burroughs' School of Dancing in Willowtree Road, Altrincham. The School was run in Frank's large, modern house, one very large room of which had been turned into a miniature ballroom, complete with a specially constructed sprung floor.

The clients would come in from the cold, hang up their hats and coats in a small vestibule and change into their patent leather dancing shoes. The atmosphere was warm and friendly. The boys looked at the girls; the girls gazed at the boys. All was innocent, shy anticipation. At the beginning of each session, Frank or his wife would ask for partners to be chosen. No-one was left out. If there *was* a spare boy or girl, then Frank or Mrs Burroughs, or another helper would serve as partner.

Frank taught primarily through demonstration. We started with the Waltz – 'one-two-three, one-two-three' – stumbling round in a clockwise direction. As the weeks went by, we progressed to the Foxtrot and the Quickstep, from Open Telemark[3] to Chassé.[4] From time to time we would learn and practise 'novelty' dances such as the 'Hokey-Cokey' and 'The Lambeth Walk'. 'The Blackout Stroll' was a favourite, first because it was easy to do and, second, because at a certain point the lights were extinguished and it was possible (briefly) to squeeze, hug or kiss. The interval was short but some made good use of it. It was all very innocent and charming in its way.

Frank was a good teacher. I found his lessons useful after I joined the Navy, in which Service all 'officers and gentlemen' are supposed to be able to dance.

– 5 –

Came the War

On 1 September 1939, Germany invaded Poland. The final preparations for this event were observed by Claire Hollingworth, a correspondent for the *Daily Telegraph* and a guest of the British Consul-General in Katowice on the Polish–German border. As she remembers the story, she had borrowed the Consul-General's car for a brief fact-finding visit in German territory. At one turn of the road she noticed that screens had been placed along the roadside. These screens concealed a mass of troops, tanks, armoured cars and field guns. The Germans were poised to strike without warning, and strike they did.

Sixteen days after Claire's adventure in West Poland and in fulfilment of a pact between the Soviet Foreign Minister, Vyacheslav Molotov and the German Foreign Minister, Joachim von Ribbentrop Russian tanks chugged into Chorostkow in East Poland. The country was now at the mercy of both the Germans and the Russians. Their unholy partnership lasted only twenty-one months until 22 June 1941 when Germany declared war on Russia.

But what of Claire Hollingworth? She has lived in Hong Kong since the 1980s. In her nineties at the time of writing and nearly blind, in ill-health but indomitable, she is often to be found in a corner of the Foreign Correspondents' Club, ready to tell her tale.

*****

On 3 September 1939, in support of Poland, Britain declared war on Germany. It was very peaceful in Sale as we enjoyed the last moments of a beautiful summer and relaxed on deckchairs in the garden. Neville Chamberlain's sepulchral broadcast seemed somewhat out of place on such a beautiful day:

> This morning the British Ambassador in Berlin handed the German Government a final note stating that unless we heard from them by 11 o'clock that they were prepared to withdraw their troops from Poland, a state of war would exist between us. I have to tell you now that no such undertaking has been received and that consequently this country is at war with Germany.

After the announcement, came a message from the King (George VI). His stutter was very pronounced.

In 1939, Chamberlain's image appeared in many newspapers and magazines. He clung to stand-up wing collars long after they had been abandoned by most men in favour of those that were easier to manage. Some commentators feel that he had also clung erroneously to the belief that Hitler could be appeased. In fairness, it is also possible that his government's policy was to bide its time until Britain's defences could be strengthened.

I was twelve years old in 1938 when Chamberlain went to Munich and I remember his claim (reported on our 'Portadyne' radio) that his meeting with Hitler had ensured 'peace in our time'. I did not know then that a distinguished predecessor, Disraeli, had made a similar announcement ('Peace for our time') when he returned to England from the Congress of Berlin.

Despite Chamberlain's assurance, gas masks were issued to everyone in Britain. The masks came in cardboard boxes which were often used for other purposes. Some people kept sandwiches and other personal items in them. There were no 'Ziplock' plastic bags then.

At first, the impact of the War was hardly felt, although precautions were taken against attacks from the air. There was a run on masking tape used to prevent windows from shattering if air raids should take place. On 8 January 1940, buff-coloured ration books were distributed and it became necessary to register with named retailers for the purchase of sugar, ham, butter and bacon. Men who were ineligible for the Army, Navy or Air Force were enrolled in a citizen's army named the Local Defence Volunteers ('LDV', later the Home Guard). The volunteers took their responsibilities seriously but very little equipment was available.

These different preparations did not seem to be particularly urgent and, for the first months, nothing of major significance happened. After all, was there not the 'impregnable' French Maginot Line, barring the path of the Germans into France? Had not the Germans settled behind *their* Line, named after Siegfried who forged the Nothung sword, slew Fafner – the dragon guarding the stolen Rhine gold – and helped Gunther to win Brunhild? As it turned out, neither fortification justified the efforts put into its construction.

The nine-month period of the so-called 'phoney' war lasted until May 1940 when, as is well-remembered, German panzer divisions, with a series of fast pincer movements, breached French and British defences and made their way through Holland, Belgium and France to the sea. The evacuation of Dunkirk followed, undoubtedly a major victory for Germany, although over three hundred thousand British troops were saved. The lines of the anti-German song could no longer apply:

> We're going to hang out the washing on the Siegfried Line.
> Have you any dirty washing, mother dear?[1]

My father and I preferred a song performed by the comedians, Flanagan and Allen:

> A. You're going across the sea, my lad.
> I wish you luck, my son.
> B. Yes, Dad.
> A. You've got a great big job to do.
> A job that must be done.
> And if you meet a lady there
> That I knew years ago.
> B. Yes?
> A. Just give her my kind regards.
> B. How will I know?
> *Refrain*:
> If a grey-haired lady says, 'How's your father?'
> That'll be Mademoiselle.
> If she smiles and says, 'How's your father?'
> That'll be Mademoiselle.
> If she says, 'Parlez Vous',
> 'Toot-sweet' tell me do.
> 'How is he after all these years'?
> If a grey-haired lady says,
> 'Don't tell your mother.'
> That's Mademoiselle from Armentieres!
>
> A. I remember one time, son.
> B. Yes, Dad?

A. We were goin' up the line near Passschendale...
   And all you could hear was the sounds of the guns and voices...
   'Shell hole on the right!' 'Shell hole on the left!'
   'Shell hole on the right!' 'Shell hole on the left!'
   'Shell hole on the right!' (in a woman's voice)
   Yes, there she was, comin' up the line with us.
   Mademoiselle from Armentieres!
B. Blimey, Dad, didn't you do any fighting at all?[2]

*****

We started to notice the war at the Grammar School when several of my contemporaries were evacuated to the United States. Without much thought as to the consequences, I envied them. I was happy at home but America seemed to be a very glamorous place. Kitchens had *refrigerators* from which people could help themselves to exotic foods and drinks. 'Teenagers' flirted at 'soda fountains' and drove battered motor cars. After some initial difficulty, Andy Hardy would invariably direct, sing and dance in a successful show and fall in love with Judy Garland (as did we all). Lewis Stone puffed his pipe and gave sage advice.

As mentioned earlier, as the months went by, Altrincham Grammar School began to lose some of its younger masters to military service. Some retired schoolmasters were brought back to fill the younger men's shoes and some women joined the staff. Following my parents' request to the school, I began to study German at the beginning of my second year (September 1938). War raged on a smaller scale in German lessons. The teacher, 'Pug' Page, sported a centre parting in his hair and wore thick 'pebble' glasses. The combination of the two made him appear quite menacing. He did occasionally resort to physical violence and we were all terrified of him. But although he was certainly a tyrant, he was nevertheless able to drive the basics of the language into the heads of his not always willing subjects.[3]

'Pug' was eventually called to serve in the Army (presumably as an interpreter) and was replaced by a young man named Higson. In contrast to 'Pug', Higson was perhaps too amiable. It was easy for a group of lively fourteen-year-olds to divert him from the main purpose of each lesson and encourage him to tell anecdotes about his relatively recent experiences as a student teacher in Germany. If suitably egged on, he would describe at length some of the duels fought by German university students and the scars they wore as badges of honour. We were fascinated by his Hitler Youth dagger with its inscription, 'Blüt und Ehre' (Blood and Honour). Higson had also replaced the school's physical training instructor, Sergeant-Major Hammond and so taught 'Gym', as well as German. Hammond favoured Army-type 'physical jerks'. Higson's approach was more up-to-date and his 'Physical Education' included a lot of work with apparatus for example the 'buck', the vaulting 'horse', the vaulting box and the parallel bars, He followed 'Pug' into the Army in 1941, joining Army Intelligence.

Another young teacher in the school, Len Bradbury, was something of a hero to the boys because he played for the first team of Manchester United Football Club. It was a surprise to many people when he declared himself to be a conscientious objector and was given a somewhat menial job at the Altrincham General Hospital. I do not remember that he was criticised at all but then there was not quite the same attitude to 'Conchies' that there had been during the First World War when objectors were denounced and white feathers were distributed to men who were vilified as cowards and treated with contempt. Only rarely were such feathers handed out during the Second World War.

At that time Manchester United was an averagely successful Club; certainly not the massive commercial enterprise that it is today. Footballers were paid very small wages for their efforts then. Who now remembers Rowley, Mitten, Pearson and others who had to get by on salaries of about ten pounds a week? In those days it was possible to enjoy the skills of one of the greatest of footballers, the late Sir Stanley Matthews, star of the Stoke and Blackpool Football Clubs; a sublime artist (with his feet) and a decent man. He was a credit to the game, unlike men such as the late George Best. It is incredible that, in Ireland, an airport has been named after that womaniser and alcoholic.

*****

Following the German successes in Belgium, France and, in particular, Dunkirk, the Grammar School authorities granted the summer holidays as usual but insisted that they should be spent at the school itself. The masters were asked to attend and find ways of occupying their pupils. They did their best by organising 'Spelling Bees', 'Brains Trusts', quizzes and word games. On the whole it was enjoyable for the boys but perhaps less so for the masters.

In both Liverpool and Sale we managed to adjust to the War reasonably well, minding our own business, eating less than we used to and, as the War progressed, bemusedly ignoring the exhortation, 'Second Front Now', pasted on the walls of many buildings.

The War intensified on 7 September 1940, marked by waves of German air attacks on the London docks. Thereafter few major cities were spared. Liverpool became one of the prime targets, suffering major raids in December 1940, March 1941 and May 1941. Manchester and its surrounding areas suffered equally. In Sale, we were issued with materials with which to build an 'Anderson Shelter', thought to provide some protection against enemy bombs. Named after the Home Secretary, Sir John Anderson, the shelter consisted of several sheets of corrugated iron. These sheets could be screwed together. Once that was done, the procedure was as follows: first it was necessary dig a deep hole at least the depth of a grave. The next step was to shore up the sides of the hole with metal sheets and then screw on the semi-circular roof. Finally the roof needed to be covered with earth and grass sods – 'convenient as a place to grow cabbages' – said one neighbour. He might have added that gas capes could be used as raincoats and that stirrup pumps were handy for watering flowers. A major air raid on Manchester took place at Christmas 1940 and then the Anderson shelters and the stirrup pumps were used for their intended purposes. The hundreds of incendiary bombs that rained down on the city created a devastating firestorm.

I cannot say that the choice of religious holidays by the Wehrmacht was deliberate but it is interesting that Manchester suffered its second heaviest air raid of the war at Whitsuntide 1941. Subsequent raids were not as frequent and eventually they seemed to peter out, at least until Christmas Eve 1944 when forty-five V1 Flying Bombs ('Doodlebugs') were aimed at the city.

One night at about eleven o'clock, my parents dragged me from bed during a particularly heavy attack. We ran down the stairs, out of the back door and into the shelter, finding our way by the light of a torch, carefully shielded as required by the Blackout Regulations. These Regulations were strictly observed and enforced by policemen and Air Raid Wardens, usually men considered too old for battlefront service. Often a cry was heard, 'Put that Bloody Light Out, or I'll Kick It Out'. The reminder was unnecessary. We had no intention of announcing our whereabouts to the enemy.

The earliest raids were carried out at first by Dornier aircraft ('Flying Pencils') and then by Heinkels. For some reason (German exactitude, perhaps?), the bombing was done on schedule. Quite convenient really. The Luftwaffe's routine became *our* routine. Each evening at about 9pm we would enter Mr Anderson's shelter. It smelt of melting candles and moist soil.

By 1941 we had all learned to adapt to different food. Dried egg powder replaced 'real' eggs. When it was available, 'Spam' took the place of fresh meat. We were glad of it and paid no heed to its carcinogenic nitrites. We were urged to eat lots of carrots because they were good for the eyesight. After all they were 'popular with the night-fighters!' (according to the government). Butchers' shops began to stock more offal and fishmongers introduced us to whale meat and to a curiously grey and tasteless fish, named *snoek*. The Ministry of Food issued 'snoek posters' and published a recipe for *snoek piquante*. We were not impressed.

I became quite fond of blackcurrant purée (strangely, no longer available), originally sold as a Vitamin C supplement for children. It was excellent filling for pies and was often given to us by Uncle Reg without the necessity to surrender any points. In fact, this was a little bit of grey-market dealing. Most farmers ate well during the war and some traded illegally on the side. Uncle Reg drove to a farm every weekend until the end of the 1940s and, in exchange for some *quid pro quo* he would be supplied with eggs, chicken parts and fresh fruit.

As the War progressed, food coupons and points became a frequent topic of conversation. This was particularly the case in 1942 when food supplies became very short. The Dutch East Indies (now Indonesia) fell to the Japanese in January. Much of Burma was snatched from the British in March. Convoys carrying precious supplies faced constant attack by U boats as they struggled through bitter seas to Murmansk, loaded with supplies for the then Russian ally, 'My Lovely Russian Rose' (as the song went).

On the credit side, Russian counterthrusts stopped the German advance at Stalingrad. The naval clash at Midway drove the first nail into the Japanese coffin.[4] 'Free French' troops,[5] with British and American troops invaded North Africa and finally prevailed against strong Italian and German forces, despite setbacks. German bombing attacks on Britain decreased whilst American and British attacks on Germany increased.

This progress was not made without heavy human cost. At Altrincham Grammar School, news of casualties among former students began to trickle in. Billy Muir – formerly a Senior Scout – was killed at sea. We heard (I don't know how) that Billy stood up in the cockpit just before his damaged plane spiralled downward and hit the water. He broke his neck.

I used to play marbles with Micky Weaver on the path outside the woodcraft room at AGS, near to the bicycle sheds. Flight Lieutenant Michael Weaver, Distinguished Flying Cross, died in action at the age of nineteen. In July 1943, I went off to a Summer Camp at Ullswater in the Lake District. Surgeon Lieutenant Malcolm Clow, an Old Boy of the School, joined us at the camp whilst on leave. Some months later, Malcolm died of exposure, swimming in the sea after his ship was torpedoed.

THE THIRD STEP

NAVY DAYS

– 6 –

Wake Up!

In 1943, after three interesting months in the sixth form at the Grammar School, I completed forms of application for the Navy under the 'Y' scheme. This scheme was devised for educationally qualified boys who were still at school but who were deemed to have 'officer potential'. After an interval of about a month I was instructed to attend for interview before a Naval Board at Crewe, Cheshire. The interview, I understood, would focus on why I wanted to join the Navy and what I had done to prepare myself. I would be asked what games I played and whether I was a member of an organisation such as the Air Cadet Corps, Sea Cadet Corps or the Boy Scouts. Since I had made a specific application to join the Fleet Air Arm, I would also be expected to be able to recognise different types of aircraft, both British and foreign.

Although somewhat pessimistic about my chances, I was successful at the interview in Crewe, even managing to recognise the Messerschmitts, Stukas and Zeros and one very odd British plane which bore the curious name, 'Walrus', officially entitled Naval D.H. 9A and manufactured by the former Westland Aviation Works. I cannot believe that at that stage the Walrus was still in use. But who knows?

I was told at the interview that I had been selected for the Fleet Air Arm and would be enrolled for six months in a University Naval Division where I would receive further academic education as well as officer cadet training. However, it would first be necessary for me to pass a comprehensive medical examination. This was particularly important because of my application for aircrew training. I was to return in two weeks. The two weeks passed quickly and once again I travelled to Crewe.

The medical examination was rigorous and unpleasant, largely because of the curt behaviour of the irascible naval surgeon who conducted it: Stand up! Lean to the right! Put your leg up! No – not that way – this way! Turn round! Lie down! Stand up! Lean to the left! Cover one eye! Not the *left* eye! The *right* eye! Wake up! Breathe into this tube and hold your breath for as long as you can! No. Not now! Wait until I tell you to begin! Wake up! Alright do it now. Yes, now! Humph! Get dressed. We'll write to you. No, not *that* door! The other door! Wake up!

The letter came about ten days later. Probably because of the breathing test, I had failed the medical examination for the Fleet Air Arm but I was accepted for a University Naval Division course leading to a commission in the Executive Branch. I accepted, attended for a further, final interview and was given the names of six universities that ran such courses. They were: Cambridge, Oxford, Edinburgh, Glasgow, Liverpool and Cardiff (University College). I contemplated the list. What little I knew about these universities I had gathered from my friend, Howard 'Joe' Curry who had been sent to Cambridge on a similar course, six months before mine would begin. During a period of leave, he extolled the virtues of his college, Jesus. Besides, Oxford and Cambridge were *the* universities, were they not? Founded in the thirteenth century, they were good enough for me. My order of preference was:

1. Cambridge
2. Oxford
3. Edinburgh
4. Glasgow
5. Liverpool
6. Cardiff.

Not perhaps paying full attention to the preferences of its new recruit, the Navy decided that I should go to *Cardiff*.

At the beginning of April – almost eighteen years old – I packed a suitcase, said goodbye to everyone and in a light spring drizzle I walked the length of Chestnut Drive to catch a Number 47 bus to Manchester's London Road Railway Station. There I boarded a London and North Eastern Railway (LNER) train for Cardiff, South Wales. In those days, Britain enjoyed a clean, efficient and (usually) comfortable rail system, operated by the LNER; the London, Midland and Scottish Railway (LMS); the Great Western Railway (GWR) and the Southern Railway (SR). Although I had been away from home before for Scout camps and holidays, I was apprehensive. There were too many unknowns. I had received some information about the course but what would it *really* be like? Could I deal with it? What would be the outcome?

The journey took only about five hours but it was an uncomfortable experience. The train was packed with servicemen and servicewomen and it was impossible to find a seat. For refreshments, I had scones (brought from home) and a cup of strong tea, snatched at one of the several stops from a trolley on the platform. At Cardiff Central Station I found a taxi and asked the driver to take me to the lodgings to which I had been assigned. I was to live in Llanishen Street for the first three months of the six-month course, sharing with Peter Meehan. Peter was a rather contemplative youth, a Roman Catholic who had attended Stonyhurst, one of the top Catholic boarding schools. The second three months were to be spent in Aberdare Hall, a residence for female students, emptied of its regular occupants for the summer.

Our landlady in Llanishen Street did her best to make us feel at home within the limitations of her household. A bath could be taken only once a week, using water derived from a boiler at the back of a fireplace in the kitchen. There was no electricity in the house and lighting was by oil lamp in the living room and by candlelight in the bedrooms. I used to read in bed. My candles never lasted long.

The day after our arrival, Meehan and I reported to the University, travelling there by bus. We assembled in one of the larger lecture rooms. There were sixty of us, all apprehensive, but nevertheless interested in the 'orientation' given by the Commanding Officer, a Professor of Physics, named Chubb. He was also a member of the Royal Naval Volunteer Reserve but with purely nominal duties. The real leader was a serving RNVR officer, Lieutenant D.G. Dodds, assisted by three serving Chief Petty Officers, CPO Hanford, CPO Thomas and CPO Rundall.

Rundall taught Seamanship and made sure that we became reasonably familiar with the *Seaman's Manual* and *King's Regulations and Admiralty Instructions.* Gunner's Mate Hanford was responsible for Field Training which he conducted in a concreted area ('The Ranch') that lay adjacent to one of the University buildings and a running track. He was a very strict drill-master, quick to spot mistakes. The first blunder was allowed to pass; the second meant that one had to run round the track with a .303 rifle held above one's head until told to stop. He would usually relent after a couple of circuits.

It was important not to play the role of superior officer cadet with Hanford. If you played square with him, he played square with you. He appreciated 'triers'. His vocabulary was rich, and served as an excellent introduction to 'the real thing'.

'All right, lads, let's be 'avin yer.'

Hanford was very smart, always immaculately turned out, with clean gaiters, well-pressed uniform and gleaming white shirt. After the War, I returned to the University College at Cardiff. I think that it was on the second or third day of my return that I bumped into former Chief Petty Officer Hanford in the corridor of one of the main buildings. He looked very seedy, with crumpled shirt, collar ends twisted, somewhat unshaven. He was wearing a brown duster coat and I understood that, as a civilian, he had been engaged as a 'porter' in the College. He had suffered much personal tragedy, and it showed. Apparently, his first wife had left him and his second had burnt to death in a fire. 'Hello, Chief,' I said. He peered at me, and then there came a look of recognition. 'Hello lad. Back then, are yer?'

He was the salt of the earth, like my friends in Ceylon, Commissioned Warrant Officer 'Shiner' Wright, Gunner's Mate 'Barney' Barnard and Chief Petty Officer Writer Freddy Hazelwood:

Barney: 'Ello, Nipper. Where yer been then? Shave orf, look at his eyes.
Freddy: What 'ave you been up to, lad?

Naval cadets at Aberdare Hall, University College of South Wales and Monmouthshire, Cardiff, 1944. The author is in the second row, 3rd from left.

Shiner: Blimey, Barney, I was at it myself, last night. I've got a taste in my mouth like the bottom of a birdcage. All shit and sand.
Barney: More like a vulture's crotch.

Strictly speaking, they were subordinate to me since by then I was a Sub-Lieutenant and they were commissioned warrant officers. But they helped me a lot. Without their support and encouragement, I would often have been lost. I was nineteen-and-a-half, or thereabouts, and they were in their forties. After over sixty years, they will have passed from the scene.

The University Naval Division course in Cardiff was divided between academic work of first year university level and naval training. My academic subjects were English, French and History. The lectures were interesting enough, even though some members of the staff were on temporary appointments. Many of the 'regulars' were away on war service. In addition to the academic and naval work each day, we were instructed to perform evening fire-watching duties on a roster system. This chore was performed once a week. We cadets would sleep on a camp bed in the porter's lodge. Before 'turning in' it was our duty to patrol the buildings, keeping alert to the possibility that incendiaries might have been dropped during an air raid (this never happened). One evening, I attempted to find my way in the dark to the lavatories attached to the men's cloakroom. I was walking quite briskly when suddenly I received a tremendous blow and found myself lying on the floor, completely dazed. I had walked into a coat peg. My mouth swelled to approximately twice the normal size and I was embarrassed for about two weeks. First, because of the jibes that came from members of the course, including the staff:

Rundall: 'Bit yer, did she lad?'

Second, because I was trying to impress a female medical student named Sally Chard. I was not at all successful.

The naval work was divided into several areas. Field Training meant formation drills and weapons training. Then there was 'Seamanship', for which the set text was the Navy's, *Seamen's Manual*. This invaluable guide included sections that were intended to be useful for all ranks. For example, it contained sections about different types of boat construction. It listed the 'Rules of the Road' and there were chapters relating to anchors and pulleys, blocks and tackle and the different varieties of ropes and hawsers. Navigation was an important subject. After the first few sessions, we were introduced to simulated 'at sea' conditions. The assumption was that a navigating officer would often have to work out the ship's position in difficult circumstances, that is, in a heavy storm or during enemy attack.

We were encouraged to work out 'fixes' as sirens screamed, bells rang and bellows were puffed.

In addition to Navigation, we were given some brief information about 'Radiolocation' (later called 'Radar'), practised knot-tying and hammock-slinging, and learned something about different types of naval dress, equipment and manners (for example, when and when not to salute). We learned that the naval salute is different from the Army and Air Force salute because deckheads (ceilings) were too low to permit of a full flourish. For similar reasons toasts were always drunk in a seated position.

The Division possessed several 12-foot sailing dinghies and also a motor cruiser. Once a week, we took these out into the harbour and imagined that we were in the open sea. Our uniforms were the regular sailor's uniforms, but we had the letters, 'UND' (University Naval Division) on our cap ribbons. If asked, we would (tongues in cheeks) tell people that this meant, 'United Nations Destroyers'.

The course at Cardiff was very packed and there was little leisure time. The evenings were occupied with preparation for the academic classes in French, English and History and by study of the books prescribed for naval training. In addition to the *Seaman's Manual*, these included the *Navigation Manual* and 'KR and AI', more formally known as *King's Regulations and Admiralty Instructions*.

Understandably, the Cardiff of 1944 was not the Cardiff of 2009. In 1944 (and indeed when I returned to the University in 1947) there was no Millennium Stadium, neither was there a Wales Millennium Centre. The National Assembly did not exist and capital city status had not been confirmed (this did not happen until 1955). The Cardiff Bay area, Bute Street and Tiger Bay were murky places to stay away from, or to pass through at speed. The docks still exported coal and they certainly did not provide a home for smart restaurants and cafes, as they do today. Sundays were usually free, and very quiet. Cardiff, like the rest of Wales at that time, was 'dry' on a Sunday and all the public houses and off-licence shops were closed.

*****

I had received no religious instruction as a child. Both my parents were brought up as low Anglicans and were forced to attend Sunday school and Bible classes and to attend church at least twice on Sundays. Their reaction to this régime in later life was a determination not to subject their own child to the same experiences. Nevertheless, whilst I was in Cardiff, I became certain that I should try to educate myself about the Church and its doctrines. I was certainly ready for some instruction, being just eighteen, away from home and becoming increasingly thoughtful about the 'meaning of it all'.

At a church in Newport Road, I attended classes for several weeks until I was ready to be confirmed as a member of the Anglican Church, in which I had been baptised as a baby. The confirmation ceremony took place at Llandaff Cathedral, one early summer evening. The cathedral had been hit by German bombs during an air raid in 1941, making it necessary for the service to be held within the roofless nave, open to the heavens. It was a perfect moonlit night, not at all uncomfortable. The organ played softly and the Bishop's voice was mellow. I was very affected by the setting.

After the ceremony, I began to attend church regularly. Sometimes, I would go to an Anglican church on a Sunday morning and to the Welsh Baptist 'Tabernacle' in the evening. Sunday night at The Tabernacle was the night for community singing by the choir, helped out by the 'WRENS',[1] 'ATS',[2] 'WAAFs',[3] soldiers, sailors and airmen who crowded the temple. The proceedings were led by a lay minister, named Richards. He was a small, red-faced, dynamic man, enthusiastic, sincere and persuasive. He would say a prayer or two and then, impresario-like, 'announce' a selection of hymns, to be sung by the choir, alone. They usually sang in Welsh and (if singers can have this) with the 'hwyl' that makes the back tingle. Following the presentation by the choir, Richards would lead the congregation in community hymn-singing. He would first ask everyone in the audience to sing; then the men alone and then the women alone. It was an emotional, uplifting experience.

Richards was a bank manager by trade but I am sure that his rewards, and those of all who met him, came from The Tabernacle. I hope that he received some national recognition for his service.

*****

As already mentioned, after a three-month stint in lodgings, we were moved into Aberdare Hall, in term-time the residence for female university students. It was a relief to have one's own room again, small though it was. The food was good by wartime standards and one could (and did) always go back for 'seconds' and 'thirds'. We were ready for it all after a gruelling day in the classroom, on The Ranch for Field Training, pulling a whaler round Cardiff harbour, or racing a 12-foot sailing dinghy.

There was one unusual incident during our stay in Aberdare Hall. The London Philharmonic Orchestra had undertaken a series of engagements in Cardiff at the City Hall, in the Temple of Peace, and at the Air Force base at Saint Athan. It was decided that, because of a shortage of conventional hotel accommodation, the members of the orchestra would be given rooms in Aberdare Hall, where the cadets were encouraged to speak to them and make them feel at home. One member of the UND's instructor staff was a certain Lieutenant Wall, a member of the University Faculty and a psychiatrist by profession. Wall had the ability to hypnotise groups of people. He had demonstrated this with the cadets in the front row of a lecture room. At his bidding the cadets performed all kinds of strange antics, including drinking from imaginary glasses of water, jumping up and down with their hands on their heads and standing *on* their hands (or trying to). But the Lieutenant failed with me. I suspect that I am a bad 'subject'.

Towards the end of the orchestra's stay in Aberdare Hall in the summer of 1944, it was decided that the University Naval Division would give a party for the musicians. Drinks were purchased, food was procured, speeches were made and cordialities exchanged. At a certain point in the party a member of the group suggested that Lieutenant Wall should be asked to hypnotise a few people. There were shouts of approval and he was urged to take action. Some thought that he should select all the violinists. Some agreed. Some disagreed. Others suggested that he should hypnotise one of the bassoon players. The chosen musician had a pronounced stutter. Could he be hypnotised so that he would, if only temporarily, lose the stutter? There was drunken agreement that this could be an interesting experiment. The bassoon player in question did not share the view of the majority. He flatly refused to be a guinea pig and was obviously embarrassed. It was all covered up with the serving of a fresh round of beer.

There is a sequel. In 1970, the London Philharmonic Orchestra visited Tokyo and the British Ambassador, Sir John Pilcher, gave a reception for the musicians. As one is expected to do, I circulated among the guests until I found myself next to a musician who had been with the orchestra for many years. I told him the story of the bassoon player who refused to be hypnotised. He said that he knew the bassoonist quite well. Apparently, the man had retired only recently.

*****

During our six months of study and training in Cardiff, we were preoccupied with anxieties and concerns that in a more global context would be regarded as insignificant. Could this essay be completed on time? Would one remember the differences between carvel and clinker? Could we explain why certain seventeenth-century poets are classified as 'metaphysical' and why? What is a 'cocked hat fix'? At the time it seemed imperative that we were able to find the correct answers to such questions but the world outside the boundaries of the University, Llanishen Street and Aberdare Hall had more serious issues to consider.

In early June 1944, Lieutenant Dodds absented himself for two weeks. When he returned to the University on or about the 12 June, he had nothing to say about what we had assumed to be his holiday. This seemed somewhat odd at the time but there was relatively little comment among the cadets. The Lieutenant was, after all, entitled to a break. It was only later in the year, just before the course ended, that he admitted off-handedly to having taken passage on one of the many naval vessels that were involved in 'Operation Overlord', the Allied invasion of Normandy which began on 6 June. Sections of the invasion fleet landed on the Normandy coast between the Orne River and Saint Marcouf, but Lieutenant Dodds did not go ashore with the invasion forces. The University Naval Division needed him in South Wales.

Our last three months in Aberdare Hall were critical ones for the Allies in the wider world. British and American armies, supported by Poles, Danes, Frenchmen and other nationalities, advanced across France from the West whilst the Russians tested German defences and continued to battle on the Eastern front.

A less crucial kind of reckoning came for us at the end of our six-month sojourn in Cardiff. This took the form of an examination in Seamanship, Navigation, Field Training, Signalling and Administration. In addition, there were examinations in academic subjects. When the results were announced, I was disappointed. I had passed in the academic subjects and I had done quite well in Seamanship, Field Training, Signalling and Administration. I had, however, achieved a poor result in Navigation and, in consequence, had 'dipped' (failed) the course. I was not alone. Over half of those on the course of sixty people had also 'dipped'. That was of little consolation and it was not comforting to hear that the reason people were being failed was because the demand for naval officers had decreased. There had been fewer war casualties than had been anticipated in recent months. I had failed the course but that did not alter the fact that I was still in the Navy. It would have been possible to withdraw but, if one did, it meant (so it was said) an immediate call-up into the Army. My very good friend, Roy Hanson, 'dipped' a similar course at Cambridge, six months after I had completed mine. Undeterred by the warnings about call-ups, he elected to be discharged. Discharged he was, with a small gratuity and a demobilisation suit. He then volunteered for the Royal Air Force and was accepted as a Russian language trainee on a course conducted at Trinity Hall in Cambridge. He qualified, was made a Sergeant, and spent the rest of his time in the service, attached to the Foreign Office as a translator of Russian scientific documents. Roy's daughter, Susan (now a lawyer in the British Civil Service) told me that Roy's written Russian was

> pretty good, but his spoken Russian was terrible. I never remember him speaking it, but I know that when it came to his mock oral, his examiner congratulated him on getting the stress wrong on every syllable of every word. When it came to the real thing, he was at his brother's wedding, and it proved impossible to re-schedule, so as he got such high marks on his written, they passed him anyway.

It was during his stint with the 'Office' that Roy met Isobel who became his wife. After his second demobilisation, he returned a third time to Trinity, to study law this time, and earned a First Class Degree. I decided to stay on in the Navy to take my chances.

– 7 –

The Holiday Camp
and Worse

In early October 1944, still in the Navy, I was posted to Skegness in Lincolnshire. The 'stone frigate' (naval establishment) at Skegness was a former holiday camp, commandeered by the Navy and re-named 'King Arthur'. Billy (later Sir Billy) Butlin founded the camp in 1936 for holidaymakers interested in an economical package holiday. It offered many facilities, including provision for the care of young children, and handsome, red-capped organisers to please the ladies. Butlin established a similar camp at Clacton and another at the Welsh resort, Phwelli. Before the War interrupted Butlin's plans, he planned to open other camps. The idea was not an original one. Butlin, who started out as a 'barker' in a circus, modelled his camps on those organised by a Mr Cunningham in the Isle of Man. These 'men-only' camps were introduced in 1894 in an atmosphere of fellowship. Butlin's was more 'jazzy' and very large, accommodating over two thousand holidaymakers. During a hot summer, Skegness – with its family chalets, its ballrooms and its swimming pools – might have been quite pleasant.

If you enjoyed sharing your annual holidays with people from different milieus and of different ages, shapes and sizes, then Butlin's was the place for you. But as a naval establishment 'King Arthur' was awful. Four to six sailors were accommodated in each unheated chalet, intended originally for two people. All items that might have provided some comfort were removed. I do not know if this paring-down was the Navy's idea, or if it was at Mr Butlin's request. Whatever the reason, the atmosphere at 'King Arthur' was more that of a prison camp than a naval barracks. When allowed out of the camp, one felt like a 'trusty' and, of course, one was always likely to be subjected to a body search at any time before departure. The naval police were looking, usually, for excessive quantities of tobacco and rum (issued duty free), to be sold on the outside. It all seems very innocent now in these days of needles and hard drugs.

We sailors ate uneasily in Butlin's empty ballrooms, defying the ghosts of the peacetime dancers. The wind cut like a sword through the open spaces between the chalets and the sea and frequent showers of icy rain lashed barbed wire entanglements on a beach that was deserted even by the birds. On the day of my arrival, I was issued with a gas mask, a hammock, a blanket and a kitbag. The hammock was not required at 'King Arthur' for we had Billy Butlin's bunks. On the second day, all newcomers were subjected to a 'short arm' inspection (a check for venereal disease) and then to a battery of psychological tests. These were intended to place recruits in different job categories: Stoker, Electrician, Artificer, Seaman, etc. It was decided that I should become a 'Writer', that is, a clerk who would normally be attached to a Captain's Office. Off came the seaman's clothing and I was issued instead with a dark blue serge jacket with matching trousers, worn with a white shirt and a black tie, instead of a seaman's jersey and collar. Then there followed some superficial training as winter announced itself earlier than usual and the cases of pneumonia increased in the sick bay.

The training did not last very long, perhaps two weeks. Then jobs were allocated. I was given the task of sweeping the lanes between six blocks of chalets, cleaning the 'heads' (lavatories), intended to serve perhaps a quarter of the camp personnel, and 'squeegeeing' the floors of the ante rooms to the gymnasium. I liked the gymnasium chores because it was warmer inside than outside, but I could have passed up the lavatory work since neither the toilets nor the seats were treated with respect. A row of eight lavatories was perched on a single drain. One day, this strange example of the plumber's art encouraged some wag to light a newspaper at one end of the row and float it down the drain, to the consternation of those occupying the eight thrones.

I disliked sweeping the road, first because of the exposure to the cruel winds of Lincolnshire and second because it seemed that as fast as I swept, another pile of refuse would form. Maddened, I attacked each layer with concentrated fury and resentment. My brush was a lance raised hopelessly against the oncoming hordes. The detritus shifted uneasily before my onslaught but still it came on. Empty cigarette packets, rotten leaves, old toothpaste tubes, spent condoms, the occasional small bottle, a dirty, gap-toothed comb or two. Thankfully, these were the days before mineral waters were distributed in cans, so there were no flip tops. In summary, 'King Arthur' disgraced its gallant namesake. This was no place for knights. It was fit only for scullions.

I was drafted to Skegness in 1944. In 1940 Cecil Day Lewis, under his pseudonym, Nicholas Blake, published a detective story entitled *Malice in Wonderland*. The book describes a series of unpleasant pranks that end in murder at a new holiday camp, obviously based on Butlin's. The setting seemed to me to be entirely appropriate.

I enjoyed only one feature of my time at 'King Arthur'. Every day, on its way to Divisions, the Royal Marine Band would swing by, and swing it did, with the raciest version of 'A Life on the Ocean Wave' that I have ever heard. Of course, there were other occasional diversions such as a trip in the 'liberty boat', that is, the barracks bus, to the small seaside town of Skegness. I attempted this on my first free afternoon. I was issued with a shore pass and after pressing my trousers and donning a clean, white shirt, I joined a queue at the camp's main exit. When I reached the guardhouse at the gates, I heard the command 'Off Caps!' I took my cap off and a member of the Shore Patrol police popped something into it. With the following command 'On Caps!' I put the cap on again and felt something soft fall into my hair. After boarding the bus, I took off the cap and inspected the object. It was a carefully wrapped rubber condom. This was one approach the Navy had adopted towards the prevention of venereal diseases. I would not, for the world, have admitted to my companions that this was only the second or third time that I had even *seen* a condom!

Skegness boasted only one or two good pubs. But it did have some Olde Tea Rooms left over from a past era. The meat-paste sandwiches were adequate and the sticky cakes were not too dry. The food was no great attraction but the place was reasonably warm and after all there was The Entertainment, a trio of elderly ladies dressed in black bombazine and equipped with 'cello, violin, piano, and a repertoire drawn from Sigmund Romberg, Franz Lehar and the like. There was one other place, a kind of snack-bar that sold rather grey sandwiches and cakes, made without butter and not much sugar. But the bar *did* have a juke box, featuring a selection of some of the popular songs of the day.

Perhaps one good thing can be said in favour of Skegness. In the 1930s, the notorious Rector of Stiffkey was unfrocked for allegedly having committed various indecent acts. After his disgrace, he joined a circus and was eaten by a lion in a Skegness amusement park.

*****

After seven weeks in Skegness, I was informed that I would be sent to 'HMS Duke' for further training. By this time, I was an expert on toilet techniques. I could handle a squeegee like a champion and I was an adept with a yard brush. I had also added considerably to my vocabulary. I noticed that the four-letter word beginning with 'f' was a favourite with all my colleagues. It was used so often as an adjective that it had almost lost its original meaning. We had been told this at Cardiff in the form of an anecdote:

> Ordinary Seaman (when bucket of water spills on the deck): 'F ... the bucket!'
> Lieutenant: 'If you can do that, lad, I'll promote you to Leading Seaman!'

Well, here I was. I had become the most efficient road-sweeper in Lincolnshire. Now I had *effing* well been transferred somewhere else for more *effing* training. Where was the *effing* place, anyway? In *effing* Malvern, not too far from the well-known public school.

Although my new-found skill would now be wasted, I left Skegness for Malvern with no great feeling of desolation. 'HMS Duke' was a much better ordered 'ship' than 'King Arthur'. In some ways, the training duplicated that given at Cardiff, but no harm in that. The course was intended to introduce all the participants to Drill, Weapons Training, Seamanship and Naval Regulations. The discipline was strict. We were under the charge of an instructor named Bell, nicknamed – naturally – 'Dingle'. A Canadian with the rank of Able Seaman, Dingle was very dapper and exceptionally clean. His jersey and trousers were always neatly pressed; his collars immaculate, in an appropriately washed-out shade of blue. When naval collars were issued by the stores ('slops'), they were dark-blue, with white edging. New recruits were advised by older hands to bleach the collar so that it assumed, as quickly as possible, the faded look that was considered *de rigeur* by members of the lower deck. It was also intended to give the impression that the wearer had 'got some time in'.

It was surprising to hear, some months after our course had finished, that Dingle had been stripped of his rank and demoted to Ordinary Seaman. He had apparently been caught with an over-supply of duty-free tobacco.

We were awakened at 5.30 every morning and at 5.45 we ran in columns up the hill to the gymnasium. There we were subjected to an hour of physical training, including what seemed like endless press-ups.

But there was also work with apparatus, particularly the climbing ropes, the beam and the box horse. My interest in and facility for physical training at the Grammar School proved to be very useful. I would not have liked to have been a weakling in that company and with those PTIs (Physical Training Instructors). After PT, we ran down the hill again and assembled for breakfast, after which the day's professional training began.

In addition to the regular training programme during the day, we were assigned 'shore duties', on a regular shift basis. In small groups we took over the duties of the naval police. Our job was to ensure that all ratings with shore passes returned on time; that there was no undue brawling in pubs; that the drunks were safely stowed away and that certain residential areas were not disturbed by over-exuberant trainee sailors. We revelled in our brief authority but knew that those we harassed could be the *harassers* on the following night when *we* were on shore leave. Hence, authority, for the sake of self-interest, was not abused.

There was little leisure time at 'Duke' but at the end of the Malvern experience, I was very fit and felt that I had learned more of the idiosyncratic ways of the Senior Service. My vocabulary had certainly become richer, containing at least some of the following words and phrases:

Chokka: Fed-up.

Two blocks: Fed-up.

Sippers: A share of someone else's rum ration. In those days, all naval ratings were entitled to a serving of rum each day. Those under the age of twenty were not allowed to 'draw'. They were written up in the records as 'UA', 'under age'. Teetotallers over the age of twenty were able to claim a small allowance 'in lieu'. The rum was served under very strict conditions under the supervision of a Chief Petty Officer. The 'tot' could not be saved, given to someone else or put into a bottle or other container. It had to be drunk on the spot, when served. Needless to say, these regulations were often breached.

Gulpers: A larger share of someone else's rum ration.

No. 1: The second in command of a vessel.

Jaunty: A regulating petty officer.

The Golden Rivet: Hypothetical rivet said to be in the keel of every ship. New recruits were given a lot of information about this so-called rivet, all deliberately misleading or scatological.

Brown Hatter: Homosexual.

Shave off: 'Oh, dear', 'Damn', 'Dear me' and other exclamations.

Permission to grow: Seeking permission to grow a beard.

Scotch Mist: Urine. This was derived from the idea that the Scots are mean. Used often in the rather meaningless sentence, 'What do you think this is? Scotch Mist?'

Dhoby: A washerman or washerwoman.

Dhoby itch: Said to be caused by excessive soap. A form of ringworm named *tinea cruris*.

OD: Ordinary deckhand, Ordinary seaman.

NAAFI (1): Navy Army and Air Force Institutes.

NAAFI (2): (But see above.) 'No aim, no ambition and f…all interest.'

Rabbits: Gifts.

Bint: Girl (from the Arabic).

Party: Girl ('I met a smashing party, last night').

Pusser: Smartly dressed. Smartly 'turned out'.

Roll on my twelve: Regular naval ratings had to sign on, initially, for a period of twelve years. This was a plea for the time to pass quickly.

Duff: Suet or jam pudding.

Aggie Weston's: A naval hostel in Chatham.

Slops: A naval clothing store.

Snottie: Midshipman.

Tailor mades: Commercially rolled cigarettes.

Oppo: Friend (as in 'opposite number').

Pigs: As in 'them pigs up aft' (i.e. commissioned officers).

*****

In late January 1945, I was transferred again, this time for specific training as a 'Writer'. Again, I packed my kitbag, folded my hammock, checked my gas-mask case and journeyed by truck and train to 'HMS Cabbala', yet another stone frigate. This one was in Lowton Saint Mary's, a small village in the Northwest of England. Here we were given a brief overview of naval accounting procedures, bookkeeping, store-keeping and inventory control.

Perhaps the most useful part for the future was the introduction to touch typing. Over the years, alas, I have allowed the technique to wither. No longer do I use the little finger of the left hand to operate *a*, or the third, second and first fingers for the remaining keys of the left sections, *d, f*. I have certainly forgotten how to use the third, second and first fingers of the right hand to operate *l, k* and *j*. I rely, mainly, on the first finger of the left hand and the first finger of the right hand, supported occasionally, by the second finger of the right hand. The little fingers never come into play at all.

*****

At the beginning of March 1945, I 'passed out' from 'Cabbala' and was given a week's leave. I was now a qualified 'Writer', attached to 'HMS Drake' in Devonport, one of the three Port Divisions, Plymouth, Portsmouth and Chatham. My number (never to be forgotten) was DMX 658773 (the 'D' in the 'DMX' signified Devonport).

'HMS Drake' was originally established as the Royal Naval Barracks in 1892 and given the name 'HMS Vivid'. In 1934 it was re-named 'HMS Drake'. The barracks was built to accommodate approximately five thousand men but, when I arrived, the many different buildings were grossly overcrowded and occupied by far more than the intended maximum. We were distributed among wooden huts and slept in hammocks, slung from iron stanchions. During the day, these hammocks were stowed at one end of each hut. The trick was to haul your hammock from the pile and sling it as soon as you possibly could in the early evening. If you were slow, then it was impossible to find a space and it became necessary to manage on the concrete floor. When slung, the hammocks were literally only a breath apart.

Overall, the conditions at 'Drake' were appalling. The only possible justification was that this was a time of War. The food was very unattractive. Eggs were fried with oil, in large metal containers. Occasionally flakes of rust would detach themselves from the sides of the containers and fall into the grease. The numbers were so large in the mess halls that it was almost necessary to fight for the food. The sanitary arrangements were crude and overworked. Lavatory doors were only *half* doors. Very few of them could be locked and there was little privacy. Heating was grossly inadequate, given that it was a cold, wet and windy February. During my time at 'Drake', I developed haemorrhoids, probably caused by constipation resulting from poor food and my reluctance to use the unpleasant 'heads' (lavatories). Next, I began to lose a good deal of hair, leading to a large, bald patch on the right-hand side of my head. It could be covered, only partially, by my cap. The barber at the barracks suggested that this baldness was the result of *scabies* and – rather ostentatiously, I thought – put his combs and brushes into antiseptic after he finished trimming what hair was left. Later, during a short leave, I saw a doctor in Sale who diagnosed *ringworm* and said that I should have my whole head shaved. Like the barber, the doctor was wrong. The condition turned out to be *alopecia*, probably caused by the poor conditions at the barracks and the nervous strain of coping with them. I remained partially bald for a year until the garden started to flourish again.

The first two weeks at 'Drake' were given over to a short training course. This included a swimming test which required that one should swim for a couple of lengths, fully dressed; a fire-fighting exercise, during which a very real and quite alarming fire had to be extinguished and a gas-mask test, which involved walking through a chamber filled with poisonous gas. The last of these three tests was treated lightly and yet this was a moment in the War when Hitler's advisers were urging him to use the 'Verzweiflungswaffe', the 'weapons of despair' (poison gases).

After the course came to an end, I was attached to the Service Certificate Office to await posting. My duties there were very light, filing certificates and updating the records of sailors who were about to be transferred to a ship or to another shore establishment. There was time for gossip when this could be carried on without attracting the attention of the Chief Petty Officer in charge. We ratings developed the technique of talking through the sides of our mouths, with minimum use of the lips. Similar techniques are employed by the inmates of such prisons as Wormwood Scrubbs, Pentonville, Strangeways and Dartmoor.

I performed my work, such as it was, at a table where sat an attractive Wren and a three-badge AB (an Able Seaman who has had over twenty-one year's service: one stripe or badge for each seven years). Oddly, I do not now remember what the Wren looked like but I do remember the AB. He was a curly-haired Irishman who, apart from the hair, looked a little like the late American actor, Barry Fitzgerald. He had the stage Irishman's stock of anecdotes, a favourite subject being what he would do when he was demobilised.

> *Paddy:* Buyin' and sellin', that's what I'm going to do, lad. And that's what you should do, too.
> *V.C.B:* But *buy* what, and *sell* what?
> *Paddy:* It doesn't matter, lad, just buyin' and sellin'.

It was possible, three times a week, to receive permission to spend the night 'ashore'. Such shore leave started at about 5pm and lasted until 7am the next morning. Sailors who returned after that time were put on a 'charge'.

These breaks, away from the barracks, were very welcome, although the accommodation available in the town was not of the finest. I would spend the night of freedom at Aggie Weston's (a seaman's hostel),[1] the Salvation Army Hostel, or the YMCA. A bunk bed and a coarse brown blanket could be hired for a very small fee. In some ways, these were really 'doss houses', but they performed a useful service.

The city of Plymouth was bombed badly in the early part of the War and there were many devastated areas, with very few places of entertainment. I do however, remember going to the cinema one Sunday. This was quite an event because, in Britain, cinemas were usually closed on the Sabbath. Exceptions were made during the War. The end result was that cinemas continued to operate on Sundays after the War was over. Giving way to television, many have now turned themselves into Bingo Halls or have become derelict.

Spring came and with it an improvement in my spirits. I discovered a baker's shop which still made good 'tiddly oggies' (Cornish pasties) and I started to develop a taste for 'scrumpy', the rough cider of Somerset. It was good to be able to walk on the Hoe, gazing at the ocean in the pale sunlight and standing where Drake is supposed to have stood.

It was during such an evening stroll that it occurred to me that I should look into the possibility of obtaining a commission. The War against Germany was about to end but there remained the struggle against Japan.

On 7 May 1945, Admiral Karl Doenitz sent General Alfred Jodl to Rheims, to offer Germany's unconditional surrender to the Allied Forces. Jodl was Chief of the Operations Section of the Wehrmacht. At the Nuremberg Trials, he was sentenced to death by hanging and Doenitz received a sentence of ten years in prison.

I was still in the barracks in Devonport, waiting for a posting. On 8 May, I joined in the D-Day celebrations on Plymouth Ho. But what next? It was up to me.

– 8 –

The Midshipman

One morning at the Service Certificate Office, I was searching for a file when I came across a collection of *King's Regulations and Admiralty Instructions* and *Admiralty Fleet Orders*. One of the Fleet Orders carried an announcement about recruitment for the Special Branch. Applications were invited for a confidential course which could lead to a commission as a Cypher Officer. With nothing to lose I applied, encouraged by the Chief Petty Officer Writer. Two weeks later I was interviewed by two officers in Devonport. The interview was successful and I was told that I would now have to go to another Port Division, Chatham ('HMS Pembroke'), for a selection board. A few days later, I packed my kitbag, rolled up my hammock and prepared to leave Devonport by naval truck. A sailor in seaman's rig helped me to load the hammock and then jumped in himself. Like me, he was on his way to the Chatham Selection Board. This was my first meeting with Anthony Weldon Tubbs, a Coder by rank and an Old Etonian by education.

On the day after my arrival in Chatham, I appeared before a Selection Board of five senior officers. Why had I made this application? Why did I think that I would be suited to the Special Branch? What was I doing now? What was my educational background? Did I play cricket? What were my other hobbies? What happened at Cardiff? Why did I 'dip'?

I was one of about thirty candidates. After the Selection Board had seen all of these, we were asked to wait in a large auditorium. An officer climbed onto the platform. 'I'm going to read out a list of names. If you hear your name, you should leave the hall and wait outside for further instructions.' He read out the list of about twenty names, quite slowly. Mine was not among them. My heart sank. Must I go back to barracks? No. Those *left in the hall* (ten people only) had been accepted.

For two weeks, we successful candidates were attached to offices in Chatham Barracks and given some make-work. Tony Tubbs had also been selected. He and I enjoyed several dinners together in a local restaurant. The wine was passable and even the wartime food was quite palatable.

At the end of the two-week period, we were issued with travel warrants and boarded a train for Alton, a market town in Hampshire, of interest to literary historians because Jane Austen's brother, Henry, had once established a bank there (Austen, Gray & Vincent).

Officially, we were attached to 'HMS Mercury', a communications centre. In fact, we were to undergo training at a large country house situated just outside Alton. It was a pleasant place with high-ceilinged rooms and a large terrace with steps leading down to the lawn and large garden. There were ten men and four women on the course. Instruction was given by a Lieutenant, Special Branch and, occasionally, by the Director, a Commander, also Special Branch. We were given intensive instruction in the use of the Morse Code by three methods – lamp, semaphore and sound – in encoding and decoding and in communications' procedures. We were (and are?) subject to the provisions of the Official Secrets Act and were obliged to sign a statement acknowledging that we had read it and would abide by its strictures.

Much of the instruction related to the use of an encryption algorithm known as the 'one-time pad', a very secure method of enciphering. The problem with the one-time pad, however, is that it is very slow. We were therefore introduced to machine cyphering. This was then done on either of two different devices, the 'Typex' and the 'CCM' (Combined Cypher Machine). We received a good deal of practice on these machines which were rotor-based and built along lines similar to the 'Enigma', a machine that since the end of the War has been the subject of many magazine articles, television documentaries and at least one film. The drums, or 'rotors' could produce a very large number of permutations calculated by one cryptographer to be not far short of six thousand million million million.

The course was very intensive – but interesting – and there were some pleasant interludes such as occasional games of croquet in the large garden of the country house. One morning, we were informed that one of the cadets had lost his file of notes which, fortunately, had been discovered somewhere in the garden. He was reprimanded immediately and sent back to barracks.

On 6 August 1945, we were still learning our trade at Alton when it was revealed on the radio and in the newspapers that a powerful bomb had destroyed the city of Hiroshima in Japan. On 9 August we were told that a second bomb had obliterated Nagasaki. Our course had come to an end and we were enjoying a short period of home leave when news came of the formal Japanese surrender that took place on the USS *Missouri* in Tokyo Bay on 2 September. Emperor Hirohito had signed the Imperial Rescript for surrender on the 'Fourteenth Day of the Eighth Month of the Twentieth Year of *Showa*' (i.e. 14 August 1945).

Without exception we were all very relieved at the news of the surrender. There is no doubt at all that if an invasion of Japan had proved necessary, the casualties on both sides would have been enormous and the fighting, city by city, town by town, village by village, might have continued for months and perhaps years. The Japanese War Minister, Rikugun Daijin, was implacably opposed to the surrender and suggested that the entire nation should fight as *kamikaze*:

> That we will inflict severe losses on the enemy when he invades Japan is certain, and it is by no means impossible that we may be able to reverse the

Cypher Group at country-house training centre in Alton, Hampshire, 1945. 'There were ten men and four women on the course.' The author is standing precariously balanced third from left.

situation in our favour, pulling victory out of defeat. Further, our army will not submit to demobilisation. Our men will simply not lay down their arms. And since they know they are not permitted to surrender, since they know that a fighting man who surrenders is liable to extremely heavy punishment, there is really no alternative for us but to continue the fight.[1]

Fortunately, the Minister's comments were ignored. We had been spared the worst.

*****

A month before our course ended in mid-August 1945, a representative from Gieves (now Gieves and Hawkes), came to the House. Gieves had for many years been tailors to the military and, in particular, the Navy. We were to be measured for officer's uniforms. There was some trepidation since the final examination had not yet taken place. What would happen to the uniforms of those who failed? Fortunately, we all passed with the exception of one man whose given name was Neville (I cannot recall his family name). He was obliged to repeat the course. I do not know whether he was successful and so able eventually to don his new uniform.

After two days' additional briefing and preparation, we were allowed a week's leave before joining the third of the Port Divisions at Portsmouth ('HMS Victory'), to await posting. I had become a Midshipman, Special Branch. The other members of the group were given the rank of Sub-Lieutenant, or the Wren equivalent of that rank. I could not be a Sub-Lieutenant until I had attained the age of nineteen-and-a-half. I was just over nineteen. I still have a rueful memory of the incredulous look cast at me at Euston Station by a grizzled 'three-badge' AB (Able Seaman) as he leaned out of the window of his train, with his cap perched at the back of his head. With a Tch! Tch! Tch! he slowly wagged his head from side to side.

*****

After my home leave came to an end, I took the train to London and celebrated success with other members of the Alton group. We were able to secure tickets for a revue at the Criterion Theatre in Piccadilly and afterwards had dinner in a nearby restaurant. It was exhilarating and very different from the barracks at Devonport where, only a few months earlier, I had learned my trade as a lavatory cleaner!

At 'HMS Victory' we enjoyed the luxury of sheets and food in the officers' mess, preceded by evening drinks in the wardroom. We were also enrolled in another field training course, supervised by a Gunner's Mate. 'Straighten your shoulders, please sir! Gentlemen, by the left, quick march!' Finally there came news of our postings. Four of the male members of the course, including me, were to be sent to Ceylon (now Sri Lanka) to await further dispersal. There followed another week's leave during which I received instructions to report to the troopship, *Athlone Castle*, at Southampton.

In September 1945, I said goodbye to my parents and set out on another journey. This time, I did not have to carry a kitbag down the length of Chestnut Drive but was equipped instead with an attaché case. A metal trunk had been sent to the ship ahead of my departure.

I shared a carriage on the train with Alan Nicholson, a Sub-Lieutenant in the Engineering branch and an Old Boy of Altrincham Grammar

Cypher Group at the House in Alton, Hampshire, 1945. 'Fortunately, we all passed with the exception of one man.' The author is standing far left, with his left foot on a step. Tony Tubbs is standing in the centre of the photo, back row. Four of the Wrens pictured were staff members at the House in Alton.

School. In addition to approximately fifteen hundred sailors, soldiers and marines, my closest companions on board the ship were Alan and three former members of the Alton course, Tom and Eric (I forget their surnames) and Tony Tubbs.

I had got to know Tony well at Alton and was invited to spend a weekend at his home. Tony lived in Chalfont Saint Giles (Buckinghamshire), in a large house of mellowed brick, with spacious grounds. We arrived after lunch on the first day. After we had changed into civilian clothes, Tony suggested that we should go shooting in the local woods. I was provided with an expensive-looking gun (a Purdey side-by-side), a pocketful of cartridges and some rudimentary instructions about what to do and what not to do. We tramped over the wet leaves and grass and poked about in the bushes in search of unsuspecting rabbits. Climbing a grassy knoll, we made our way down a narrow path quite close to the Clivedon Estate.

We had just circled a cluster of young saplings when I thought that I detected some movement to my left and then, suddenly, to my right. Startled, I discharged my gun involuntarily, to my chagrin and to Tony's disgust. He would not be mollified until, after thirty minutes or so, he caught sight of a rabbit that was too slow off the mark and managed to shoot it. This was unfortunate for the rabbit but fortunate for me.

The highlight of my visit to the Tubbs was each morning's breakfast. It was served as one might expect in a house with that style. Despite the War, there were maids to serve, fetch and carry. One could come down to the dining room at any reasonable time. The food was laid out in silver dishes over warmers on the sideboard. There was always a choice of boiled, poached or fried eggs, sausages, bacon, kippers and haddock, supplemented by crisp rolls and ample supplies of toast. The lavishness of the Tubbs's breakfast table was an example of the family's affluent way of living – uninterrupted, it seemed – by the War.

In 1947, after we had been demobilised, I was invited to Tony's engagement party at the Dorchester Hotel. Unfortunately, I lost contact with Tony after that and have not met him since.

*****

The *Athlone Castle* was commissioned by the British government early in the War to move troops from zone to zone. For this particular voyage she was to skirt delicately through the mined waters of the Bay of Biscay and then proceed via Port Said to Aden and Colombo. Although she had been converted for the mass transportation of troops, she bore some signs of her earlier – more pampered – existence. The saloons were still panelled with mahogany and cherry-wood veneer and it was possible to guess where the swimming pools had been.

I was very pleased to be allocated a cabin to myself. In the ship's cruising days the cabin probably served as second-class accommodation, being on the starboard (right-hand) side of the ship, supposedly the hottest side for the outward voyage. Nevertheless, I found my quarters to be quite comfortable.

It was a long voyage but the monotony was relieved by the ship's radio with its announcements about various activities, punctuated by music that came from its limited supply of gramophone records. There was a small ship's library stocked with old novels by writers such as Alexandre Dumas, Baronness Orczy and Eden Phillpots. These 'hardbacks' were shelved side-by-side with fairly up-to-date Penguin books, received as donations to the Navy. Penguins cost only sixpence in the old currency and, being more or less pocket-sized, they could be carried very easily.

I had packed a thin anthology of contemporary (i.e. 1940s) poetry which included a short poem about the War. John Pudney's, 'For Johnny', was used as a theme in a popular wartime film, *The Way to the Stars*, featuring among others the actress Jean Simmons in her first role and Bonar Colleano, a gifted American actor. Given the heavy casualties suffered among RAF pilots during the so-called 'Battle of Britain' (and later during bombing raids over Germany), 'For Johnny' tugged at the emotions:

Do not despair
For Johnny-head-in-air;
He sleeps as sound
As Johnny underground.

Fetch out no shroud
For Johnny-in-the-cloud;
And keep your tears
For him in after years.

Better by far
For Johnny-the-bright star,
To keep your head,
And see his children fed.[2]

Tombola was another diversion for those who did not care to read. Now called 'Bingo' (at least by civilians), Tombola has been played in the Navy for many years. It was only after the War had ended that the game became popular throughout Britain. Tombola and Bingo have similar rules but the language is different. No doubt the modern Navy has been obliged to update some of this language because of rising inflation:

Eyes down!
Eleven! One! One! Legs Eleven!
Eyes down!
Seventy-Six. Seven and Six.
Was she worth it?

Reading, Tombola, cards, self-improvement. Entertained by these various diversions, we enjoyed a calm and uneventful passage through the Bay of Biscay and the Mediterranean. Then came a one-day stop at Port Said with an opportunity to go ashore; enjoy the conjuring of the *gully-gully* man with his day-old chicks and haggle for camel-skin pouffes at Simon Artz, an emporium visited through the years by legions of tourists and servicemen and -women. After Port Said, we cut through the Suez Canal, still a joint British and French possession, and on into the slate-blue 'Red' Sea before entering the Indian Ocean and sailing towards Ceylon, arriving alongside at the port of Colombo in the early morning.

I had never been 'abroad' before. Ceylon was to provide me with my first experience of another country and another culture.

*****

Once ashore, I was met by a naval rating with a truck and driven to the shore establishment, 'HMS Lanka', to await further posting. 'Lanka' consisted of a number of long low 'basha' huts. Some of these served as barracks for ratings. Others were divided into one-room chalets, accommodating one or two officers. In contrast to my experience at 'Royal Arthur', I did not have to share a room and the temperature was in the plus eighties rather than in the minus nines. I forgot the inadequate heaters of the Skegness mess halls and welcomed Colombo's warmth. The cold, salt smell of the North Sea was replaced by the sweet odours of frangipani and coconut oil.

I saw everything in dazzling colours. The lush vegetation around 'Lanka' was emphatically green; the mellowed Dutch colonial buildings of York Street were a startling white and the skies a perfect blue.

*****

I can't remember that I had many official duties at 'Lanka' for the first
two weeks, except to attend morning Divisions, the daily parade. At the
beginning of the third week however, I was ordered to report to the
Captain's Office dressed in 'No. 10s', the Navy's tropical dress uniform. This
'rig' consisted of white trousers and a long, white, brass-buttoned tunic,
fastened at the neck. I had been chosen to take a bag of confidential
papers to Admiral Lord Louis Mountbatten's Southeast Asia Command
(SEAC) headquarters in Kandy.

On the next morning, feeling somewhat self-important, I collected a
sealed canvas bag and was then taken by car to Colombo Railway Station
where I boarded a train for Kandy. We arrived in the early evening and
there I was met by a fierce-looking, moustachioed Sikh sailor who drove
me in a well-polished jeep to the SEAC complex. I delivered the papers and
– receipt in pocket – was then driven to a large hotel. After registering, I
had a welcome drink and an equally welcome dinner before retiring early
to my room where I undressed and crawled under the mosquito net to
ponder, before sleep, the events of the day.

The next morning, I enjoyed a splendid breakfast and then, shortly
afterwards, I took the lift down to the lobby, to be met again by the Sikh
driver who led me to his jeep and drove me to the station to catch my
train back to Colombo. All very simple and efficient.

I understood that couriers travelled to and from Kandy on a regular
basis and that they were always booked into the same hotel. I assumed
therefore that the hotel charges were contracted for by the Navy. I was
wrong. Two or three days after my return to 'Lanka', I was summoned
again to the Captain's Office. Why had I not paid the bill? Did I not know
that I should have paid it and then claimed the amount back on Form
Number So-and-So? Did I not know that the hotel had made a complaint?
No sir, I did not. Sorry sir.

As a new boy, I had learned the hard way one of the rules of naval
bureaucracy. Without money of my own except for my Midshipman's pay,
it was occasionally going to be difficult to be an officer and a gentleman.
This lesson was to be reinforced a week later when I was informed that I
had been posted to Bombay and that I should travel there by train from
Colombo. Funds were very low.

With some trepidation, I made my way, for the second time, to
Colombo Railway Station and boarded, first, a train for Dhanushkodi
in the northwest of the island and then, second, a ferry to Vizak in the

southeast of India. From there I climbed aboard another train which puffed up the Coromandel Coast, passing through Trichinopoli, Cuddalore and Pondicherry en route to Madras. I had been provided with a day compartment, converted at night into a sleeper. At a price, the usual meals were provided in the dining car and these could be supplemented at the frequent stops en route where it was necessary to fend off hawkers selling bananas, mangosteens, papayas, peanuts, water melons, chapatis, betel nuts and sundry other delectables.

Before I left Colombo, I was given a travel advance of ten pounds. I spent a substantial amount of this on food during the journey of one night and one day to Madras, the oldest of the three Presidencies.[3] The rest of the money had to be used at an Officer's Club in Madras where I needed to spend the night, waiting for a connection to Bombay. I had no other money and was apprehensive about the rest of the journey. This was to last another three nights and two days, and would take me across India westwards through Sholapur and Pune to Bombay itself. Fortunately for my dignity – and my stomach – I met another naval officer in the Club. Lieutenant Phillip Hodge lent me sufficient money to carry me through to Bombay. Hodge became a good friend and adviser and we had many pleasant evenings together before he left India for demobilisation. He wrote to me once after the War, suggesting that I might apply for a post in the Bank to which he was attached in one of the Latin American countries, but I did not follow this up.

Bombay was a British possession long before Britain extended her control over the rest of India. The city came to Britain in 1662, not as the result of conquest but as part of the dowry brought by the Portuguese Princess, Catherine of Braganza, to the Stuart King of England, Charles II. The dowry also included Tangier, two million Portuguese crowns (foreign coins) and access to trade routes in the East Indies and Brazil.

I am not certain that in 1945 its occupants were aware of its history. But 'Braganza' was the name given to the naval establishment to which I was to be attached. Situated on the Colaba Causeway, it was established before the Second World War began, next to the barracks of the Royal Indian Navy, the 'RIN'.

After a few days in a transit hut at the barracks, I was informed that I was to share a flat with two other officers, the Captain's Secretary, 'Smithy', and a naval accountant, named 'Jock' (I have forgotten his family name). Owned by a rich Parsee family, the flat was one of a number of 'walk-ups' in Meyer Mansions, also on the Colaba Causeway. There were three bedrooms and this meant that I was able to have a room of my own.

Smithy, Jock and I usually breakfasted and dined together and we were looked after by a young 'bearer', a Madrasi who sported magnificent black moustaches. He was a fine chap who, when appropriately encouraged, could perform a rather startling trick. He would bend forwards with his head almost touching the ground. Then he would slowly 'unroll'. When he had regained an upright position, there would be a huge lump on his forehead, approximately the size of a squash ball. After a few minutes, the lump would disappear.

The bearer cleaned most of the flat, laid out our clothes and served the meals that were carried up from a central kitchen. The rough and dirty work in the flat – for example, the cleaning of the lavatory – was done by another servant called the 'hamal', a class of person in the Indian caste system expected to do such jobs. I reflected occasionally that, only a few months before, I had myself become a specialist in the same kind of activity. Conclusion: one British naval rating in training = one Indian hamal.

After working at 'Braganza' for two or three months, I became a member of the choir of the Afghan Church situated at the end of the Causeway. Choral singing relieved the monotony of my work at 'Braganza'. Other activities were tennis at the International Club and visits to the cinema, followed by 'sticky cakes' and tea at the Taj Mahal Hotel, or Green's Hotel or at one of the two long-established department stores, the Army and Navy and Whiteway Laidlaw. Occasionally it was possible to book naval transport to take several of us for a picnic on Juhu Beach or sometimes for a swim at the (now exclusive) Breach Candy Club, founded in 1875. In 1928, according to the Club's written history, '13,600 rupees was sanctioned for the construction of the present outside pool in the shape of British India.' I was able to frolic in that pool and indeed, it was at Breach Candy that I learned to swim more than a length or two of breaststroke and make some crude 'overarm' movements. To my regret, I have made little progress since then.

*****

In March 1946, a rare opportunity came my way. I was present at a large football stadium when the Aga Khan was weighed in diamonds on the occasion of his Diamond Jubilee. He weighed 243 lbs. The diamonds were valued at two million American dollars, but the Aga Khan kept only one stone as a souvenir. The pro-British Aga Khan the Third (Aga Sultan

Sir Mohammed Shah) was hereditary head of the Ismaili Muslims. In 1937 he became President of the League of Nations. He owned several Derby winners.

*****

The commanding officer of 'Braganza', Captain Farquhar, was a disgruntled man in his early fifties. He longed to be at sea again, instead of on shore. He was tall and thick-set with a florid complexion and a snarl that resembled that of the late General Sir Gerald Templar (of whom more later), except I suspect that Farquhar developed his snarl first, as befitting a member of the Senior Service.

Months before 'Braganza' paid off ('closed down'), Captain Farquhar moved into a hotel. On one occasion I was summoned to the hotel and to his room to receive instructions about some relatively unimportant matter. He was suffering from *tinea pedis* (vulgarly known as 'foot rot'). He received me while still in bed or, rather *on* his bed. His thick, fleshy legs were painted purple with potassium permanganate and there was a container of 'Whitfield's Ointment' (another standby) on his bedside table. The irritation that resulted from his ailment did not improve his temper.

I had been in Bombay for about six weeks when – on some matter or other – I made the mistake of sending a signal direct to 'C in C E I' (Commander-in-Chief, East Indies), instead of through FOB (Flag Officer, Bombay). Captain Farquhar was informed of this. He hauled me over the coals and insisted that, as a punishment, I should move out of the Colaba Causeway flat into a Naval Mess. This I did and spent about two weeks in the Mess contemplating my sins. It was whilst I was living in the Mess that I began to suffer from tropical boils. These sprouted from various parts of my body but were particularly noticeable on my legs. The doctor attached to 'Braganza' recommended hospital and so I was incarcerated for three days and subjected not only to injections of the relatively new drug, penicillin, but also to the discipline of a military hospital. Each evening, the officer-in-charge visited every ward in the hospital. The patients who could manage it were obliged to sit *at attention* as he passed through.

*****

Shortly after my discharge from hospital the whole of Bombay erupted. Twenty thousand sailors from seventy-eight ships of the Royal Indian Navy mutinied on 18 February 1946. The sailors were supported by some NCOs in the Indian Army, local police forces and large numbers of civilian factory workers who declared a strike. This soon spread to other parts of India. The causes of the mutiny and the strike are still being debated. One story has it that a certain Commander F.W. King, RIN (Royal Indian Navy), used 'uncouth language' whilst dressing down a group of naval ratings who had 'wolf-whistled' a parade of WRINS (female naval ratings in the Royal Indian Navy). Another story tells of the resentment caused by the incarceration of a Royal Indian Navy Captain, held in solitary confinement for scribbling 'Quit India' and 'Jai Hind' ('Victory to India') on the deck of HMIS (Her Majesty's Indian Ship) *Talwar*, in which frigate the Commander-in-Chief was to take the salute. What is certain is that the White Ensign was hauled down in many RIN shore establishments and ships and HMIS *Narbada*'s guns were trained on the Bombay Yacht Club. In response, the British Prime Minister, Clement Attlee, ordered Royal Navy and British Army personnel to put down the rebellion. British destroyers took up positions off the Gateway of India and the British Royal Air Force flew planes over Bombay harbour in a show of strength. Very different estimates have been given of the casualties that were suffered. It does seem, however that civilian deaths exceeded those of the mutinous sailors.

Both the strike and the mutiny came to an end following a meeting between the Central Strike Committee and Vallab Bhai Patel, a representative of the Indian Congress. Patel urged the strikers and the mutineers to end their action and his plea was endorsed by Mohammed Ali Jinnah of the Muslim League. Despite this intervention at a high political level, many of the mutineers paid for their actions at courts martial and none were reinstated into the Pakistani or Indian Navies after partition a year later. It may, however, be of some consolation to those who are still alive, or to their families, that a monument has been erected in Mumbai (formerly Bombay) in their honour.

Whilst the strike and mutiny were in progress, Captain Farquhar was in his element. Action at last! He increased street patrols by naval shore police and provided all passenger-carrying naval vehicles with hastily formed escorts, armed with axe helves. Signals flew back and forth. I carried messages about the city. Farquhar to Flag Officer Bombay. Farquhar to Commanding Officer Marines. Farquhar to General Officer Commanding Bombay. It was all very dramatic. But it did me some good. For after it was all over Farquhar allowed me to move out of the Mess and back into the Colaba Causeway flat again. He was a hard man and I thought that he disapproved of me. But he gave me a good report before he left 'Braganza' on completion of his tour of duty.

Shortly after the mutiny, the news came that most of the British naval bases in India were to be paid off, including 'Braganza'. Officers and ratings were to be dispersed; some to return to the United Kingdom, some to join the crews of ships and others to be transferred to different naval establishments in the SEAC region. I was informed that I had been posted back to Ceylon and that I was to join the shore establishment, 'HMS Lanka'.

I left Bombay with a feeling of regret. I had had little time or opportunity to get to know any of the local community or even the civilian 'Europeans'. But long after I had departed, I thought of the efficiency of the *dabbawallas* as they distributed their tiffin boxes to hungry office workers.[4] I recalled the mewing of seagulls and the strangled cries of vultures, hovering over the remains of the cremated dead laid out upon the *ghats* near Malabar Hill. I remembered the grimaces of the gaunt prostitutes in their Grant Road cages; the bones of the emaciated ponies that pulled my gharrys along and the bright-coloured skirts, oily hair and ankle ornaments of street-corner dancers.

I served in India before 1954 when the independent government banned the import of cars. Although there were very few of these on the streets in 1945, it was possible occasionally to catch a glimpse of a Rolls Royce, a Daimler, a Bentley or a Jaguar. Who owned these cars? Maharajahs perhaps, for *Nano*, the People's Car – and Democracy – had still to come.

On 16 August 1997, *The South China Morning Post* printed a feature about the destruction of colonial-era statues in India. A politician in that country had formed a lobby group with the aim of removing from the streets or at least decapitating statues that might remind passers-by of the days of the Raj. When I read the article, I was comforted by the knowledge that, during my short time in India, the great Lord Wellesley (or rather his statue) was still wearing his head. Prince Albert Edward, astride a black horse, continued to greet visitors at the gates of the Zoo and the statue of Lord Cornwallis was still being treated with respect. Of course, I served in India before it became an independent nation.

THE FOURTH STEP

BACK TO REALITY

– 9 –

Return to Ceylon

The year 1946 was a year to remember. An out-of-office Winston Churchill warned of an 'Iron Curtain' descending across much of Europe. The League of Nations was dissolved and replaced by the United Nations. Terrorists blew up the King David Hotel in Jerusalem, killing nearly a hundred people, an indication of what was to come in Israel and in Palestine. American physicians suggested that cigarette smoking could cause cancer. Good grief! Did anyone ever believe that a 'smoker's cough' was a good thing? (Cigarettes were not sometimes called 'gaspers' for nothing.) A new London airport was under construction in the London borough of Hillingdon. It was named Heathrow.

Where was I?

In early March 1946, I took passage back to Ceylon in the aircraft carrier, *Formidable*. It was an uncomfortable voyage in a vessel so overcrowded that I was obliged to sleep on the deck in someone's cabin. This was just a temporary discomfort and certainly not comparable to the distress that must have been felt by the ship's officers and crew in May 1945. On the 4th of that month, two Japanese *kamikaze*[1] aircraft struck *Formidable*, causing major damage to the flight deck and the centre boiler room. Eight crew members were killed and twenty-seven were wounded. On 9 May, *Formidable* was again the target. Once more the flight deck suffered, as did the after aircraft park, destroying twenty-three US Chance Vought F4V Corsairs and seven Grumman TBF Avenger aircraft.[2]

In Colombo once again, I was accommodated at first in a house near to the University. After two weeks I moved into shared accommodation in

'Flagstaff Mess', situated across the street from 'HMS Lanka', a short walk from the War Memorial. My companions were Commissioned Warrant Officer 'Shiner' Wright, Gunner's Mate Barney Barnard and Chief Petty Officer Freddy Hazelwood. As mentioned earlier, I benefited a great deal from the sagacity of each of these three men.

Shortly after I had settled in, I was told that there was little cypher work to be done. I would therefore be given the task of supervising the demobilisation of Goanese cooks and stewards. Over the years, the Royal Navy had recruited hundreds of Goanese citizens to staff its catering facilities ashore and to serve as cooks and stewards at sea. Now each was to be released in Colombo and Trincomalee and provided with a gratuity and other benefits, including a passage back to Goa.

*****

At some time in late 1946, I visited Trincomalee to discuss ways in which the demobilisation process might be speeded up. My work in 'Trinco' finished, I was driven to the railway station, boarded the train and settled comfortably into a closed first-class carriage, book in hand. We chugged along for about an hour when the train stopped suddenly, not at a station but somewhere in the countryside in an area decorated with rice fields. Half an hour went by. Then two hours. After the third hour had passed, I got out of the carriage and walked alongside the train towards the engine to discover, to my astonishment, that the driver, guard and attendants had disappeared. According to a fellow passenger who poked his head out of a window as I walked by, the crew had gone on strike. This was evidently one of a number of protests against colonial rule that were to become more frequent as the independence movement gathered strength in Ceylon and in neighbouring India.

I returned to my carriage and sat there for a while, wondering what to do next. Another hour passed and it seemed that some kind of action was necessary if I was not to be stranded for the rest of the day and the night as well. I decided to walk to the nearest village, hoping to find alternative transport. After walking for about half-a-mile, I came across some small houses and shops and I was fortunate to find a telephone that worked. I managed to contact Flagstaff Mess, Colombo; explained the situation and asked for help. After some hesitation, it was reluctantly agreed that a naval truck would be sent to pick me up, a drive of about seventy miles that would take the driver about two-and-a-half hours. I was told to return to the train and wait for the driver to arrive. Obediently, I returned to my carriage and sat down to wait as instructed. After about ten minutes, I felt a faint vibration; then a whistle blew twice and the train began to move, slowly at first and then eventually at full speed. We were under way again. The crew had returned. The strike was off.

I found it difficult to explain the situation to the Transport Officer when I arrived back in Colombo. The truck had left on its journey, to search for me and for a train that was no longer there.

*****

Colombo was more 'manageable' than Bombay for both vocational and recreational purposes. It was a smaller place. I managed to scrounge a bicycle and found it useful for short journeys after working hours. It was also possible to reserve a Navy car and driver. I took advantage of this privilege occasionally to visit Negombo beach and the hotel at Mount Lavinia. Negombo is about thirty-five kilometres from Colombo. Many of its inhabitants (the Karavas) were converted to Catholicism during the

Author and fellow officer outside the Naval Distributing Authority Building, Colombo, Ceylon, 1946.

Portuguese occupation and the town is sometimes tagged with the name 'Little Rome'.

Formerly the official residence of the British Governor, the hotel at Mount Lavinia now has a third life as the much-altered and upgraded Mount Lavinia Hyatt Hotel. It was fortunate to survive, with only minor damage, the devastating *tsunami* that struck on Boxing Day 2004.

It was a pleasure at weekends to stroll in the comparative cool of the evening along the Galle Face Green, a long stretch of open land extending back from the seafront. Sometimes the stroll could turn into a purposeful walk. Drinks and dinner tempted at the Galle Face Hotel, built in 1864 and then somewhat faded. I am told that it has now enjoyed a 'make-over' and is doing relatively good business as the 'Regent of Colombo'.

On some occasions, it was possible to leave Colombo and its delights and venture further afield. One weekend, I was able to pay a visit to Sigiriya, the Lion Rock, a fortress of the ancient Sinhalese kings. I climbed up the Rock, treading gingerly in crevices made slippery by countless feet. At the top, the panoramic view is magnificent. Here is a place where present meets past and history encounters myth.

In 473AD (so the legend goes), King Dhatusena was forced by his son, Kasyapa, to abdicate. Afraid that attempts might be made to rob him of his newly gained powers, Kasyapa built a fortress on the massive Rock of Sigiriya. Eighteen years later, the fortress came under attack. All might have been well but Kasyapa made the mistake of riding out to face his opponents. He lost his way and became mired in a swamp. Deserted by his army, he committed suicide. Many years later Sigiriya became a monastery but eventually the monks departed and the buildings crumbled.

Half way up the Rock, a stairway leads to a sheltered gallery, embellished with frescoes, mainly of beautiful women and mostly created *circa* the fifth century AD. A high wall beyond the frescoe gallery is decorated with graffiti. Many of these have been listed and explained in a book published in 1956 by Dr Serenat Paranavitana.[3] According to Dr Paranavitana, one typical inscription reads: 'By means of the splendour of the mountain side, I saw the manner in which nymphs stood in heaven. My hand jumped up with the desire of grasping their girdles in dalliance.' Unfortunately, I was there in 1946, ten years before the publication of Dr Paranavitana's book and so was unable to enjoy his translations.

At the time of my visit to Sigiriya, Ceylon was still a British colony. The government had established a number of 'rest houses' in each town, to serve the needs of District Officers and other peripatetic civil servants. The food served in rest houses was often a local version of the worst of

British cooking; overdone watery cabbage, leathery 'rissoles' and similar gastronomic delights. The Sigiyra rest house was no different. Meat, vegetables and gravy were unpalatable, as expected. But then! Wonders! The dessert was served. Gracing my plate was a magnificent, flaming rum omelette that, as a speciality pudding, has only been matched in my experience by the lemon meringue pie produced by the original proprietors of 'The Willows' restaurant in Hausten Street, Honolulu.

It was evident from the anticipatory gleam in the waiter's eye that I was not the only person to give thanks for the yellow and brown delight. After I had consumed two portions and was contemplating a third, he drew my attention to a framed notice on the wall of the dining room. The notice turned out *not* to be a notice but rather a poem, written by a previous guest in an elegant script. It was entitled, 'An Ode to a Rum Omelette'.

*****

Two weeks or so after my return from Trincomalee, I received an invitation to a party in a fellow officer's 'quarter' in Colombo. A number of the guests were dressed in civilian clothes, including a man named David Jacobs. He was of medium height, with black, shiny hair and a waxy complexion. He told a long string of anecdotes with polished ease, many of them to do with the theatre and with radio 'bloopers'. I discovered later that, despite his 'civvies', he was a Chief Petty Officer, attached to Radio SEAC (Southeast Asia Command). He encouraged me to visit the radio station and, although I did so one afternoon, it did not occur to me then to offer my services. I would have enjoyed such an experience. Who knows? If I had taken the plunge, and if my performance had been acceptable, I might have been able to claim, as Jacobs has, that I had been in the radio business since the age of twenty.

I lost track of Jacobs until 1948 or 1949 when I heard his voice on BBC Radio. In 1955, when I was on leave in London, I saw him, fairly often, on television. By this time, he had become a freelance broadcaster and had achieved a considerable reputation as a 'TV personality' on such shows as 'Juke Box Jury' and as a presenter at beauty competitions, ballroom dancing exhibitions and ice-spectacles.

At the party I met a girl named Pamela Garvin. She was two years younger than me and came from a Burgher family. Pamela's father came from Ireland. Her mother was a Van Langenburg and her uncle, Dr Van Langenburg, had the distinction of being physician to the last British

Governor of Ceylon, Sir Henry Monck-Mason Moore. Pamela was a sincere, somewhat intense girl addicted to the novels of Angela Thirkell. I knew nothing about the author's work at the time and assumed that her books were cheap romantic novels of the type offered by publishers such as Mills and Boon. I was wrong. I did Pamela an injustice. I have learned since then that Thirkell was the grand-daughter of the Pre-Raphaelite painter, Edward Burne-Jones and the cousin of Rudyard Kipling. The novels that she published in the 1940s have been said to provide a vibrant picture of the attitudes and struggles of women during the Second World War.[4]

Pamela and I were good companions until a natural parting took place when I left Ceylon to return to Britain. I was tempted, but after much thought I opted not to be demobilised in Ceylon although there was some possibility of a civilian job ashore. The offer was made by a Lieutenant Commander, RNVR who had asked to be released locally. He was a tea planter before the War and offered me a job on his plantation as a 'creeper' (*sinna-dorai*), a kind of trainee manager. I thanked him for his offer but did not accept it.

After I had served in Ceylon for about six months, the British Navy handed over Flagstaff Mess to the Ceylonese authorities. I moved into the Grand Oriental Hotel ('GOH') and shared a room with another Sub-Lieutenant, named Alan Loxley. Eventually, I became one of the last six naval officers to remain in Ceylon.

The Grand Oriental was very comfortable as befitted a building re-named *Taprobane*, following the departure of the British. The entire island was once known as *Tambappani*, a name shortened by the Greeks and the Romans to *Taprobana*. 'Taprobane' may have failed to attract foreign tourists and so the name 'Grand Oriental' has been restored. Built in 1837 to house British soldiers and converted into a hotel in 1875, the Grand Oriental now advertises itself as a 'colonial' three-star hotel, relying on its 'ambience' to attract custom.

The Christmas of 1946 passed very pleasantly. The GOH was decorated for the occasion and there was dancing in the ballroom and in The Silver Faun night-club.[5] I was comfortable and my pay was adequate. I had few real responsibilities and was filling in my time in the office of the Navy's Distributing Authority, responsible for the safe handling of confidential books, documents and other materials.

One night, during Christmas week – perhaps the 27 or 28 December – I was invited to dinner by Dr Van Langenburg and Mrs Garvin. Pamela would be there, and there were to be other guests. I arrived at the Regent flats about ten minutes after the designated time in the belief that this was the polite thing to do. As I was ushered into the dining room by Mrs Garvin, I saw that the first guests had already arrived and were being supplied with drinks by Dr Van Langenburg. Whilst accepting these, the two guests gazed at me, beady-eyed, across the gin bottle and glasses. One guest was Sir Arthur Palliser, CB, DSO, the Commander-in-Chief, East Indies, a Vice-Admiral, and the other was the Flag Officer, Ceylon, Rear Admiral J. M. Mansfield, CB, DSC. I was a very junior Sub-Lieutenant in the Royal Naval Volunteer Reserve. Fortunately for me, Dr Van Langenburg was an assiduous host with a good cellar and, in particular, a large supply of Beefeater Gin, to which all hands applied themselves purposefully and frequently. The occasion gradually became more relaxed so that, by the time we had reached the savoury stage, we were all wearing paper hats and pulling crackers. The two senior officers loosened their cummerbunds as the conversation became more and more anecdotal.

After the brandy and cigars arrived and Mrs Garvin and Pamela had withdrawn, the fumes seemed to clear for a moment. Flag Officer, Ceylon fixed me with a cold stare across the littered table. We were back to the beady-eyed look. He challenged me with what then seemed to be a non-sequitur. 'Well, subby, you're Special Cypher.' 'Yes, but I'm not actually doing that work now, sir. I have another job.' 'What job?' 'The Distributing Authority, sir.' 'Mmn, not much to do there, is there?' 'Frankly, no sir' (I was emboldened by the gin). 'Don't you think it's time for you to go home?' 'Well, yes sir, but I've applied for a transfer to the BPF' (the British Pacific Fleet, based in Singapore). 'The BPF is paying off its officers.' 'Yes sir.' 'Mmn, I see.'

It may have been only a coincidence but, two weeks later, I received news that people in my 'age and service group' category – number 62 – were to be posted back to Britain for leave, prior to demobilisation. Three weeks after that, I was one of four naval officers sharing a cabin on an Army troopship, *The Monarch of Bermuda*, bound for Liverpool.

The voyage home was without incident. There was a one-day stop in Aden with a chance to buy some 'rabbits' (gifts). As on the voyage out, we made our way through the Suez Canal, but now the banks were lined with jeering German and Italian prisoners-of-war. We occupied ourselves with reading, card games, watching occasional films and walking the deck. I noticed how the large number of Asian wives, accompanying their soldier husbands, became obviously and understandably apprehensive and miserable as we passed through the rough waters of the Bay and approached the snowbound city of Liverpool. They were to be introduced for the first time to a new country and exposed to a new culture. I, too, was to suffer some culture shock. No longer would I enjoy the status of a naval officer or the comforts and pleasures of the Grand Oriental Hotel. I was to find myself back 'on the market' again with minimal qualifications and very little money.

At Liverpool docks, I completed negotiations with a sour-faced Customs Officer and at St James Street Station boarded a train for Manchester. As I settled into my seat, I reflected on the War. I had joined the Navy fourteen months before the War came to an end. More than 35 million people had been killed. I was lucky. My War had not been very adventurous, although there had been a few moments of drama. To adapt what the dying writer and poet, Lady Mary Wortley Montagu (1689–1762) is said to have exclaimed, just before she expired: 'It was all very interesting.'

– 10 –

Back to Wales

The winter of 1947 was very severe with heavy snowfalls, finger-numbing frosts and icy rain.[1] Although the War was over, food rationing was still observed strictly in Britain and there was a critical shortage of coal, then the most important fuel for domestic heating purposes. In those respects, conditions in the country were similar to those that existed when I left for South Asia two years earlier. In other respects, profound changes were taking place in British society.

On 1 January, every coal-mine in Britain displayed a plaque announcing, 'This colliery is now managed by the National Coal Board on behalf of the People.' In the 1940s, the Labour Party commissioned the socialist film-maker, Humphrey Jennings, to make a propaganda film in favour of the Labour Party. Released in 1944, *Diary for Timothy* extolled the value of a welfare state and the benefits it could bring for the children of the future.

Following the General Election of June and July 1945, the wartime political coalition of Liberals, Conservatives and Labour was dissolved. Despite his massive, morale-boosting efforts during the War, an aging Winston Churchill suffered rejection (much to the bewilderment of many, including my family). Labour gained 203 seats from the Conservatives and overall won 394 seats to the Conservatives' 210. Clement Attlee, the wartime Deputy Prime Minister, became Prime Minister. 'After this what?' said James Griffiths, a new Labour Minister. Part of the 'what' that came was the controversial nationalisation of the coal and other industries in 1947; the desirable introduction of the National Health Service in 1948 and the undesirable devaluation of the pound in 1949.

Two weeks after my arrival back in Britain, I was asked to report to a demobilisation centre to be 'processed out'. After the paperwork had been completed, I received a small gratuity payment and was asked to choose between a blazer or a cheap brown suit. I asked for, and received, the suit. I should have chosen the blazer.

In February 1947 I received the following letter:

ADMIRALTY

S.W. 1

C.W. 601/R.A.

25th February, 1947

Sir,

On the occasion of your release from Naval Service, I am commanded by the Lords Commissioners of the Admiralty to convey to you an expression of their recognition of your services in the Royal Navy during the war.

The good wishes of Their Lordships go with you on your return to civil life.

I am, Sir,
Your obedient Servant,
W.A. Medrow

In March 1947, I received confirmation that I had been accepted once again as a student at University College, Cardiff. In early April, I attended a 3rd Altrincham Scout Troop Easter Camp at Sandoway in Cheshire and on another occasion acted as Master of Ceremonies at a dance sponsored by the Rover Crew and held in the Altrincham Grammar School Hall.

It had all been fun, but I still had six months to wait before returning to the University and funds were very low. I needed some money, even though I was living at home. The only course, it seemed, was to report to the government department that was then entitled, 'The Labour Exchange' but is known today as the Department of Social Security. I had some hope that the Exchange would provide me with unemployment pay and so allow me the opportunity to prepare for re-entry to University.

But I was out of luck. Instead of an allowance, I was offered a choice of two jobs, onion picking or postal work, both obviously regarded as eminently suitable for an ex-naval officer – the proletariat strikes back? Remembering with some displeasure my previous experience as a potato picker, I decided to throw in my lot with the Post Office.

A week after my visit to The Labour Exchange, I reported to the Head Post Office in Sale where I was to be employed as a temporary postman from April until September 1947. Every morning, I got up at 4am to report for duty at 4.45am. This proved difficult at first, for the mornings were cold and dark and the journey by bicycle was unpleasant. Nowadays I might find it easier, but then youth needs its rest.

Once at the Post Office, the first job was to 'sort out' and then 'face up' the letters and small packages which were to be delivered in my delivery area (the 'route'). 'Sorting out' meant placing the letters in separate piles for each street on the route. 'Facing up' meant arranging the letters in each pile according to the odd and even numbers in each street. Those houses without numbers but with names such as 'The Larches' or 'Mon Repos' could only be identified through familiarity with the route. After the 'sorting out' and 'facing up' was complete, I would collect registered letters from the supervisor and then at about 6am set out by bicycle, bag on shoulder.

What did I learn from this experience as a temporary Post Office employee? Well, there was, it seemed, a 'them' and 'us' attitude among the postmen in their relations with members of the public. I quickly began to understand why this was so. The public complained a lot, sometimes with justification but often without. For example, of two complaints against me, one had to do with a letter that, according to the complainant, was delivered in a damp condition. I was indignant since I remembered that it had been a particularly cold and rainy morning. As I put my numbed hands through the slits in my gas cape the rain dripped from the roof of the householder's porch onto the corner of the envelope just before I slipped it into the letter-box.

Another – this time legitimate – complaint was that I was observed reading the backs of postcards. I pleaded guilty to this charge. One had to do something to relieve the boredom of the round. If I were to be spotted committing this heinous crime today (2009), I might be reported by a dustman or a street cleaner to a Police Community Support Officer, no doubt with the full approval of the Audit Commission.[2]

Registered letters had to be delivered into the hands of the addressees and a signature obtained on a receipt. What lay behind those closed doors that were opened so reluctantly? Occasionally, fresh smells of Mansion polish but, more usually, the repellent, stale odours of cooking, last night's scent, bodies, cigarettes and bad breath. What sights did I see? There were stained dressing gowns, collarless shirts, grey underpants and vests, hair curlers and – very occasionally – a business suit.

After the last envelope had been delivered, it was back to the Post Office, to begin sorting out and facing up for the lunchtime delivery. At that time of day there were few letters but, instead, a large number of advertising leaflets and football coupons produced by such companies as Vernons, Littlewoods, Copes and Shermans. At the Post Office in Sale, these coupons were known as 'totes', or as pronounced in the local accent, 'torts'. Occasionally, the shelves would contain packets of Manx (Isle of Man) kippers, two fish per package, and small white boxes of wedding cake addressed to friends and relatives. Not infrequently the boxes would break open and the sorting had to be carried out among cake crumbs and fish bones. Fish bones that smelt. This was the situation in 1947. Today, in at least one Post Office, the problem is *cheese*. It was reported in the 27 May 2006 edition of *The Spectator* that the Clapham Sorting Office smelt of drains, largely because a customer failed to collect a large ripe Camembert.

In September, my temporary job with the Post Office came to an end and I went on my first trip to Paris in the company of my life-long friend Roy Hanson and his then fiancée (later wife) Isobel Biddulph. There was a fourth member of the party, Peter Marychurch, Roy's and Isobel's colleague when each was attached to the Foreign Office.

Sir Peter Marychurch retired some years ago from his post as Head of 'GCHQ', in Cheltenham. He is referred to in laudatory terms in Peter Wright's book, *Spy Catcher*, notorious because it exposed details of the internal operations of the intelligence agency, MI5. Lamenting GCHQ's insufficient coverage of Moscow's broadcasts to illegal agents in the field, Wright recalls that:

> The intelligence was processed by the section supporting the counterplan committee. A young GCHQ cryptoanalyst named Peter Marychurch transformed my laborious handwritten classifications by processing the thousands of broadcasts on computer and applying 'cluster analysis' to isolate similarities in the traffic, which made the classification infinitely more precise. Within a few years this work had become one of the most important tools in Western counter-espionage.[3]

Before leaving for Paris, we were given some information about cheap accommodation which could be reserved during the summer at the Cité Universitaire, a hostel complex built for university students enrolled in courses at the Sorbonne and associated colleges. We sent letters, completed the necessary forms, and eventually received confirmation of our reservations. I met Roy, Isobel and Peter in London and we left for Calais by ferry from Dover. From Calais, we travelled by train to Paris and then by Metro to the Cité Universitaire at Number 14, Boulevard Jourdan.

The Cité Universitaire is an extraordinary place with many separate dormitory buildings, each representing an architectural style that is supposed to be characteristic of a particular country. The Franco-Britannique building is constructed of red brick and is covered with ivy. The Japan House has a pagoda-like look. And so on.

We used the Cité as a base from which to visit Versailles and to explore the capital, the Louvre, the Left Bank, the Bois de Boulogne, the Champs Élysées and various restaurants and bistros. In the evenings we bought cheap tickets and were able visit the Opera, the state-owned Comédie Française (starring the inimitable thirty-nine-year-old actor and director, Jean Louis Barrault) and the Folies Bergères music hall which is still going strong at 32 rue Richer (and still attracting large audiences in 2009). We were all short of cash but somehow managed to eke out our thin resources by careful daily accountings and some self-denial; wine every *other* day and only a very few thirst quenching glasses of sherbet despite the humidity of early September in Paris.

*****

The visit to France had been an interesting prelude to the resumption of my university studies. On a grey day in October 1947, I travelled once again

Calais to Dover Ferry, 1947. Peter (later Sir Peter) Marychurch (left), Isobel Biddulph (later Hanson) (centre) and the writer.

to Cardiff by train from Manchester Central Station. Through a friend of my mother's, I had managed to find accommodation with Reg and Hilda Taylor and in fact I was their first lodger. The Taylors lived in a small, neat bungalow at 10 Heol Carne Street, Whitchurch. This was quite accessible to the University by bus or by bicycle, my usual modes of transport.

Hilda presided over a sales counter at Boots the Chemists, in Queen Street, Cardiff, whilst Reg laboured as a boatman at Cardiff Docks. He had previously seen a good deal of the world as a seaman in the merchant navy and had given the name 'Socotra' to his bungalow, to remind him of past voyages and adventures. (As he told me, Socotra is an island in the Arabian Sea near to the mouth of the Gulf of Aden.)

Reg and Hilda were a friendly couple who did their best to make me feel at home and who gave me good value for the agreed rent of two pounds and ten shillings per week. This paid for my bedroom; the use of the 'front room' for studying purposes and two good meals a day, breakfast and supper.

The couple did not deserve the misfortunes that were to come. In 1949, whilst I was on vacation, they went to a baseball match on Reg's motor bicycle. On the way home, after a good evening's entertainment, Reg swerved to avoid a dog and the motorbike crashed against a kerb. Hilda was thrown clear of the crash but Reg was trapped underneath his bike and suffered a fractured femur. He was taken by ambulance to Llandough Hospital, just outside Cardiff, and languished there for some weeks with his thigh secured by a metal pin and suspended from a pulley. Isolated – apart from regular visits by Hilda and occasionally by me – his mind began to deteriorate in the over-antiseptic surroundings of the relatively new hospital which, apparently – at least in his case, as it seems – paid insufficient attention to occupational therapy. Never much of a reader, Reg lay with his leg skewered, brooding about Hilda's difficulties, the possible loss of his job, the household chores that were being neglected and other matters, until his mind exploded and he screamed to be released from what for him had become a prison. His state of mind was such that a transfer to a mental hospital became necessary and he was moved to Whitchurch Mental Hospital in Cardiff itself where I visited him several times.

I do not wish to do Whitchurch Hospital an injustice. Much good may have been done for many of its mentally ill patients. Conditions may now be much improved. But then – at least to the outward eye – it had a 'snakepit' look. The buildings were old and seemingly neglected. Inside, the dark brown and cream-painted walls were chipped. The wards were very overcrowded. Ambulatory patients leaned against pillars and in corners, some gibbering, some slavering, some moaning, a few chirpily repeating mantras from the past.

Reg's condition deteriorated shortly after he was admitted and there were two or three violent episodes, including his attempt to smash his way to freedom through one of the windows of his ward.

After Reg had spent about two months in Whitchurch, it was decided that a weekend at home might help his condition. Hilda collected him from the hospital in a taxi one Saturday morning and he seemed to be quite normal when I met him at the front door of 'Socotra'. He was cheerful enough throughout the morning until we sat down for lunch, during which he and Hilda began to reminisce about times past and to recall some of the tunes to which they had danced. Then, suddenly, one memory proved too painful for him. He leapt up from the table, ran out of the back door of the bungalow, seized an empty milk bottle from the step, smashed it against the wall and declared that he was going to kill himself. Hilda, who had followed Reg out of the kitchen, shouted for help. I rushed into the kitchen, to find that the next-door neighbour, Mr Handy, had climbed over the low dividing fence and was struggling with Reg and attempting to wrest the bottle from him. I joined in the fray gingerly and grasped Reg's trunk-like arm. After a short struggle, he went limp, handed the bottle to Mr Handy and walked back into the bungalow. Within a few moments, we were back to a kind of normality and we resumed our lunch.

After the meal, I retired to the front room to study whilst Reg remained in the living room with Hilda. Later that afternoon, he was visited by his two brothers, both of whom were policemen. Their part was to comfort their brother and his wife. Mine was to leaf through my copy of Grant and Temperley's, *Europe in the Nineteenth and Twentieth Centuries*, recommended reading for my forthcoming degree examination in History. In the circumstances, I found it difficult to concentrate. Questions ran repeatedly through my mind. What, if anything, would happen next? Was the lunchtime incident an aberration or would something similar happen again? It seemed unlikely since all was quiet and there was only a low muttering to be heard through the closed living-room door.

Just as I was settling down to read the same page for the third time, there was a desperate shout and the sound of furniture being knocked over. The living-room door opened and, clutching a kitchen knife, Reg jumped out and ran to the bathroom, exclaiming, 'I'm going to do it! I'm going to do it!' The two brothers rushed after him but he had locked himself in. They pleaded with him to come out but he refused and continued to shout,

'I'm going to do it. I'm going to do it.' In fact, he did *not* do it and, after spending about an hour in the bathroom, he unlocked the door and came out quietly, handing the knife to one of his brothers.

That evening, before the brothers left, they and Hilda decided that it would be in Reg's best interests if he were to be taken back to the hospital the next day, Sunday. The evening passed without incident and the three of us retired at about 10:30. I could hear Reg and Hilda talking softly in the adjoining bedroom and I found it difficult to drop off to sleep, wondering what Reg, in his disordered mind, thought about *my* position in the household. Hilda told me later that Reg continued to remind her of their past life together and she encouraged him to talk about it. He undressed, hung his jacket in the wardrobe and placed his trousers on a hangar. There on the top shelf was a packet of razor blades. Reg fingered it and then suggested to Hilda that they should commit suicide together. She told him not to be foolish and he did not pursue the suggestion.

On the next morning, Reg was driven back to the hospital in a taxi. All was well as the taxi drove into the grounds until it stopped at the Patients' Entrance. An attendant walked down the steps towards the car and spoke to Hilda through the open window, informing her that, as a voluntary patient, Reg would have to be re-registered and that he would need to complete some admission forms. It was at that point that Reg seemed to realise where he was and he struggled so frantically to escape that it proved necessary to put him under restraint.

Shortly after Reg returned to the hospital, I left Cardiff for the summer vacation. I decided not to return to the Taylors after the break was over, although I liked both of them and they had treated me with great kindness. I had now reached a crucial stage in my studies and was convinced that, as the examination season approached, I should keep myself as free as possible from outside distractions. I wrote to Hilda and told her that I would not be returning for a third year. She accepted this decision philosophically and replied to say that Reg had made a good recovery, following electric shock treatment. He had been discharged from hospital. I continued to visit both of them during the rest of my stay in Cardiff and when I left that city for Singapore in 1951, Reg was back to his old self and had received some compensation for his accident. He had been able to find another, lighter job. All seemed set fair for the future.

But the gods had not finished with the Taylors. The tragedy was to continue. For me the last act was played out twenty-seven years later. In 1978 I accompanied my twenty-one-year-old son, Simon, from Hawaii to Britain to look for opportunities to continue his education. We journeyed down from London to Cardiff so that he could enroll in a College there. On the second day after our arrival, I decided to telephone the Taylors. I thought it would be very interesting to see them again after such a long interval. I could not find their name in the telephone book, nor could the operator at Directory Enquiries help. Finally, I decided to try to call the neighbour, Mr Handy. Somewhat to my surprise, I found him at the other end of the line. I said that I would like to contact the Taylors and asked if he could help me to do this. There was a silence. Then Handy said, 'I'm sorry that you hadn't heard. Hilda died some years ago of cancer and shortly afterwards, Reg killed himself. He jumped off a bridge.'

– 11 –

A Study Regimen

At the beginning of the twentieth century, according to Stephen Inwood,[1] some Londoners enjoyed centrally heated houses, received their post over breakfast, answered the telephone, paid their cleaning ladies, summoned petrol-driven taxis, took the Underground to their offices served by electronic cables, read daily newspapers, and shopped in department stores. In Cardiff in 1944, we were certainly able to enjoy daily newspapers and shopping in department stores; the post was delivered twice a day and affluent homeowners were able to employ cleaning ladies. But very few homes were centrally heated. There was no Underground Railway and there was a chronic shortage of taxis. Even when I returned to the city in 1947, very few advances had been made. It is true that 'The Ranch' was now used as a practise running track, rather than for cadet Field Training, and Chief Petty Officer Hanford now appeared in brown overalls, rather than in blue serge. Rationing was, however, still in force. Dried egg was still a regular item on the menu of the Student Union refectory and only occasionally were the new detergents – such as 'Stergene' – available to help with the washing of encrusted plates. Mr Birdseye had not yet introduced his frozen foods to South Wales and shopping for groceries was done in small shops, rather than in supermarkets. Dairies sold milk, cream and eggs but there were no yoghourts as yet, at least not in South Wales. Butter was carved from large butter 'wheels' and weighed into one pound chunks. Bacon slicers were used to meet customers' preferences – streaky or 'back' – 'Number five, please!' There were still no fast food outlets of the McDonald's type. The pubs in Wales served faggots and peas and 'laver' bread (made from seaweed). Fish and chip shops flourished, despite shortages of fish and fat. Coupons still had to be exchanged for clothing purchases but this was not much of a problem for students. A large number of us were ex-servicemen and -women and we made innovative and possibly illegal use of former military uniforms; the duffel coat and the balaclava helmet being particularly popular. Undergraduates did not have cars. Instead we used bicycles, the bus and the train. Books were in short supply and were hoarded carefully. The age of the photocopier had not begun. Essays were written in longhand rather than typed. Although there were no pocket calculators, mobile phones or microcomputers, there were plenty of slide rules. People took baths instead of showers. In the winter, they were grateful for the comforting warmth of rubber (and sometimes stone) hot water bottles. Central heating was very rare and coal fires polluted the air. For physical recreation, there were walking, athletics, rugby, cricket, tennis, squash and horse-riding. Soccer was played in heavy, studded boots that had to be dubbined regularly. There were no compact discs or DVDs, but the radio, the cinema and the gramophone provided canned entertainment. Twelve-inch and ten-inch gramophone records were sold in paper covers – cardboard 'sleeves' cost extra – and issued on labels such as Brunswick, Columbia, Parlophone and HMV (His Master's Voice). Television was generally unavailable, although in existence. There were no tape recorders. Pastimes included making music, playing cards, the cinema and the theatre. Cardiff was fortunate enough to have two professional theatres, the Prince of Wales and the New Theatre. In addition, there was the University's Reardon-Smith Theatre and an open-air stage in the grounds of Cardiff Castle.

It was in Cardiff that I became a theatre-going addict and usually sat in the one shilling and ninepenny 'gods' for shows at the Prince of Wales Theatre and the New Theatre. Binoculars clipped to the back of every seat could be hired for sixpence and made it possible to observe the actors' facial expressions. There were performances of local origin, but also many visiting companies. I particularly remember the American film actress, Margaret Sullivan, in Van Druten's *The Voice of the Turtle*, and other plays featuring actors such as Margaret Rutherwood, Roger Livesey and Michael Redgrave.

Occasionally, when I seemed to be 'flush', I would buy a seat in the stalls of the Prince of Wales. No binoculars were necessary. During intervals, it was pleasant to be served pre-ordered tea and biscuits. These were passed along the rows on trays. Originally named the New Theatre Royal, the Prince of Wales opened in 1878. Alas, the grand old theatre closed for ever in 1957. In 1999 – final humiliation – the building was converted into a pub.

In 1949, I was fortunate enough to be able to visit the then Shakespeare Memorial Theatre (re-named the Royal Shakespeare Theatre in 1964) in Stratford, for a splendid production of *Macbeth* directed by Anthony Quayle. The cast included such distinguished actors as John Gielgud, Leon Quartermaine, Godfrey Tearle, Diana Wynyard and Harry Andrews.

Theatre-going was a delightful addition to my education and it reinforced my resumed academic work in Cardiff. I had been awarded a government ex-serviceman's educational allowance of four pounds a week for living expenses. Tuition fees and other academic bills were paid for by the government. Registration for a particular degree course was of course necessary and I did this during the first week of October. As a naval cadet, I had already completed a compressed year's work during my six months in the University Naval Division and so could finish a Final Degree in two years or an Honours Degree in three years. I chose to read English and History again because I enjoyed both subjects and had done reasonably well in these at school, and later at college. The addition of Education was necessary in order for me to complete the degree requirements.

English Literature was a comparatively new subject of study at university level, finding a sturdy advocate in Sir Arthur Thomas Quiller-Couch ('Q'), one of the founders of the English Faculty at Cambridge. By 1947, English Literature and Language was a recognised subject of study in most British universities, as was History, studied often through what were regarded as significant time periods. At Cardiff, this meant beginning at Subsidiary level, with Mediaeval History and early Welsh History (a separate course). At the Final level, 'Modern' European History was read, plus an optional subject such as Economic History or Colonial History. I chose the latter and as a result, became interested in Britain's colonial policies and, in particular, those that affected Asia. After all, I had spent a short time in that part of the world.

By the end of the first week of October 1947, I had completed college and university registration procedures and was already attending lectures in my three selected subjects.

The Head of the Department of English Language and Literature was my erstwhile firewatching companion, Professor E.C. Llewellyn, who lectured on Anglo-Saxon and Robert Browning, with the assistance of a senior lecturer, George Thomas. In a sense, the language section of the Department was also the secular side. Both Llewellyn and Thomas were *bon viveurs* and appeared to be as interested in good ale as some of the characters in *The Canterbury Tales* of whom they spoke. The staff of the literature section – in particular the Rev. Moelwyn Merchant and S.L. Bethell – argued that literature should be analysed in terms of the religious and social background of its time. They believed that some appreciation of the nature of grace and evil, sin and remorse, the influence of churchmen philosophers such as Richard Hooker, an understanding of the Divine Right of Kings and of the hierarchical nature of the universe was necessary in order to be able to interpret (for example) Shakespeare:

Take but degree away
Untune that string
And hark what discord follows...[2]

The approach through religious belief was fortunately not a narrow one. Both the senior lecturers responsible had wide-ranging interests. Contrary to the recommendations of scholars such as G.E. Saintsbury, S.L. Bethell was of the F.R. Leavis School of structural criticism, focusing on what is *actually said* in a text, that is, on the 'words, words, words', rather than speculating about what might have been, and so going beyond what was actually written. The work of the Leavisites is well illustrated in the title of L.C. Knights' well-known essay, *How Many Children Had Lady Macbeth?*[3] The point of the title is that there is no reference in the play to Lady Macbeth's progeny, except the lines:

I have given suck and know
How tender 'tis to love the babe that milks me.[4]

Bethell was fascinated with the *how* of sixteenth-century play production and wrote a stimulating treatise on stagecraft in Shakespeare's time entitled *Shakespeare and the Popular Dramatic Tradition*, a book long out of print and from a now defunct publisher (Dobson), but a gem of its kind. Bethell also had an engaging interest in films, particularly those of the Marx Brothers. He was often to be seen at the Globe Cinema in City Road, Cardiff, a House that specialised in foreign films and classics. There are now very few 'Globes' left in British cities. They were built originally as local cinemas, to show the latest products of Hollywood and Elstree but, as times and tastes changed, a few of them found fresh niches by presenting what might now be called 'up-market' productions. This gave people like me a chance to enjoy films such as *La Ronde, Les Enfants du Paradis* and *Open City*. Occasionally, such cinemas would arrange 'classic' seasons, with showings of such films as *The Blue Angel, The Cabinet of Dr Caligari* and *All Quiet on the Western Front*.

Clad in dinner jacket and dark trousers and with a small rose in his buttonhole, the affable manager of 'The Globe' would appear in the lobby just before each programme began, to greet members of the audience as they came in from the street. The atmosphere was almost club-like for regulars such as we became.

Moelwyn Merchant shone as the other senior lecturer on the literature side. A full-time member of the Department, he was also an ordained clergyman who held a living at a church in Caerleon, a village situated not far from Cardiff and a centre for archeological exploration. Merchant lectured and conducted tutorials on the Romantic poets and also led seminars on the History of Ideas. Never idle, he had three interesting side interests: landscape gardening and the work of Capability Brown; engravings, particularly mezzotints and aquatints and – like Bethell – stagecraft. Long after I had left Cardiff, he was invited to the Folger Library in Washington, DC, to conduct research into Elizabethan stage design and to catalogue paintings, engravings and drawings that had some connection with Shakespeare. The product of his research was a book, *Shakespeare and the Artist*, his magnum opus, superbly produced by the Oxford University Press.

It was through Moelwyn's connections that the English Honours group was invited to spend some time at Cumberland Lodge, now known as 'The King George VI and Queen Elizabeth Foundation of St Catherine's'. Formerly a royal residence in Windsor Great Park, the Lodge served as the venue for several meetings between the Prime Minister, Stanley Baldwin and the King's Private Secretary. These meetings were significant in that they led eventually to the abdication of King Edward VIII.

In 1947, the late King George VI offered the then empty Lodge to Miss Amy Buller, the daughter of the Boer War veteran, General Sir Redvers Buller. For many years, Amy had nursed a desire to establish a new kind of religious college in which students could discuss social and ethical issues that were not normally part of their regular degree courses. Now the opportunity had come. Accepting the King's offer with alacrity, she moved into the Lodge, and took the title of Warden of St Catherine's. She was supported by a Bursar and a Tutor, Roger Young, later Headmaster of George Watson's College in Edinburgh. There were also some volunteer helpers, including Lady Isabella Elphinstone of the distinguished Scottish family.

Sir Walter Moberly, the author, *inter alia*, of *The Ethics of Punishment*[5] and *Crisis in the University*[6] was named Principal and it was under his overall direction that students from the University of London and other universities were invited to spend weekends at the Lodge. There, in comfortable sylvan surroundings they were able to study and debate issues of the day with guests such as the well-known philosopher, C.E.M. Joad. Many years after the régime of Miss Buller and Roger Young ended, I received a letter from the then Principal of the Lodge, Timothy Slack, a former colleague in the British Council. Timothy told me that Sir Walter Moberly's son, Sir John Moberly, had become a frequent visitor to Cumberland Lodge.

During the period that separated the end of term and our final Honours examinations, my good friend, Alan Morgan and I were invited to spend two weeks at the Lodge. We travelled from Cardiff by train in a closed carriage. Alan munched a 'Spam' sandwich, and offered me one. I accepted. By the time we reached London, Alan had fallen ill. On the train from London to Windsor, he felt worse. At Windsor Station we were met by a car and driven to the Lodge. There, outside the entrance to the Lodge, the senior staff assembled to greet us. Miss Buller stepped forward, hands outstretched. Roger Young stepped forward, hands outstretched. Isabella Elphinstone stepped forward, hands outstretched. Alan and I climbed out of the car. We moved slowly towards the entrance, bags in hands.

Then poor Alan vomited at Amy Buller's feet.

There is a sequel to this story. In our shared bedroom, Alan was put to bed to recover. Lady Elphinstone acted as nurse and administered cool hands, soothing words and camomile tea. I watched, almost enviously, from my own bed. Later in the week, when Alan was on the mend, but before he was up and about, we were joined for a day by a large contingent of students from the University of London. They represented different Christian groups, Protestant, Catholic and Non-Conformist. After lunch on that day, I was talking to members of one of the groups when I myself began to feel ill. I rushed apologetically from the room, vomited and then took to my bed. The Spam had struck again. It was my turn.

Alas, Lady Elphinstone never came my way. Perhaps she was at Court.[7]

*****

After a month or so at the University, finding my feet again in 1947, I fell into a work–leisure routine which I found to be congenial. Each weekday would begin with breakfast at my lodgings, usually porridge, with Tate and Lyle's Golden Syrup and milk, followed by fried bread and egg, sometimes with bacon or kippered herrings.

After breakfast, I would don a long-sleeved white shirt, with separate 'Van Heusen' collar and thin tie, and cover these with a greenish-coloured Harris Tweed sports jacket (my only jacket) and raincoat. Then I would cycle, or take the bus to the University buildings at Cathays Park, to attend lectures that were later rehashed in long and sometimes vehement discussions over Heinz spaghetti on toast or cottage pie in the Students' Union refectory. These might be continued in the 'Rhondda Corner', an area in one of the cloakrooms where a small group of students from the Rhondda Valley congregated every day. Although I was an Englishman and a foreigner (a 'Sais'), I was accepted as a kind of honorary member of the group, largely because I was introduced to them by John Davis (known as John 'Trombone' Davis, to distinguish him from the other Davis's in the Cwm Park Brass Band). I first met John at Devonport Barracks where, like me, he was awaiting a posting to a ship or another shore establishment.

Most of the members of the Rhondda Corner came from mining families and were united by their fierce interest in education, their passion for Rugby football, their determination to succeed ('Christ, boyo, I finished sixty pages of that piss-pot, Kant, last night') and their left-wing political affiliations. It was in the Rhondda Corner that I heard Winston Churchill criticised for the first time. I was shocked since, like many English people, I considered him to be the wartime saviour of the country (and I still do). The boys of the Rhondda Corner saw him in a different light. They had not forgotten what they had been told about Churchill's decision to confront a crowd of coalminers with troops during the General Strike which took place in the year of my birth. 'The murdering bug-ger', they called him in English but I am sure that their epithets were much more imaginative in Welsh.

The study regimen was severe but stimulating and there were opportunities for relief in soccer games, Saturday-night dances at the Union, singing in a choir conducted by Alan Morgan, cinema-going and visits to the theatre, not only the Prince of Wales and the New Theatre, but also the Reardon-Smith Theatre where plays of quality were presented by the University Dramatic Society.

In June 1948, I sat examinations at the Subsidiary level in English and History and at Intermediate level in Education. The results could mean that one might have to repeat a year at one's own expense, for the government grant did not allow for failure. In early July, the Pass Lists were pinned to a notice-board in the lobby of the main University building and I noted thankfully that I had passed successfully.

In August 1948, I received a letter from the Head of the English Department at Cardiff, notifying me that I had done well enough in the Subsidiary examinations to be enrolled in the two-year Honours course organised by the Department. Did I wish to be accepted? I replied in the affirmative.

So the summer of 1948 was satisfying. I had earned a little money and was accepted into the English Honours School. There remained only one highlight to cap the vacation and this was the Australia–England Test Match held at Old Trafford, the Lancashire county cricket ground. I had not been able to reserve a seat and I went to the ground without much hope that I would be able to get in, consoling myself with the possibility that at home I would be able to listen to the flamboyant radio commentaries of John Arlott, supported by his more conventional partner, Rex Alston. Fortunately, after a long wait in a cheerful queue at Old Trafford, I was able to buy a ticket and found myself a place on the grass, with an up-and-down view of the wicket.

Australia's team was formidable. Donald Bradman – that great cricketer of the 1930s – led the side, and played some fine innings for it, supported by Barnes, Brown, Harvey, Hassett, Morris, the all-rounder Miller, and the wicket-keeper batsman Tallon. The attack was equally menacing, with pace bowlers Lindwall and Miller supported by the medium pace and spin of Johnston, Johnson and Loxton.

A few years ago in *The Daily Telegraph*, I saw a photograph of the then sixty-one-year-old Lindwall 'turning his arm over' with some difficulty for an Old World XI, in competition with an Old England XI. The caption referred to him, quite incorrectly, as the 'former bodyline bowler, Ray Lindwall'. Either the caption writer had mistaken Lindwall for Harold Larwood or his ignorance of the game was so profound that he was unable to distinguish between a bowler who bowls an occasional 'bouncer' and the bodyline tactics worked out by the England side that toured Australia in the early 1930s and which relied on Larwood, Allan and Voce to execute them.

In 1948 the twenty-six-year-old Lindwall was sometimes unplayable. He was very fast and able to maintain an immaculate line and length. But it was the beauty of his action that I remember, with his fluid lope to the wicket, the rhythmic flow of his shoulders and the final, graceful delivery of the ball that immediately became a deadly missile.

The late Keith Miller, Lindwall's regular partner for the opening overs, flew Mosquito fighter-bombers over Germany during the Second World War, an experience that he never forgot. 'When athletes these days talk of pressure,' he once declared, 'they only reveal what they don't know of life. They've never had a Messerschmitt up their arse. That's pressure.'

One incident in the match was unforgettable. The Lancashire fast bowler, Dick Pollard, was playing on his home ground. Good pace bowler he was. Batsman he was not. There came the moment when Dick was at the wicket, facing Johnson at one end and Keith Miller at the other. Bradman was applying pressure and had a ring of fielders round the bat, with Barnes at the silly mid-on position, very close in. Dick had scored a few, using the 'eyes shut, nothing to lose' principle.

From the Old Trafford end, Johnson delivered a tempting full toss on the leg side. Dick's startled response was to open his vast shoulders and, cross-batted, attempt to swipe the ball over the scoreboard. Unexpectedly, he connected and, caught in the meat of the bat, the ball shot rocket-like to the boundary. Unfortunately, Barnes was in the way of the cannonball that struck him in the middle of the stomach. He jackknifed and lay folded on the ground until he was carried off the field like a broken reed.

*****

On 24 June 1950, two years almost to the day after the Old Trafford Test Match, I received a telephone call confirming that I had been awarded a Second Class Degree in English. I decided, there and then, to return to Cardiff to study for a Diploma in Education. I knew that I would continue to receive my personal allowance from the government and that my tutorial and other university costs would be met.

Punctuated by (unsuccessful) applications for employment in schools and other educational establishments, my Diploma year passed very pleasantly. In the second term I spent four weeks as a student teacher at a primary school and in the third and final term a similar six weeks at a grammar school in Penarth, Glamorgan, a school previously attended as a pupil by a future Governor of Hong Kong, Sir Edward Youde. When not engaged in teaching practice or in attending lectures on different aspects of education, I was developing an ever-growing interest in drama. I played small roles in College productions of plays such as R.C. Sherriff's, *Badgers Green*, Shakespeare's *Troilus and Cressida* and John Dryden's, *Marriage à la Mode*. Later, I was given somewhat larger roles in T.S. Eliot's *Sweeney Agonistes* and George Bernard Shaw's play for two characters, *A Village Wooing*.

It was all excellent preparation for what was to come.

THE FIFTH STEP

SINGAPORE: LION CITY

– 12 –

The Undelivered Message

With some regret, I left the University at the beginning of June 1951 and took a summer job for one month at a Home for elderly men (known in those days as an 'Old Men's Home'). My job each morning was to stoke the boiler; make about thirty beds; damp-mop the linoleum floors; dust the furniture in all the rooms; clean the windows in the bedrooms and common rooms; assist with the dish-washing that followed breakfast and lunch; and when these chores were finished hold myself ready to take on any other tasks that needed to be done.

During my first week at the Home the Warden was rather hostile. It was obvious that he had little time for university students, believing them to be effete and incapable of hard manual work. He could not have known then that he was supervising the finest lavatory-cleaner and the most experienced 'squeegee' artist in Lincolnshire! I am happy to say that his attitude changed at the beginning of my second week at the Home and our relationship became quite cordial.

The men who were admitted to the Home were more or less destitute. Those who had a little money were obliged to surrender it to the authorities. Part of this money was handed back to them on a Saturday night when they were allowed out of the Home and given permission to visit the local 'pub'. Although the Warden did not object to the men leaving the Home, he imposed a strict curfew and declared that any man failing to return to the Home after 10.30pm would be locked out. This happened on only one occasion during my short period of employment. One old man broke the curfew and sure enough he was forbidden entrance. He spent the night on a bench in the garden of the Home. It did not seem to do him any harm.

Men were not allowed to die in an 'Old Men's Home'. If an inmate was found to be seriously ill and at the point of death he would be taken out of the Home and transferred to a hospital. The system was different in the Death Houses of Singapore, in which city I was to spend the years 1951 to 1959. In contrast to the British system, Chinese families of humble means would bring their elderly and infirm to the 'Houses' of Sago Lane to live out their last days. Each person in a 'House' was allocated a living space and shared sanitary arrangements. A number of shops in nearby Sago Street sold funeral artifacts such as flowers, clothes and paper money to family members. Their relatives could take these to the next world.

The Death Houses were closed down in 1961 and since then the street and the entire area has been redeveloped. It incorporates what is now weirdly named 'Chinatown' – weirdly since the Chinese are in the majority in Singapore, despite the presence of other, smaller, ethnic groups such as Malays and persons of Indian and Sri Lankan origin.

But – back in South Wales – the time came for one hundred-year-old George to end his days outside the Old Men's Home. As in all closed communities, rumours spread very easily. Someone said (and he was believed) that George had kept some money back from the Warden. He had hidden this money somewhere in the wall that surrounded the Home.

During the last week of my stay, I observed little old men furtively poking their sticks in places where they thought hidden treasure might be concealed. I hope one of them found it.

*****

From July to September 1951, I was employed as a clerk by Cambrian Airways, a regional airline based in Cardiff. My multi-faceted job was to issue the tickets, weigh the passengers, serve them with sandwiches and tea and then escort them out to the aircraft. The Company owned five outdated but sturdy De Havilland Rapide planes, each seating seven passengers. The only routes operated by the Company were Cardiff to Jersey, Cardiff to Weston-Super-Mare and Cardiff to Liverpool (to connect with Aer Lingus flights to Ireland).

I was so impressed by the short and tall tales told by the five Cambrian pilots (each of whom had served in the Royal Air Force during the Second World War) that I toyed with the idea of applying to BEA (British European Airways) for a more permanent job which would offer long-term career prospects. At the beginning of September, however, I was informed that my application to join the Colonial Education Service had been successful. I would be posted to Singapore, dubbed in a dispatch of 18 September 1820, 'The Emporium and the Pride of the East', by its founder, Sir Thomas Stamford Raffles: 'My settlement of Singapore continues to thrive most wonderfully. It is all and everything I could wish, and if no untimely fate awaits it, promises to become the Emporium and the Pride of the East.'

My appointment came about in a somewhat bizarre manner. After completing my Diploma course, I sent job applications to a number of organisations and government departments, including the Colonial Office. After some weeks, I received a summons to attend an interview at Great Smith Street, London. The interview was scheduled for 12 noon. In those days the train journey from Cardiff to London took about three hours. It seemed to me that I would arrive in good time for the interview if I left Cardiff by the train scheduled to leave at 7.30am.

At 6.45am on the appointed day, I left my lodgings in Kimberley Road and boarded a tram. Unaware of the importance of my journey, the tram chose to break down about a quarter of a mile from the railway station. I waited for some minutes and then needed to make a quick decision. Stay with the tram or abandon it? I decided on the latter course, jumped off and ran towards the station. As I entered the concourse, the barrier gates were closing. 'Please let me through. I have an important appointment in London,' said I, to a grim-faced railway official. 'Can't do that,' he said. 'Take the next train.' 'When is the next train?' 'Oh, about ten o'clock, I think, boyo. Ask at the ticket office.' In despair, I sped to a taxi rank at the entrance to the station. 'Can you race the 8 o'clock London train to Newport?' (an important stop on the way). 'No, I can't do that, lad, more than my license is worth.'

There was no alternative. It would have to be the ten o'clock train. I would not arrive in London for my interview until at least one hour after the scheduled time. Somewhat depressed, I decided to telephone the Colonial Office at the first stop, Newport. The telephone was conveniently placed on the station platform. I made contact very easily and was able to give my message to a clerk. Could he please convey my apologies to the interview board; explain that I had been delayed, but that I was on my way? 'Yes sir. I'll do that.'

I arrived at Great Smith Street at 1.20pm. In 1951, the security of office buildings was often made the responsibility of retired military men. In this particular case, the 'guard' was a former naval petty officer: 'Ooo, you're very late, sir. They've been waiting for you for a long time.' This comment was disheartening, to say the least, and I felt distinctly apprehensive as I entered the interview room:

You're late. *Very* late

Yes, I must apologise, sir. I'm afraid that I missed the train. But I hope that you received my message.

Message? What message?

I telephoned the station from Newport, sir, to explain that I would be late.

Just a moment. [The Chairman made a telephone call.]

OH, I SEE. YOU STILL HAVE THE MESSAGE! WHY WASN'T IT SENT UP HERE? OH [*irritably*] VERY WELL.

[I stood in front of the Chairman's desk.]

Do sit down. Do sit down. Let me take your coat. Now, let me see. You have applied for a post in Cyprus. How old are you?

I'm twenty-five, sir.

Twenty-five. Mmn. I see. Cyprus is a small place. There would not be many opportunities for you to make your way up the ladder. We strongly recommend that you should apply for Malaya. Would you be interested?

That's very kind of you, sir. Yes, I believe I would.

Good, good. Thank you for attending this interview. We will let you know.

I would like to believe that the selection board had my best interests at heart. Untroubled then by EOKA separatists, Cyprus in 1951 was regarded by ill-informed outsiders as a peaceful place, a land of unadulterated milk and honey, blessed by plenty of sunshine and not too long a flight from Britain. Malaya, on the other hand, was in the throes of a dangerous 'Emergency'. Was it possible that I was being penalised for arriving late for the interview? Surely not!

Several weeks after attending this interview, I received from the Colonial Office the offer of a position as an Education Officer in the Malayan Education Service. My appointment would begin from the date on which I would be expected to leave for Malaya on 10 November 1951. There would be a three-year period of probation from the date of my arrival in Malaya, that is, from the 13 November 1951. I would be granted two years six months and fourteen days war service credit and would be permitted to draw an initial salary of 470 Malayan dollars a month, proceeding to $500 a month on 27 April 1952. A cost of living allowance and an expatriation allowance would also be payable.

The Malayan Education Service made no deductions of salary for British National Insurance and indeed I was not asked to contribute to the British scheme during my entire service in Singapore, from 1951 to 1959. I was later to regret this omission since a portion of my social security pension was reduced for lack of sufficient voluntary contributions.[1] Although the British Social Security system did not apply in Malaya, a pension scheme was in place which, '(was) permitted or (might be) ordered at any time on or after attaining the age of 55 or, in special cases, with prescribed approval, on attaining the age of 50'. Compulsory contributions had also to be made to a Widows' and Orphans' scheme. Male officers were required to contribute four per cent of salary (including Expatriation Pay) to a local scheme, set up to provide for the payment of pensions to widows and orphans.

*****

On Tuesday, 10 November, my wife, Lois and I enjoyed a farewell dinner in London with our friends, Brian Seymour and Alan Hansen before boarding a British Overseas Airways (BOAC) 'Argonaut' propeller-driven aircraft at the then modestly-sized Heathrow Airport. We were bound for Singapore in search of a new career rather than the Golden Fleece, and we certainly had no desire to meet Jason's fate with the wreck of another Argo. Although calmed by the elegant and 'well-spoken' hostesses (not 'stewardesses' or 'flight attendants') it was something of a relief to arrive at our first stop, Rome. There we were each provided with a cardboard box containing a sandwich, a piece of cake and a peach. Deprived of our passports but fortified by the snacks, we were driven round the city until the time came for our plane to begin the second leg of the journey, to Pakistan, a new country that had not yet been divided. At that time Bangladesh did not exist.

In Karachi, we were allocated a chalet for five hours of uneasy sleep before we were asked to re-board the plane for the final leg of the journey to Singapore.

Originally a Mon-Khmer settlement and later a colony of the Buddhist Srivijaya, a vassal state of Siam and a thriving sixteenth-century port-of-call, Singapore was mainly inhabited in the early years of the nineteenth century by Malay fishermen who, under their chief, the 'Temenggong', were subjects of the Sultan of Riau. The city is said to have been named Singapura ('Lion City') by a Sumatran ruler, Sri Tri Buana, who saw a tiger and took it to be a lion.

After the intervention of Sir Stamford Raffles in 1819 and the signing of the Treaty of London in 1824 which gave Singapore and Malacca to Britain, the island flourished as a busy, free entrepôt port. The social changes which accompanied this development came about largely because of the growing demand in 'Western' countries for the raw materials (such as rubber and tin) of Malaya, marketed largely through Singapore. They were affected also by an influx of South Indian Muslims, Hindus, Jews of Sephardi descent and individuals from different Chinese dialect and language groups: Hokkien, Teochew, Cantonese, Hainanese and Hakka. Although some parts of the growing city were recognised as areas that were predominately Malay, Chinese, Indian, Jewish or 'European', there was no area that was ethnically sealed off; there were no ghettos. As the years went by, the threads of what had become a pluralistic society were more and more drawn together by English, the link language.

In 1951 Singapore Airport was situated in the Kallang district and it was there that we were met by Arnold Halliday, a Senior Education Officer based in the Education Department. Nothing if not bluff, Arnold drove us to The Cockpit Hotel, all the while dispensing trenchant advice about Singapore, the Education Department and Raffles Institution where I was to teach English (and Physical Training!).

The hotel was situated then at Number 6 Oxley Rise, a narrow street leading off Orchard Road and Oxley Road, the latter named after a Dr Thomas Oxley. Orchard Road owed its name to a nutmeg plantation owned by William Cuppage, a postal clerk, in the 1830s.[2] Oxley Road is perhaps better known today as one of the homes of Singapore's Senior Minister, Lee Kuan Yew.

Orchard Road had developed hardly at all when we first arrived, boasting only a few shops, the well-frequented Princes' Restaurant, and the Indonesian Consulate. Today, The Cockpit Hotel has been re-located to Number 115, Penang Road and Orchard Road is a major thoroughfare lined with shopping malls and luxury hotels such as The Marriott, The Mandarin and Le Meridien. It has been described recently by an ecstatic real estate developer as 'one of the world's greatest shopping streets'. Hyperbole aside, it certainly attracts many 'shopaholics'.

Very soon after the Second World War, The Cockpit at Oxley Rise became popular with airline employees. This accounted for the strings of model aircraft which decorated the hotel bar. Guest rooms were situated in the main building and a group of chalets provided additional accommodation. We were allocated one of these chalets and were comfortable enough during our four-month stay.

Although the Second World War had come to an end only six years before our arrival, Singapore had made a remarkable recovery if one was to judge by the variety and quantity of food available at the hotel. Full 'English Breakfasts' were followed by piquant lunches and dinners. On Saturdays, a splendid Indonesian *rijstaffel* (several different curries) was served on the outside terrace by a line of waiters, each carrying a separate, aromatic dish. Every evening, in the main hotel building, Charlie Lazaroo played dinner music on the piano. During the day, for five and a half days a week, Charlie taught English at Raffles Institution.

*****

In 1951, Singapore was ostensibly at peace although there had been riots a year before our arrival, sparked by the 'Hertogh' case. In 1942, during the Japanese occupation of Hong Kong, a Dutch woman, Adeline Hertogh, handed her over her baby to a Malay woman, Che Aminah, for protection since she (Adeline) and her husband believed – rightly – that they were about to be interned by the Japanese in Java. The parents survived the Japanese internment camp and in 1950 came to re-claim their child. The foster family objected. The child was now *their* child. Stirred up by the Malay Nationalist Party, the argument became a racial matter: Malays versus 'Europeans', and blood was shed. Eighteen people were killed and 173 persons were injured in the rioting. Eventually, judgement was given in favour of the natural mother.

With the riots over and order restored, Singapore appeared calm but there were worries below the surface – and here I quote from my book, *Searching for Frederick* [3] –

> In 1948, the Malayan Communist Party ordered the Malayan Peoples' Anti-Japanese Army (MPAJA) back into the jungle. The intention was to declare Malaya a Communist Republic in August 1948 and oust the British. Under the command of Chin Peng, Secretary-General of the Malayan Communist Party, the MPAJA was re-named the Malayan People's Anti-*British* Army (MPABA). [4] Hostilities began when a squad from the fifth Regiment of the revived force murdered five persons at Sungei Siput in Perak in June 1948.

Several more murders followed and as a result, a state of emergency was declared on 19 June 1948.

The so-called 'Emergency' was actually an unpleasant and violent *war*, as is clear from the casualty figures. During the three-year period 1949–51 alone, over one thousand police and soldiers lost their lives and two thousand communist guerillas were killed.

A controversial film released in 2006 has stirred up old memories. Entitled *Lelaki Komunis Terakhir* ('The Last Communist'), it has been described as a 'semi-musical road movie that traces the towns in which Chin Peng lived'.[5] The film has been banned for general viewing although a special screening was arranged in May 2006 for members of the Malaysian Parliament, senators and the media. In a letter to *The Sun* newspaper on 19 May the same year, an indignant Hamdan Ibrahim of Kuala Lumpur deplored the ban and claimed:

> We should be proud that we are the only nation that managed to win the war against the communists, not through battles alone but most importantly, by winning [sic] the hearts and minds of the people. This resulted in their sympathisers abandoning the communist struggle as it is unsuitable in this multiracial country of ours.[6]

Some re-writing of history there. The late General Sir Gerald Templar would have corrected Mr Ibrahim – politely – I hope.

The seriousness of the Malayan situation was brought home to us by one of the guests in The Cockpit, a rubber planter by profession. He was spending a few days in Singapore before returning to his estate in Malaya, following a spell of leave in Europe. He was a frightened man, understandably. The dangers were very real. To quote just one case, referred to in G.E.D. Lewis's memoir, *Out East in the Malay Peninsula*,[7]

> (Mr) Stuchbury had been preparing to set out with a police escort on the Bentong–Kuala Lumpur road. Mrs Stuchbury, perhaps rather recklessly, decided to go ahead with a Chinese interpreter and stopped on the way in a most unfortunate place. It was the very spot where the Communist terrorists had set an ambush. They therefore had no difficulty in abducting both Mrs Stuchbury and the Chinese interpreter, and then murdered them both in the nearby jungle. She was shown no mercy. The insurgents cut her throat.

We arrived in Singapore on 13 November 1951, thirty-nine days after the British High Commissioner was assassinated. I referred to this, now well-recalled, event in *Searching for Frederick*:[8]

> Sir Henry Gurney, British High Commissioner in Malaya, had been ambushed by a band of thirty-eight terrorists while driving up the

winding road to Fraser's Hill, a hill resort favoured by residents of
Kuala Lumpur. When the terrorists began to shoot, Sir Henry got out of
the car to divert fire away from his wife. He was successful. Lady Gurney
survived, a miracle, since the unarmoured official car (a Rolls Royce) was
punctured by thirty-five bullets, mostly fired from the guerilla band's two
Bren guns.

The MPABA's activities were not restricted to the Malayan peninsula.
The organisation was also prepared to challenge the British in Singapore.
This was done in various ways. In April 1955, for example, the MPABA may
have been behind the riots that took place between strikers of the Hock
Lee Amalgamated Bus Company and the Singapore police. In the middle
1950s, evidence emerged that covert cells had been established in Chinese-
medium middle schools. In October 1956 more than four thousand
students assumed control over two of the Colony's largest middle schools,
Chung Cheng School and the Chinese High School. Following that action,
142 students from eight Chinese schools were expelled. Two teachers were
dismissed and seven others received warnings.

*****

Singapore began to 'grow' its own politicians after the Second World War.
Two of the most prominent of these – the charismatic Eurasian lawyer,
David Marshall and the trade unionist, Lim Yew Hock – pressed for
'Merdeka' (self-government) but not through the methods advocated by
the MPABA. They preferred negotiation with the British. These tactics
were partially successful in that limited self-government was achieved in
1955. David Marshall became Singapore's Chief Minister after taking his
Labour Front party to victory in a territory-wide election. He resigned
the following year (May 1956) after leading a thirteen-man delegation to
London where negotiations for full self-government failed. According to
Lee Kuan Yew, Marshall, supported by another member of the delegation,
Lim Chin Siong, rejected the British offer of a self-governing constitution
by which the Singapore government would have control of internal
security but Britain would retain power to override this constitution if it
proved to be necessary.[9] Lim Yew Hock took over from Marshall who, on
his return from Britain, spoke movingly on the radio about his decision
to resign. I happened to be using a studio in Radio Malaya (now Radio
Singapore) on the day of the resignation and found the following notes
scribbled on a piece of wafer-thin paper:

I would like to mention the conduct of one delegate from the Opposition, Mr Lim Chin Siong. Although we disagreed at times and once he was quite angry with me, he displayed so deep an urge for the welfare of the people of Singapore, ignoring personal and party considerations, that the whole delegation was impressed and he was a real help in maintaining the unity of the delegation. On your behalf I thank this true patriot for his sincerity and his courage.

Lim Chin Siong was a pro-Communist, a member of the Singapore Bus Workers' Union and a markedly left-wing group known popularly as 'The Big Six'. In October 1956, he was detained by the British authorities, together with fellow members, Fong Swee Suan (paid Secretary of the Bus Workers' Union), Devan Nair (Secretary of the Singapore Teachers' Union), Sandrasegeram ('Sandra') Woodhull and James Puthucheary (both Marxists of a kind) and Chan Chiaw Thor. All were released in June 1959.

In August 1958, the British Parliament changed the status of Singapore from a colony to a state and elections were scheduled for May 1959. Ten parties contested the election, won easily by the Peoples' Action Party. In June 1959, Lee Kuan Yew was sworn in as Prime Minister of the self-governing state of Singapore. In August 1963, Singapore declared its independence and in September of the same year it became part of the newly-formed Malaysia which comprised Singapore, Malaya, Sarawak and Sabah. The link with Malaysia lasted for only two years and in August 1965, Singapore separated from Malaysia.

These facts about the political development of Singapore can be extracted from any written history or web site. However, I feel justified in reiterating them, since I was present when many of the events took place. During a riot in 1956, I was obliged to duck into a side street to avoid a mob and I remember how alarmed we were when extreme left-wing politicians such as James Puthucheary and Devan Nair joined the PAP. With hindsight, it seems that our worries were groundless since their cards were neatly trumped by Lee Kuan Yew. Independent Singapore has flourished although it has a reputation as a 'nanny state'.

Despite occasional journalistic statements to the contrary, there is no doubt that Mr Lee and his supporters benefited from the excellent infrastructure that they inherited. Singapore has not been transformed, as has sometimes been said, from the 'third world' of the 1950s to the 'first world' of the twenty-first century. To take just one example, the Housing and Development Board established in 1960 was built upon the firm basis inherited from its predecessor the Singapore Improvement Trust, an organisation established by the British shortly after the Second World War. Other modern civil institutions have developed from similar strong foundations.

I lived in Singapore from 1951 to 1959. Much was done during those years to reconstruct the Colony after the depredations of war. In the early 1950s, the roads were excellent and the public services and utilities operated smoothly. Educational institutions recovered rapidly although much remained to be achieved in the Chinese-medium schools. The University of Malaya in Singapore successfully revived its intellectual traditions through the medium of English. In contrast, as we shall see later, a controversial new Chinese-medium university named Nanyang was opened in March 1956.

On my second day in Singapore, I was driven to 'Raffles' by Donald Darke, one of the few other Education Officers recruited after the Second World War. Donald arrived in Singapore *circa* 1948 and so was a comparatively old hand. The poet and novelist, Seamus Fraser, was another outstanding early arrival. Seamus was an enthusiastic poet. Posted to a government secondary school, Victoria Institution, he passed on his love for poetry to pupils such as Edwin Thumboo who later became Dean of the Faculty of Arts at the National University of Singapore and a pioneer of the 'Asian Writers in English' movement.

A year before I arrived in Singapore, two other Education Officers had been appointed to Raffles, Geoffrey Rutt, an historian, and David Hughes, an anthropologist turned geographer.

Raffles Institution was founded by Sir Stamford Raffles in 1823, 'for the cultivation of Asian languages, the education of the sons of Malay rulers and the moral and intellectual improvement of the peoples of Asia'. When I was there, the school was housed in an elegant (although crumbling) colonial building, part of which faced Bras Basah ('Wet Rice') Road and Raffles Hotel, described by Ilsa Sharp as 'a marvellous French Renaissance-style wedding cake'.[10]

In addition to my duties as an English teacher, I was given the task of running the school library on the first floor of the building. It was possible to peep through the gaps in the floorboards of the library to the floor beneath and there were other structural faults. Despite these problems, the decision to move the school to another site was a mistake. Part of Singapore's heritage was obliterated, smothered by yet another ugly commercial complex (designed by I.M. Pei) comprising two hotels, an office tower and a shopping centre, all at an estimated cost of one billion Singapore dollars.

121

On my first morning at Raffles, I introduced myself to the Headmaster, Mr Philip Howitt, and then met Mr Ambiavagar, a colleague in the English Department. He ignored the preliminaries and went straight to the point with the question, 'How important do you believe Milton to have been as an influence in English literature?' I was startled and somewhat bemusedly rehearsed in my mind my superficial knowledge of Milton. *Samson Agonistes? Paradise Lost* and *Regained? Comus?* Was this a trick question? How should my answer be structured? Before I could offer a stumbling reply, Mr Ambiavagar floated away, satisfied (I hope) with the impression that he had certainly made.

I believe it is true to say that Raffles Institution was and still is the premier secondary school in Singapore, the equivalent of Queen's College in Hong Kong, described in my wife, Gillian's, book, *The Golden Needle*.[11] How could Raffles *not* be the top school? It was attended by the former Chief Minister, Harry Lee (better known as Lee Kuan Yew) from 1936 to 1939 and, as a history of the school notes,[12] the first two Presidents of Singapore, the first Chief Minister and two Prime Ministers were pupils at the school. In 1983 twenty members of Parliament were Rafflesians, of whom eight were Ministers.

As I 'write', I have in front of me a photograph of the staff taken in 1954. I see in the front row Mr Wee Seong Kang, a father figure in the English Department and a former pupil at the school; next to him Mr E.W. Jesudason, Mr V. Ambiavagar and Mr Philip Liau. (Each of these would later become Principal of the school.) Then there are Lian Fook Shin (later Head of the Visual Aids Department at the Singapore Teachers' Training College and at the University of Singapore), M.A. Mallal, a distinguished historian, and myself.

Missing from the photograph is my friend, Kwan Sai Kheong, a graduate of Raffles Institution. A teacher of mathematics, painting, calligraphy and music, Sai Kheong was made Vice-Principal of the Singapore Teachers' Training College in 1957. In 1961 he was named Director of Education and Permanent Secretary in the Ministry of Education. In 1975 he was appointed Vice-Chancellor of the University of Singapore and after retirement became Singapore's Ambassador to the Philippines.

Sai Kheong was an inventor as well as a scholar-administrator. Four of his inventions were registered with the Patents Office in London. He also designed the well-known Merlion Statue, sculptured by a local craftsman, Lim Nang Seng. This statue has now become a national icon, visited by thousands of tourists each year. Originally placed on a site at the mouth of the Singapore River, the statue has now been moved to 'Merlion Pier', near to the Fullerton Building, originally a post office and now a luxury hotel.

It has to be reiterated that when I began to teach at the school in 1951, only six years had passed since the Second World War and the Japanese occupation of Singapore had come to an end. Some members of the staff had suffered considerably during the Occupation, although few were willing to talk in detail about their experiences. One colleague, Mr Yapp Thean Chye, told me that he had worked as a rickshaw driver for several years. In his new role as a teacher at Raffles, Mr Yapp was usually given the responsibility of organising celebratory staff dinners. Often these were held at one or other of the 'Worlds' in Singapore, the New World, the Happy World or the rather risqué Great World. Today, these 'Worlds' might be labelled 'Theme Parks'. Each park occupied what was considerable acreage in Singapore and included restaurants, cabarets with 'taxi dancers' (girls who would dance with customers for a set fee), Chinese theatres, food stalls, photographic studios, small booths with trinkets for sale and platforms for *joget* folk dances. These last are graceful dances performed to a particular tempo (the *ronggeng*). The male and female partners do not touch each other.

It was invariably the custom at Chinese banquets for bottles of (duty free) brandy to be provided on the table and Shark's Fin and Birds' Nest soups were mandatory.

– 13 –

Friends and Acquaintances

In 1951, the Malayan Emergency had reached a critical phase. The rubber plantations and tin mines were under siege, the economy had been seriously disrupted and there were several 'incidents' (mainly ambushes), each day. Drastic remedial action was necessary and so the decision was made in Britain to turn the High Commissioner's job over to a soldier. The story went round that, at the conclusion of a dinner party in London, Winston Churchill suddenly raised his head from his wine glass and addressed a relatively junior army officer seated at the other end of the table. In that familiar rasp that was almost a snarl, he said, 'Templar, Malaya.'[1]

Tony Beamish, later to be a Director of Radio Malaya, served as Sir Gerald Templar's ADC during the War. In an interview with *The Straits Times* in Singapore,[2] he described Templar as a man of action and a soldier-administrator of the highest quality. 'He (has) a sense of humour, but no patience with incompetent people... he did not hesitate to remove those who showed inefficiency... He is restless, always wanting to move forward and very optimistic.'

I remember Templar's flat and somewhat menacing voice well for, from time to time, I read news bulletins for Radio Malaya. Often a bulletin would include a pre-recorded interview between Templar and a journalist, or an item like the following:

The time is 9.30pm. This is Radio Malaya. Here is the news, read by Verner Bickley. Three terrorists were captured today by security forces, following an ambush near Kuala Lipis... In Kuala Lumpur last night, General Sir Gerald Templar said that final arrangements had been made for him to meet the terrorist leader, Chin Peng. The meeting would take place in the village of Yong Peng...

It is quite possible that the Templar/Chin Peng interview was arranged by Alec Peterson whom I was to meet on several occasions after I left Singapore. Who was Peterson?

After service in Intelligence during the Second World War in the Propaganda Branch of the Special Operations Executive, Alec returned to his pre-war occupation as a teacher and from 1946 to 1952 served as Headmaster of Adams' Grammar School in Shropshire. After Templar had been in Malaya for about three months, he invited Peterson to visit Malaya in a consultant capacity. Peterson accepted and spent a couple of months in Malaya, considering ways and means by which covert propaganda work might be strengthened. His recommendations were accepted by Templar who then challenged Peterson to return to Malaya to implement them. Not one to resist a challenge, Alec obtained the blessings of his wife and his school and returned to Kuala Lumpur in July 1952, to begin a two-year contract as Director-General of Information Services. I did not know Alec then but many of the news bulletins that I read must have had Alex's hand behind them. His role in the winning of the propaganda battle must have been quite significant.

Alec never returned to Adams' Grammar School. After his return from Malaya, he became Headmaster of Dover College and then Head of the Department of Education at Oxford University.

In 1962 I attended a conference in Cambridge organised by the British Council. The conference itself was not particularly interesting but the conferees were. I met I.A. Richards who worked with the late C.K. Ogden on Basic English, Edmund Blunden, the Romantic poet and at that time Head of the Department of English at the University of Hong Kong, E.M. Forster, the novelist and Alec Peterson. Alec had recently published a seminal history of British education, named *A Hundred Years of Education*.

My next meeting with Alec was in Honolulu. I invited him as a consultant to my Institute (The Culture Learning Institute) at the East–West Center and he was able to make some very useful suggestions for the improvement of our various educational projects and to discuss his new responsibilities as Director of the International Baccalaureate organisation. He stayed with us in our home in Kahala Avenue and was a courteous and thoughtful guest. Why do I write of Alec now?

When I was in Jeddah, Saudi Arabia (from 1981 to 1983), I borrowed a paperback book from a 'book exchange' in Saudia City. The idea was that you would put 'x' number of books into the kitty and in return you could borrow a similar number of books. One Thursday evening, I came home with what I thought might be a good adventure 'yarn', entitled *The Sea Wolves*, by James Leasor. The book turned out not to be fiction but an entertaining account of an actual clandestine operation carried out in India and Goa during the Second World War. Alec Peterson played a major role in planning the operation which is referred to in some detail in the daily newspaper, the *Calcutta Telegraph*, in two articles published on 21 August and 28 August 2005.

Three German ships led by the flagship *Ehrenfels* had taken refuge in Goa (then still a Portuguese colony). One of the ships was a 'Q' ship with a radio transmitter on board used by a German spy, code-named 'Trompeta', to convey information about allied shipping to German and Japanese submarines. Forty-six allied ships were sunk in six weeks, a total of 250,000 tons. Something needed to be done, and done quickly, if more losses were to be avoided.

After so many years, it is difficult to verify where and when planning for the operation took place or how many people were involved. What does seem certain is that, with Peterson's help, eighteen officers of an irregular cavalry unit named the Calcutta Light Horse were recruited for the mission. The men were drawn largely from Calcutta's business community.

There were two phases to the operation. Two men journeyed to Goa by train. Acting 'on information received' (from Peterson?), the men seized 'Trompeta' and took him to Belgaum in India where he was promptly gaoled. The men then returned to Goa and persuaded members of the local population to organise a party in the town for the crews of the three German ships. Despite receiving strict instructions not to go ashore, the sailors seized the opportunity and joined the party. Only a few guards were left on each ship.

The timing of the mission was crucial to its success. Before the party began, the remaining sixteen warriors had commandeered a ship named *Phoebe*. In this vessel they steamed through the Bay of Bengal and arrived in Goa when the party was in full swing. As the merrymaking continued, the men of the Light Horse boarded the *Ehrenfels* and engaged the crew successfully in hand-to-hand combat. The gallant sixteen then set fire to the ship and made their escape. Caught ashore at a party that they should not have attended, the crews of each German ship made their way back to their vessels and scuttled them. It would be interesting to know how their actions were received by the German High Command.

There is no doubt that the irregulars of the Calcutta Light Horse made a significant contribution to the Allied war effort in South Asia and saved a good many lives. Today, Calcutta's Saturday Club has a facility named 'The Light Horse Bar'. I understand that the medals on display were earned by some of its long-departed members, none of whom was a regular serviceman.

*****

In 1952, I suggested to Philip Howitt, the Principal of Raffles Institution, that I might work with some students on a short play. Howitt agreed and I chose Anton Chekov's, *The Proposal*. The cast was selected and I included a girl from Raffles' sister institution, Raffles Girls' School. Rehearsals went well. The actors worked hard. Their performances were well received and the play was adjudged to be the winner at the annual Singapore Schools' Drama Festival.

Success in the Drama Festival emboldened me to recommend that the school should combine with its sister school, Raffles Girls' School, to stage a full performance of Shakespeare's *As You Like It*, a text set for study and examination in 1953 for the Cambridge School Certificate examination. I was given permission to go ahead and set about the task of interpreting, managing and directing the play. My colleague, David Hughes helped in the construction of an apron stage in the school hall and did sterling work as Stage Manager. Evelyn Norris, a senior mistress at Raffles Girls' School (later appointed Principal) designed the costumes and had these made locally. Paul Abishegenaden, of the Education Department's music department, gathered together an excellent student orchestra which accompanied each performance. A week or so after the last night, Philip Howitt received a letter of congratulation from Professor Roy Morell, the Head of the English Department at the University of Malaya (Singapore). He said that he had thoroughly enjoyed the production.

*****

In Singapore I had now enriched my taste for the theatre and looked for other opportunities to perform, or direct. Such an opportunity soon presented itself at an audition held in 1953 for Shakespeare's *The Merchant of Venice*, also a set Cambridge Certificate text. This was to be a production of the Singapore Arts Theatre, directed by its founder, Donald Moore. I was selected to play Shylock and the rest of the cast was drawn from several different racial groups. To judge by the enthusiasm of the crowds of schoolchildren who attended the play, it was a great success.

To quote Donald:

> We played for three nights, and gave four matinee performances. The matinees were an attempt to cope with the four thousand Asian children who tried to book seats. It was a terrible pity that we still had to turn 2,000 of them away. The children's audiences, as always, were magnificent; always a jump ahead of the adult audiences, they were sharper, more responsive, clearly understanding the whole play far more intelligently than their elders, and obviously deriving far more enjoyment from it.

I have sometimes said that if I could gather all the necessary archival material, I would like to write Donald's life story. An ambitious, energetic man, bubbling with ideas, he was also generous to a fault. When his assistant, Geoffrey Penny, fell ill with tuberculosis, Donald gave him generous leave and paid his substantial medical bills. When my wife and two children were evacuated to Singapore from Jakarta, following the riots of 1963, Donald put them up for several nights and later made sure they were comfortably accommodated in a hotel.

Donald Moore was born in Leicestershire in 1923. After leaving school he worked for a short time in a bank until the beginning of the Second World War when he joined the Royal Navy and served mainly in Capital Ships and Aircraft Carriers. After the War, Donald exercised the option to be demobilised outside Britain. He chose Singapore and for a while worked in the 'Lion City' as a representative of the banknote makers, Waterlow and Sons. In 1947, he established an agency for British publishers in Singapore with the long-established company, Hodder and Stoughton, as his principal backers. According to the Company Director, John Attenborough (brother of the naturalist, David and the actor, Richard):

> Donald, and his wife, Joanna, who had worked in Simpkins, were well equipped for the job. They shared a zeal for British books... Donald combined the priceless gift of enthusiasm with a most attractive personality and, once the Moores reached Singapore in 1947, he showed a real gift for picking men of high quality to be his associates, irrespective of their Chinese, Japanese, Indian or English origins... in conjunction with Leo Timmermans, Donald began to explore and exploit the educational opportunities. His problem was a shortage of capital to support expansion. Beyond the phrase 'export or die,' was the ever-threatening presence of a

ghost rider whispering 'expand and die.' ... In the fifties however, the danger was still invisible to the young agency as it expanded its offices and warehouses to Kuala Lumpur, Penang, Hong Kong and Tokyo.[3]

I benefitted personally, albeit to a modest extent, from exploitation of 'the educational opportunities' when the University of London Press, a subsidiary of Hodder and Stoughton, published my anthology, *Poems to Enjoy*, as well as *A New Malayan Songbook*, jointly edited and written with my colleague Francis Mace, and the textbooks *Twentieth Century English* (with Kenneth Methold), *Systematic Composition*, (with Kenneth Methold), *Progressive English Exercises* (with Kenneth Methold), *Reading and Interpretation* (with Clarice Godfrey) and *Reading and Understanding* (also with Clarice Godfrey).

In 1960, John Attenborough visited Singapore, following a visit to New Zealand and India. He found Donald 'depressingly and inextricably involved in far too many local commitments... he listened to the warnings of the bank manager and hurriedly dictated firm guidelines for cutting one's publishing according to one's cloth, but the lesson was never learnt.'[4]

'Too many local commitments.' That was certainly true. These commitments stemmed from Donald's almost irresistible enthusiasm and perhaps the lack of a business partner willing to pour cold water onto some of his more innovative ideas, and say, 'No!'

By the early 1960s, Donald had accepted the representation of several British and American publishers. He started a Book Club and a Record Club. He opened a shop that sold Scandinavian crystal and teak products and he functioned as an impresario, bringing professional pianists, violinists, orchestras and actors, such as Sybil Thorndike and Lewis Casson, to Singapore.

There was the heady occasion when he served as the local agent for a United Services Organisation (USO) sponsored performance by the Benny Goodman Orchestra. Donald told me later that Goodman would under no circumstances allow his players to take alcoholic drinks before a performance. Answering a plea by a few of the musicians, Donald smuggled in some liquor in a set of thermos flasks. The contents were represented as containing coffee.

Not content with these various preoccupations, Donald became a published writer as well as a publishers' representative. His first book – *Far Eastern Agent* – gave a true account of the life of a representative of the book trade and became a best-seller. There followed, among others, a short story collection, *The Sacrifice*; a documentary, *We Live in Singapore*; an anthology, *Where Monsoons Meet* and two novels, *The Striking Wind* and *All of One Company.*

But the clouds – first observed by John Attenborough in 1960 – were thickening. In 1967 another representative of Hodder and Stoughton, Leo Timmermans, visited Singapore and thereafter submitted to the directors of Matthew Hodder a factual report on Donald's financial situation:

> Within seven days, John Attenborough was on his way to the Far East with carte blanche from the London publishers to take whatever steps seemed right to him to recover a collective debt in the region of Five Hundred Thousand Sterling Pounds and to reconstruct the agency if any reform seemed viable. The outcome was extraordinary. Donald and Joanna Moore resigned from the company within six hours of John's arrival in Singapore having decided to concentrate on their other local activities, ranging from bookshops to show business.[5]

Donald and Joanna now had to rely on their businesses in Singapore, but these were ultimately unsuccessful. Part of the trouble was that they were ahead of their time. They were pioneers in English language publishing and retail book-selling in Singapore, activities now conducted there by multi-national publishing companies and bookshop chains, such as Borders, Waterstones, Dymocks and Page One. Donald and Joanna's non-profit dramatic activities, professional 'show business', and music presentations appealed largely to an expatriate or British-educated audience in a city which, like Hong Kong, was once labelled a 'cultural desert'. Business was so bad for the Moores in the 1970s that nothing remained of their many enterprises except their theatrical agency. This too failed after it became necessary to 'paper the seats' for a Spanish Circus.

Then tragedy of a more personal nature struck. Joanna Moore and their eldest daughter, Sarah, were killed in a motorway accident whilst driving a 'camper' in Italy. A few years later, Donald – hounded by the tax authorities – left Singapore for good. I have not been able to trace him since that time, although it is possible that Karen, one of his other daughters, lives in Honolulu. I have made a few attempts to contact her, but without success.

– 14 –

Sarawak and Broadcasting Days

In early 1953 I was summoned to the Headmaster's study at Raffles Institution to be informed that I had been chosen with David Hughes (my colleague at Raffles) and Cicely Hinchcliffe, the Headmistress of Raffles Girls' School, to visit Kuching in Sarawak. We were to spend a week there, running a teacher training course. Cicely would travel separately.

The two-day voyage to Kuching on the SS *Rajah Brooke* was most pleasant, with calm seas. On arrival, David and I were met at the dock by a representative from the Education Department. He spoke with a soft Norfolk burr and (unnecessarily) attempted to justify this homely accent by claiming that it earmarked him as a 'Raja's Man'. During the short car ride to our hotel, he told us that the way to distinguish between a 'Raja's Man' and a Colonial Civil Servant was by the person's English accent. He asserted that Raja James Brooke (1803–68) and his successors, Charles Johnson Brooke (1829–1917) and Charles Vyner Brooke (1874–1963) had recruited most of their employees from Norfolk since the first Raja had been educated at Norwich Grammar School in Norfolk, England, although born in Benares, India.

I doubt that our host's assertion was correct but it was indicative of the resentment felt by those civil servants who had been recruited by the Brookes. The 'Raja's Men' were now obliged to work alongside officers who were appointed directly by the Colonial Office after Sarawak was ceded to Britain by Charles Vyner Brooke in 1946, only seven years before our visit. This resentment was also felt by nationalistic Malay activists who opposed the secession and, in December 1949, one of these, a young man named Rusli Dhobi, stabbed the second Governor, Sir Duncan Stewart, to death with a Malay *kris*. As the story was told to me, the stabbing took place just outside the Governor's temporary home in Sibu. Holding his stomach, the Governor maintained his dignity and walked back into the house, from where he was flown to Kuching and then to Singapore for treatment. But to no avail. He died a week after the stabbing took place.

Sir Duncan Stewart was succeeded in post by Mr (later Sir) Anthony Abell who, in 1950, set out for Sarawak by sea. It was a somewhat macabre voyage since Abell was accompanied on the ship by the gallows meant for his predecessor's murderer. Dhobi was hanged on 2 March 1950, together with two other conspirators, Awang Ramli Mohd Deli and Bujang Sunton.

But yesterday's villain sometimes becomes today's martyr. Dhobi's body was exhumed and re-buried in 1993 and his name is inscribed on the Sarawak Warrior Monument, near the Sarawak Museum tourist complex.

*****

We had been in Sarawak for only a few hours when we were told that the anthropologist, Tom Harrison, lived in Kuching. 'You must meet Tom Harrison' was a refrain repeated by every person whom we met. We were impressed and, eschewing the opportunity to make a second visit to an Iban (Sea Dayak) longhouse, we made several efforts to find Harrison, then Curator of the Kuching Museum. We got as far as the entrance to the museum but it was closed. Security was maintained outside the main door by a large chattering gibbon, Harrison's pet.

Before the Second World War began, Harrison turned his attention to the people of Bolton in Lancashire. Together with a poet, Charles Madge, and the previously mentioned socialist film-maker, Humphrey Jennings, he organised a survey of ordinary people's lives. This was accomplished by sending out detailed questionnaires to a large number of volunteers who were asked about their attitudes, opinions, habits and possessions. The results, entitled 'Mass Observation' (MO), are now archived at the University of Sussex where they sit, having given way to the more rigorous annual British Social Attitudes Survey.

In 1939 the MO survey was featured in an edition of the colourful magazine *Picture Post*, but it was soon supplanted by the more serious business of the War. Harrison put Mass Observation on one side and joined a special branch of the Armed Forces. This took him by parachute behind the lines in Sarawak and Borneo. At the conclusion of the War he remained in Southeast Asia and was eventually appointed as curator of the museum in Kuching. He took a particular interest in turtles, as well as gibbons. But we never did meet Tom Harrison. In January 1976, he died as the result of a traffic accident in Thailand.

*****

Two weeks or so after I first arrived in Singapore in 1951, I was informed that I must learn and pass examinations in one of three languages, Chinese (Mandarin), Tamil or Malay. Although there seemed to be three possibilities, I was not given a choice. I was instructed to learn Malay. The wisdom of this puzzled me somewhat since there were relatively few opportunities to use the language in Singapore except as the language of the bazaar.

I understood that I must pass the Malay examination at two levels – or 'Standards' – before I would be given permission to take my first overseas leave. There was a third 'Standard' but I was told that this would be very difficult to achieve in Singapore's urban setting in which English flourished as a link language among different racial and ethnic groups.

My timetable at Raffles Institution (8am to 1pm) made it possible for me to teach in the mornings and study Malay in the afternoons two or three times a week. I joined forces with a new female Education Officer, Margaret Shattock, and we shared a *munshi* (language teacher), a gentle Malay gentleman who taught at a Malay-medium primary school.

The Standard One examination focused largely on pronunciation and lexis and these posed few problems. Malay is however, a subtle and elegant language. It is not difficult to acquire the bastard language of the bazaar but 'Raja Malay' is much more of a challenge. In English, for example, water is water. In Malay the word is qualified more frequently according to the specific meaning. Water for washing one's hands is *ayer basoh tangan*, whereas water for religious ablutions is *sembahyang*. For explanations of such subtleties as these, we found Sir Richard Winstedt's English–Malay and Malay–English dictionaries invaluable.

After a distinguished career in the Malayan Civil Service, Winstedt (1878–1966) became Reader in Malay at London University, publishing grammars, dictionaries, a book of Malay proverbs and the seminal study, *The Malays: A Cultural History*. We particularly needed the latter publication because the Standard Two examination included a General Paper on Malay history and customs. There was also an oral examination and written papers, requiring an ability to translate from and into Malay and to read and write Jawi – that is Arabic – script.

I had completed three years continuous service in Singapore before I sat for my Standard Two examination. I found the translation paper, history and culture papers and the Jawi paper to be manageable. In the translation from Jawi paper, we were presented with a rather faded letter, rescued for examination purposes from a District Office in one of the Malay States. It was very difficult to read. But I managed this adequately too.

The oral examination was much more of a challenge. There were three examiners. One was a British administrative officer, a former wartime army officer and prisoner-of-war, later honoured by the Malay government and subsequently known as Tan Sri Dato Haji Mubin Sheppard. Sheppard was flanked by a Malay gardener and a Malay teacher. I was 'floored' at the beginning of the examination when asked in Malay whether the Singapore Teachers' Training College (to which I was then attached) possessed a library. I replied in the affirmative, referring to the têmpat buku' (a place for books). These words were too colloquial for the examination board which demanded the Arabic version, 'kutub khanah', which I did not know. Thereafter, it was all downhill and I failed to pass. Fortunately, I did not have to repeat the other parts of the examination. The oral section remained the only challenge.

David Hughes (my friend and colleague at Raffles Institution and later at the Teachers' Training College) also failed the oral examination and so he and I decided to enlist the help of a senior Malay teacher who lived in a *kampong* (village) on the outskirts of Singapore. At our first meeting, this austere gentleman informed us that he had tutored many government officials in the past. Then, with satisfaction, he announced that he had reduced Tuan 'So and So' (a distinguished civil servant) to tears. He would do the same for us if we failed to do our homework. The medicine seemed to work for we both passed on the second attempt.

In 1954, after two-and-a-half years as a master at Raffles Institution, I was transferred to the Singapore Teachers' Training College as a lecturer in the College's Education Department. My duties included lecturing to full-time and part-time students on educational methods and on the teaching of English. The curriculum had been determined before I joined the College. I was therefore somewhat startled to be presented with an interesting, but hardly appropriate, reading list (for the English courses) which included Apsley Cherry-Garrard's book, *The Worst Journey in the World* (a description by a member of Captain Scott's ill-starred expedition to the South Pole in 1912), Sir John Vanbrugh's seventeenth-century comic play, *The Relapse, or Virtue in Danger* and Norman Douglas's novel, *South Wind*, an account of the curious behaviour of certain people in pre-war Capri. These books were selected by my colleague, Shamus Fraser, who had enjoyed them himself. I enjoyed them too but doubted that they were suitable for study by Chinese student teachers.

*****

In 1953, I summoned up the courage to telephone Radio Malaya (now Radio Singapore) to ask for an audition. After some uncertainty on the part of the receptionist, I was able to speak to a Miss Marjory Morris, one of the producers in the Schools section. Following our telephone conversation, Marjory invited me to the studios where I read a short announcement on microphone, and also spoke my party piece, an extract from George Bernard Shaw's play, *A Village Wooing*. The audition was successful and thus began a relationship with Radio Malaya which lasted until I left Singapore in May 1959. From 1952 until 1959 I performed in programmes for schools and in Radio Theatre. From 1956 onwards, I

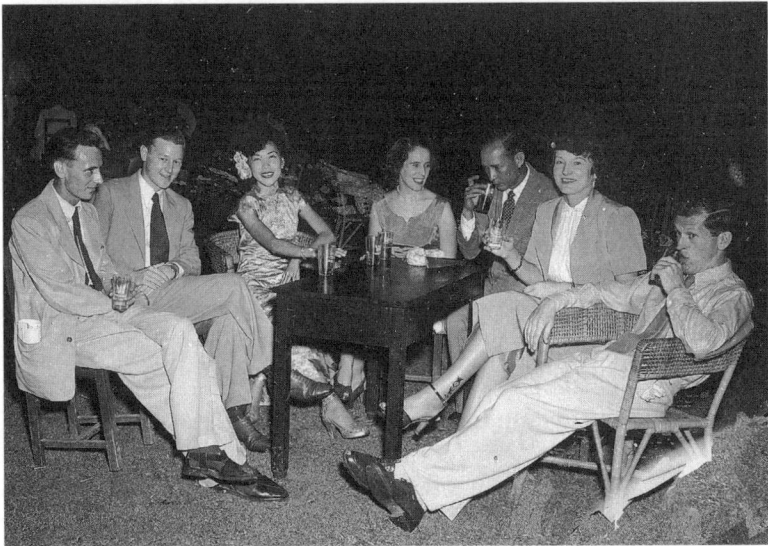

Evening Garden Party in Singapore, c. 1952. From left: Willis Hall (newspaper in pocket), the author, Rosalie Hernon, Lois Bickley, Henry Hockstadt, Dorothy Atherton, John Flak.

135

combined work in schools' programmes with sessions as a part-time newsreader. In the same year I began to perform continuity duties with the BBC Far Eastern Station, now re-named the BBC World Service.

I still possess copies of the scripts of the first few Radio Malaya programmes in which I participated. The first script is dated, '1st Term 1952' and entitled, 'Felix Mendelssohn Bartholdy', a programme in the series, 'Adventures in Music and Poetry', written by Annie Chang. I was chosen for the part of Felix. In the same series I played Joseph Haydn's young brother, Michael and in another broadcast was entrusted with the role of Narrator in 'Marco Polo, the Venetian'. There followed several other broadcasts in the 'Scenes from Asian History' series, mostly written by Marjory Morris. These included, 'Whampoa' (1952), 'Malayan Aborigines – a Negrito Group' (1953), 'Sir Frank Swettenham' (1953), 'Thailand – We Visit an Ancient City' (1953), 'Legends of Malacca' (1953), 'The Voyage of the Pluto' (1953) and 'The Japanese in Malaya' (1953). The last two were written by Professor C. Northcote Parkinson, then a Professor of History at the University of Malaya (Singapore). I played the young Frank Swettenham in 'The Voyage of the Pluto' and the Japanese 'A' character in 'The Japanese in Malaya'.

> A: Singapore is ours. All Malaya now belongs to our sacred Emperor. But this is only the beginning. We must conquer Sumatra, and Java and all the islands. Then Ceylon and India and Australia. The whole of Asia must come under our rule.
>
> B: No doubt. But shall we leave the question of our future glories for the moment, and come back to Malaya? Malaya is our task at the moment. What is our policy to be?
>
> A: Quite simple. You have heard of the phrase, 'Divide and rule?' We will divide – we will set Chinese against Malays – Malays against Indians, Indians against Chinese and so we will rule. If they are busy hating each other, they will never combine to drive us out. It is as simple as that.

Parkinson – or 'Parky', as he was familiarly known (by some) in Singapore – taught at the University of Malaya (Singapore) for some years, and specialised in the study of conflict and trade in Southeast Asia. His book, *Britannia Rules: The Classic Age of Naval History 1793–1815* and a dozen other works of military and naval history earned him considerable academic respect. But then he changed course. In 1954, to the delight of colleagues at the University and elsewhere, he published an amusing article in the *Economist Newspaper*. This mocked the world of business management by stating that 'work expands so as to fill the time available for its completion'. The article was reprinted in 1958 in the book,

Parkinson's Law: The Pursuit of Progress which became a bestseller and (because it was so profitable) changed Parkinson's life. There followed other books in the same mocking genre, in addition to serious books about business practices and some historical novels.

I met Parkinson several times, usually in relation to educational matters but sometimes on social occasions. I remember talking to him once at a party held on someone's roof. He told me that he *never* read newspapers, no matter where published. I could not quite believe him.

Dr Wang Gung Wu – well regarded now as a historian and former Vice-Chancellor of the University of Hong Kong – studied under Parkinson at the University of Malaya. I met Gung Wu first when he was a student at the University of Malaya and a keen amateur actor. We performed together in one of Radio Malaya's broadcasts for schools.

*****

John Burgess Wilson, an English teacher working in the Federation of Malaya, was another contributor to Radio Malaya's broadcasts to schools. Later, commonly known as Anthony Burgess, he achieved best-seller status with his Malayan trilogy *Time for a Tiger, An Enemy in the Blanket* and *Beds in the East*. It is said that he published under a pseudonym because he felt that the Colonial Office might object to certain passages in the Trilogy. A recent biography paints a vivid picture of the tempestuous nature of the life that Burgess and his first wife Lynne led in Malaya; Lynne addicted to gin and drunken scenes, and Burgess alienating colleagues and officials with his arrogant behaviour.[1]

*****

One afternoon at Radio Malaya I was introduced to a young National Serviceman named Willis Hall. Encouraged and tutored by Marjory Morris, Willis began to write scripts for schools' programmes as well as pieces for the *Singapore Standard* newspaper. His adaptation of the Malayan *Father Molecricket* folk-tales was broadcast as an adult programme series by Radio Malaya. The broadcast – with a different cast – was later repeated on the BBC World Service. I played the part of an Emperor in the Singapore version.

137

After leaving Singapore the demobilised Willis Hall took to writing as a full-time occupation and – among others – wrote the successful play, *The Long and the Short and the Tall*, described as 'an army episode'. The title was taken from a line in *Bless 'Em All*, a song that was popular during the Second World War. Willis also wrote the play, *Billy Liar*, in partnership with his friend, the novelist, Keith Waterhouse. *Billy Liar* was eventually made into a film (1963), directed by John Schlesinger and starring Tom Courtenay and Julie Christie.

*****

In 1956, I was invited to audition as a newsreader for Radio Malaya. The audition was successful and thereafter I read the evening news on a fairly regular basis. Newsreaders were supposed to arrive at the studio at least half-an-hour before the scheduled broadcast. The purpose of this rule was to give the reader the opportunity to rehearse the pronunciation of any 'difficult' words. 'Kruschev' and 'Nagy'[2] caused some initial difficulty, as did the family name of the first Malayan Prime Minister, Tengku Abdul Rahman. Some readers found it difficult to manage the glottal check in 'Rahman'.

On one occasion, I arrived late at the studio and plunged straight into the reading ('This is Radio Malaya. Here is the News, read by Verner Bickley'). The civil rights movement was gaining momentum in the United States. The state of Arkansas was in the news. I pronounced it as one might pronounce 'Kansas' in 'Kansas City'. This was a mistake, as several irascible gentlemen from 'Arken-saw' informed me by telephone, immediately the broadcast was over.

My year for broadcasting was 1956. In addition to work as a part-time newsreader and actor for Radio Malaya, I was recruited by a Senior Programme Assistant, Brian Denney, to serve as a part-time continuity announcer for the BBC Far Eastern Station (today's BBC World Service). During most of the day, I carried out my work as Head of the English and Speech Training Department at the Singapore Teachers' Training College. Then, for two or three nights a week, I would work a 5pm to 8pm shift at Radio Malaya and an 8pm to midnight shift at the Far Eastern Station. I do not remember ever feeling tired, perhaps because the work was so interesting. How often does one have the opportunity to announce the achievement of a country's independence (Malaya in 1957), or the first launch of a rocket into outer space (the 'Sputnik'), or the sad news of the devastating air crash at Munich on 6 February 1958, a crash that resulted in the deaths of eight members of Manchester United's football team.

In 1985, in Hong Kong, I toyed with the idea of making an application for an 'on mike' position with Radio Television Hong Kong. In this connection, I asked my friend, Brian Denney, for a recommendation. Brian was kind enough to write the following letter but I did not use it.

BBC TV
British Broadcasting Corporation
Television Centre, Wood Lane, London W12 7RJ
25 August, 1985

I have known Verner Bickley since 1956, both in a professional capacity and as a friend.

From 1956 to 1962, I was Senior Programme Assistant at the BBC Far Eastern Station in Singapore. During that time Verner Bickley worked regularly for the BBC as a continuity announcer whenever his professional responsibilities permitted. He also worked as announcer, newsreader and actor for Radio Singapore (now the Singapore Broadcasting Corporation).

I have a high regard for Verner Bickley's professionalism both in and out of the studio. He has a good microphone voice and can quickly adapt to the technicalities of broadcasting.

Also, I know that he has had considerable experience in production during his long involvement with education and the dissemination of modern communication skills.

Brian B. Denney
Head of Television Liaison

– 15 –

The Railway Victims

After six pleasant months as guests at The Cockpit Hotel, Lois and I were offered the opportunity of sharing a flat in Nassim Hill with Ralph Ince, the Deputy Director of Education. A refusal was out of the question since accommodation was difficult to find and there were few government 'quarters' to be had in a Colony still engaged in post-war reconstruction. Nassim Hill is in the Tanglin ('Eastern Peaks') District of Singapore.

We moved from The Cockpit in the Spring of 1952. We had our own bedroom and bathroom but shared the living room and meals prepared by a Chinese amah, always immaculate in her black trousers and white top. Ralph, our co-occupant, had survived the notorious Burma Railway (the 'Railway of Death') as a forced labourer.

There is now a substantial number of books that focus on the ordeal of confinement. An example of one of these is *Out East in the Malay Peninsula*,[1] in which Ralph's former colleague, G.E.D. Lewis, records in considerable detail his own trials as a virtual slave on the Railway.

Such trials were also undergone by Francis Thomas, missionary teacher and later Headmaster of St Andrew's School in Singapore. I met Thomas first in 1952, in connection with the Singapore Teachers' Union Youth Drama Festival. His school was the winner in the Senior Section, with a play named *Such Vain Keeping*. Raffles Institution won the Open Section with my production of Chekov's *The Proposal*.

In his autobiography, *Memoirs of a Migrant*,[2] Thomas takes the reader from Changi prison in Singapore to Kinsayok in Siam (now more frequently referred to as Thailand) and from Kinsayok to Kanu where his fellow prisoners, suffering from beri-beri, malaria and dysentery 'began to earn our name, Death Camp'. One day, the prisoners heard that some of them were to be selected for work in Japan. Thomas was among those chosen to join over twelve hundred other prisoners on a captured American ship, *The President Harrison*. Re-named *Kachidoki Maru*, the ship joined a convoy of about fifteen ships escorted by two Japanese destroyers. At this point in his life, Thomas must have felt that enough was enough, for the ship was torpedoed. Thomas survived the water and was taken to Japan with other rescued prisoners. There he was to labour in a factory in Omuta, a small industrial city in Kyushu, until he was freed and able to return to St Andrew's School after Japan surrendered.

During the year that we shared a flat with Ralph Ince, he spoke very little about his experiences. There was one thing, however, that he was quite certain about. He never wanted to be hungry again. Every day the amah was instructed to prepare and serve a full, cooked breakfast, a three-course lunch (we both came home for this meal, Ince from the Education Department and me from Raffles Institution), late afternoon tea and biscuits. At about 8pm each evening we addressed a three-course dinner.

Apart from food, Ince derived considerable pleasure from his efforts to mend and service the organ in St Andrew's Cathedral. St Andrew's was built by government engineers between 1856 and 1864. A stained glass window in the apse commemorates John Crawfurd who, as Resident, obtained the treaty that ceded Singapore in perpetuity to the East India Company and its successors and heirs. It hasn't happened.

*****

From time to time, we heard tales of other survivors from the Japanese prison camps. It was said that some returnees found themselves unable to function in their former positions in the Civil Service. A few became alcoholics. To protect their pension rights (so it was rumoured), they were discharged as suffering from 'tropical neurasthenia' (whatever that is). Perhaps the saddest of a number of sad tales was that of the Education Officer who had completed a doctoral dissertation, immediately prior to the British surrender in Singapore. He had entrusted the only copy of his manuscript to his wife who was evacuated from the Colony on one of the last ships to depart for Britain. Unfortunately, the vessel was torpedoed. She survived but lost all her possessions, including the manuscript. The man and the woman were parted for three-and-a-half years. The man suffered many privations as a prisoner but survived by holding on to the memory of his future academic triumph. When the war was over (so he thought) he would be able to submit his dissertation to the University and engage in its defence.

The day finally came when the pair were re-united. They approached each other shyly. He was the first to speak but not with the words she expected. Not 'My darling, I have missed you so much. I love you' but rather, 'Is my manuscript safe?' She had to confess otherwise. This was too much for the man. Shortly after their meeting, the pair divorced.

Well over sixty years have passed since the Second World War came to an end and yet books still continue to appear that refer to the sufferings of Allied prisoners of the Japanese Forces. Some 125,000 of these prisoners were civilians. For nearly two years, I was privileged to share a home with one such (Ralph Ince) and to serve under another (Philip Howitt, Principal of Raffles Institution). Never once did they speak of their sufferings.

Philip Howitt was my first boss in Singapore. Philip and his brother Charles, the latter an Administrative Officer in the government – arrived in Malaya *circa* 1928. They both lived life to the full. When captured and put to work in the jungles of Siam they could not have been completely fit. Against some odds perhaps, both survived.

Philip was an encouraging leader, always ready with sound advice and tolerant of the ambitions of callow youth. In 1957 prior to his retirement, he was attached for a short time to my own Department. I was then Head of the Department of English and Speech Training at the Teachers' Training College in Singapore. Despite the reversal of roles, Philip continued to be supportive and never caused me the least embarrassment, although I was now *his* boss.

I have mentioned the Chinese amah who cooked and cleaned for us in the flat in Nassim Hill. She remained with us in the flat after Ralph Ince was allocated another government 'quarter', a house befitting his status in the government. I am afraid that on one occasion, I may have offended her. On the eve of a Chinese Festival, she presented me with four 'moon cakes'. I dislike these delicacies, perhaps because of the egg yolks placed inside them. Unwilling to offend the amah, I accepted the gift and then hid the cakes in a bathroom cabinet, intending to smuggle them out of the flat for disposal on the same evening. Unfortunately I forgot to carry out this task and failed to remember the cakes until several days later. When I did look for them, they had gone without even a crumb to remember them by. No doubt the amah found them and my action may have confirmed any sentiments that she might have had about the eccentricities of 'Europeans'.

*****

In mid-1954, we moved from Nassim Hill to a small bungalow in Goodwood Hill. Among a number of similar bungalows, it had been built to relieve an acute shortage of quarters for government officials. Sir Franklyn Gimson was Governor of Singapore at the time and, inevitably the bungalows were dubbed 'Gimson Shelters'.

On transfer from the Ceylon Civil Service, Gimson arrived in Hong Kong on 7 December 1941 to take up the post of Colonial Secretary. His timing was unfortunate, for the Japanese Air Force bombed Pearl Harbour on the same day and repeated the action over Hong Kong the day after. On 18 December, Japanese troops attacked Hong Kong and on Christmas Day 1941, the Colony surrendered to Japanese forces and was re-named by them, 'Captured Territory Hong Kong'.

Gimson remained in the City for a few weeks and was allowed to attend meetings in the newly established internment camp at Stanley. In March 1942 he was obliged to move into the camp himself and functioned there as 'Representative of Internees'. Three years and five months later,

Rashid and Mina in the grounds of 7A, Goodwood Hill, Singapore, 1954. 'Rashid in his best sarong and songkok and Mina resplendent in *her* sarong with silk jacket and scarf and high-heeled, gold-coloured shoes.'

in August 1945, it became apparent that the Japanese surrender to Allied Forces was inevitable. However British naval forces, commanded by Admiral Harcourt, were unable to relieve Hong Kong until 30 August. Still resident in the camp on 16 August, Gimson assumed the title of Officer Administering the Government. On 23 August, he left the camp. In the following week, under the most difficult circumstances and with the Japanese occupying force still *in situ*, Gimson took charge of the Territory, working from the French Mission Building in the City (now the Court of Final Appeal). Gimson's prompt action contributed substantially to the resumption of British control in Hong Kong. This took place despite the ambitions of a Chinese faction led by the late Chiang Kai Shek, supported by the American government.

I met Gimson very briefly at the Victoria Memorial Hall in Singapore. In 1953, as already mentioned, I played Shylock in the Singapore Arts Theatre production of *The Merchant of Venice*. Just after curtain time on the opening night, the Governor and his entourage came backstage to congratulate the players. He was in full dress uniform, in sharp contrast to the Commissioner for Southeast Asia, Malcolm Macdonald, who came to the theatre on the following night dressed in slacks and an open-necked shirt.

Given his rank, Malcolm Macdonald was certainly unconventional. In his lively book, *People and Places*,[3] he mentions an evening spent in 'Concubine Street' with the world-famous cellist Pablo Casals. At some point in the evening Casals said that he had heard someone say that Macdonald could walk on his hands. Macdonald confirmed that this was true and promptly demonstrated by standing on his hands and walking upside down along the street. He repeated the feat when Casals shouted 'Encore!'

*****

My daughter, Karen, was born on 31 December 1954 after we had moved into Number 7A, Goodwood Hill. We now needed more help in the house. The amah – mooncakes rejected – took employment elsewhere. I do not remember now how we managed to find willowy and gentle Mina but she quickly became an indispensable part of the household. Soon, she was joined by little Maria and the wash-amah, Mousse. We were very well looked after by the three 'Ems'.

Elegant Mina and her husband Rashid, a driver, had no work obligations on Fridays and it was a pleasant sight as they left their 'quarter' for the day – Rashid, in his best sarong and songkok and Mina resplendent in *her* sarong with silk jacket and scarf and high-heeled, gold-coloured shoes.

*****

I was extraordinarily busy during our first 'tour' of Singapore. I had a full-time job teaching English and Physical Training at Raffles Institution. I conducted 'Normal' classes for in-service trainee teachers on two afternoons and I met my Malay 'Munshi' (teacher) two evenings a week. I became very involved with the affairs of the Singapore Arts Theatre, serving on the Board of Directors and appearing in five productions, including Shakespeare's *Macbeth* and George Bernard Shaw's *A Village Wooing*. In May 1953, I appeared as a solo act in a Coronation Fun Fair held for '4,000 poor children' at the Victoria Memorial Hall.[4] (I believe that I performed some readings from Dickens.) On that occasion the Patron was Franklyn Gimson's successor as Governor, Sir John Nicoll. In the same month I directed a production of Shakespeare's *As You Like It*, for Raffles Institution ('The Raffles Players') and followed that in March 1954 with Sir John Vanbrugh's play, *The Relapse, or Virtue in Danger* for the Arts Theatre.

*****

We were pleased to be visited on the last night of *The Relapse* by the novelist, Graham Greene. Under the pseudonymous by-line, 'Vic Mem', a review in *The Straits Times* stated that Greene

> had a special reason for attending the Arts Theatre's performance of *The Relapse*. It was the Arts Theatre which in 1953 presented Greene's only play, *The Living Room*; the only amateur company to do so while the play was still being shown in the West End. Greene appeared to enjoy the show (*The Relapse*). In a backstage chat with the players, he suggested that William Wycherley's play, *The Country Wife*, might be the Arts Theatre's next venture.

Greene's appearance at a performance of the the Arts Theatre's play must have taken place during the period when he was visiting Southeast Asia to gather material for a novel, *The Quiet American*, and perhaps also to carry out some Intelligence activities. His visit to Singapore took place in March. Two months' earlier he had been in Dien Bien Phu where the French were defeated in 1954 after a battle that lasted from March to May of that year.

– 16 –

There Was Still
an Emergency

The 'emergency' continued in Malaya during the whole period of my stay in Singapore (1951–59) but people seemed less anxious about this after 1956. General Sir Gerald Templar's anti-communist measures had begun to bite and constitutional progress appeared to convince at least the Malay population that the colonial period was coming to an end. As noted earlier, Malaya was granted independence and became Malaysia on 31 August 1957. The new country remained within the Commonwealth. I announced this in a news bulletin on Radio Malaya.

After two somewhat uneasy years of cooperation, Singapore severed its connection with Malaysia and became an independent Republic. It, too, remained a member of the Commonwealth.

Mr Lee Kuan Yew gave the title, *From Third World to First*, to the second part of his memoirs, published in October 2000. The title is misleading unless only narrow economic measures are used. There is no doubt that there was considerable human discomfort in Singapore in the late 1940s and early 1950s, mostly as a result of the devastation caused by the Japanese occupation, but the post-war colonial government made strenuous efforts to improve the people's lot. Considerable progress had been made by the time self-government was granted. My own main contacts during the seven-and-a-half years that I spent in Singapore were with Chinese, Indian and Malay colleagues. They certainly did not give me the impression that they were living in a 'Third World' territory.

Mr Lee's book contains many valuable insights into the recent growth and undoubted success of Singapore as a sovereign nation. I hope, however, that the statement on the dust jacket of the book was imposed on Mr Lee

146

by his publisher, Harper Collins, and is not a reflection of his own opinion. It is simply not true that 'few gave tiny Singapore much chance of survival when it was granted independence in 1965'. This is a sweeping over-generalisation. I risk such an over-generalisation myself but I maintain that most of us who worked with the multi-racial peoples of Singapore would have been astonished if the territory had not prevailed.

*****

From the end of the Second World War until some years after independence, Singapore served as a springboard for British, Commonwealth and American Forces. The soldiers who rested or drilled in Tanglin Barracks, the airmen who flew in and out of Seletar Airfield and the sailors who operated from the Naval Base were involved in two conflicts. Many came for 'Rest and Recreation' from the jungles and villages of Malaya; others came from the battlefields of Korea.

A war of words – that led eventually to actual war – began when Korea was divided into American and Russian zones of occupation after the Japanese surrender. Hostility between the two powers became active when the Communist North invaded South Korea. This is not the place to attempt to describe the different retreats and advances of the ensuing war. It is sufficient to say in the present context that Singapore derived some economic benefit from it. The transvestites of Bugis Street, the whores of noisesome Lavender Street and bars such as the Savoy in Orchard Road and the Washington in Bras Basah Road welcomed clients from Britain, the United States, Turkey and from eleven other member countries of the United Nations. Hundreds of mixed grills must have been served in the Stamford Café in Bras Basah Road whilst there was surely a strong demand for the fragrant curries of the Islamic Restaurant and others of its type. Tailors in South Bridge Road and Coleman Street sewed twenty-four-hour tropical-weight civilian jackets and trousers for troops to wear during visits to the amusement parks, New World (Jalan Besar Street), Great World (Kim Seng Road) and Happy World (in the Geylang district) with their 'cabarets', 'taxi dancers', food stalls and repetitious 'musak' – 'Rose, Rose, I Love You, Da Dee Dah Dee Dee Dah'.[1]

Perhaps more *louche* than Disney, these 'parks' were invented whilst Mickey was still a tiny mouse on the cinema screen, attempting (successfully) to oust Felix the Cat ('who kept on walking')[2] and long before the creation of 'Disney Worlds'.

On 27 July 1953, an Armistice was agreed in Korea, although even at the time of writing (2009), there are still occasional clashes between North and South, and a peace treaty has yet to be signed.

*****

In 1955, we had lived in Singapore for over three years. It was now time to enjoy our first home leave. In August of the same year, we flew by a 'Lockheed Super Constellation' aircraft to London and, after visiting my parents in Cheshire, settled into a flat in Edith Grove, Worlds' End, Fulham, not then (as now) a dangerous place at night. We rented the flat from my good friend, Roy Hanson, for the entire period of our stay in England. The leave was uneventful, made pleasurable by frequent visits to the theatre in London and in Stratford and interesting by my studies for the Licentiate Diploma Examinations in Speech and Drama offered by the Royal Academy of Music and the Guildhall School of Music and Drama. I was successful in both examinations, thanks both to my personal experience and work with the Singapore Arts Theatre and Radio Malaya and to excellent tuition provided by Greta Colson, author of an excellent primer, *Voice Production and Speech.*[3]

It seems strange to report this now but it was not until 1955 in London that we became television viewers for the first time. On a 14-inch set leased from 'Radio Rentals' we watched news broadcasts and a variety of black and white features, including some very satisfying discussion programmes, for example, *Free Speech* featuring such luminaries as the then Independent MP, W.J. Brown, Labour MP Michael Foot, historian A.J.P. Taylor and Conservative MP Robert Boothby. Boothby was once asked by an interviewer about his romantic attachments. He replied with the patrician comment, 'You can whistle for that,' presumably not being willing to discuss his ongoing affair with the wife of Harold Macmillan, then British Foreign Minister and later Prime Minister.

*****

In February 1956 we boarded the passenger cargo ship *Glenearn*, bound, once again, for Singapore. The journey passed slowly but pleasantly enough, partly because we were entertained at all meal times by our fellow passenger, Paddy, a purser of Irish descent who possessed an apparently inexhaustible stock of amusing (and 'clean') stories. After just over a month at sea we arrived back in the Colony and were fortunate to be accommodated at the Goodwood Park Hotel, formerly a German Club and regarded today as one of the finest hotels in Singapore.

The turbulence experienced in 1955 in Singapore continued in 1956. Student demonstrations and strikes began, sparked off by the Chinese Middle Schools Students' Union which encouraged students to boycott classes in several schools:

> Through the textbooks in use in Singapore Chinese-medium schools from the primary level upwards and influenced by the teachers directly and recently arrived from the ideological turbulence which was twentieth century China, Chinese Middle School children in Singapore were encouraged to identify themselves politically with institutions and ideas of relevance in the context of China's internal affairs.[4]

An issue with explosive power and sometimes neglected in accounts of the strike and riots was the resentment caused by the government's well-meant attempt to introduce additional English lessons in the Chinese-medium schools. On the one hand, such lessons were welcomed secretly by students who were aware that English language skills were necessary in higher education and in the job market. On the other hand, many of the same students were encouraged to believe that the increased attention paid to English constituted an attack on Chinese culture.

On one occasion, I had the direct experience of facing a mob in Singapore. Returning from a meeting at the YMCA, I walked along Orchard Road in the hope of catching a taxi outside Amber Mansions, the office of the British Council and home to its Director (then known as the 'Representative'). Suddenly, I heard shouting in the distance that soon became a kind of *baying*. Very shortly afterwards I spotted the leaders of a host of screaming rioters. On this occasion they were Chinese rather than Malay. I chose discretion instead of valour and darted down a parallel road to avoid being spotted. From there I made my way cautiously – on foot – to what was then home, the Goodwood Park Hotel.

This was my second of three experiences of a riotous mob. The first was in Bombay in 1945 (see Chapter Eight above). The third was in Jakarta in 1963, but that is a later story.

*****

In 1953, the first step was taken to establish a Chinese-medium university in Singapore. It came about as the result of a proposal made in 1953 by the Chinese Chamber of Commerce, the prominent Chinese businessman, Mr Tan Lark Sye, and other members of the Hokkien Huay Kuan, a social organisation founded in 1840 to 'preserve and promote Chinese language and culture'. The new institution, named 'Nanyang' got off to an unsatisfactory start even before it offered its first classes in March 1956. The novelist, Lin Yu Tang, was appointed as its first Chancellor but resigned in March 1955 after a disagreement with the University's financial backers. After the appointment of a new Chancellor, the University continued its controversial way after its official opening in March 1958.

In 1963, under Lee Kuan Yew's leadership, the PAP decided to 'deal' with 'prominent figures who had acted as front men for the communists'. Number One on the list was Tan Lark Sye. His Singapore citizenship was cancelled. 'He had gambled and lost. He never regained his prominence.'[5]

On 8 August 1980, with little opposition, Nanyang University was merged with the National University of Singapore. Kwan Sai Kheong (my former colleague at Raffles Institution and at the Singapore Teachers' Training College) was entrusted by Lee Kuan Yew with the task of overseeing the successful merger.

By 1980, Sai Kheong had risen to the rank of Permanent Secretary of Education. On one occasion, when he was still in that post, he told me that his son had disappointed him, at least for a time. The boy refused to follow in his father's academic footsteps and would not consider a university education. Now here I have to be careful because I am simply reporting one conversation with Sai Kheong and my memory of it could be wrong. What seems to have happened is that the younger Kwan became something of an entrepreneur; made some money in various enterprises and was then offered the opportunity to attend the so-called 'Hamburger University', a training school operated by the food chain, McDonald's, in the United States. After that experience, he returned to Singapore and opened the first McDonald's restaurant in the city-state. How could McDonald's possibly succeed in Singapore, a place admired for its superb mix of Asian cuisines? But, of course, it *did* succeed and the younger Kwan has succeeded with it.

There was no McDonald's in Singapore in 1956 but it was customary after a theatrical performance to dine on succulent, although not elegantly served Chinese food at the open market in Bugis Street or at the 'Car Park'[6] in Orchard Road. Such delights became increasingly rare because I ceased (at least as an actor) to 'tread the boards' and took to directing, 'front of house', instead. There were other time-consuming reasons for this self-denial. First, I was appointed Head of the Department of English and Speech Training at the then Teachers' Training College. This meant overseeing the work of both full-time and part-time trainee teachers and supervising approximately thirty-five full- and part-time staff. Second, on the intervention of Derek Cooper, I became a regular part-time newsreader at Radio Malaya and, on the recommendation of my friend Brian Denney, I also became a part-time continuity announcer for the BBC Far Eastern Station. Third, I collaborated in February 1957 with my colleague, Francis Mace, in a Teachers' Training College production of John Gay's *The Beggars' Opera* and in 1958 in a production of Benjamin Britten's delightful, *Let's Make an Opera*. These diverse activities took place against the backdrop of a Singapore that was beginning to earn its title, 'Emporium and Pride of the East'.

*****

In the 1950s, 'Le Shopping' had not been developed into an art form in the Colony and there were relatively few 'smart' shops and no shopping malls, the cathedrals of the 'developed' world. Change Alley at Collier Quay was, however, a useful shopping lane and the shoemakers in Middle Road made excellent leather shoes for relatively low prices. In Orchard Road, the 'Cold Storage' store and Teck Joo's small grocery shop (and many other small businesses) provided us with an adequate variety of foods and frozen goods. Tailors and dressmakers in Coleman Street and South Bridge Road sold fine silks and cottons and in Raffles Place the three rather grand but somewhat faded department stores, Whiteway Laidlaw, John Little and Robinsons, competed fiercely for a relatively small market, largely 'expatriate'. The principal bookshops were Kelly and Walsh and the Malayan Publishing House, backed up by a row of small shops along Bras Basah Road, catering mainly for the second-hand textbook market. A few shops specialised in *objets d'art*. In particular, I remember Tang's small, overcrowded emporium then situated in River Valley Road, now grown into a modern air-conditioned department store in Orchard Road. In Tanglin Road, Helen Ling's small shop was crammed with small items of teak and cherrywood furniture, fragrant smelling chests, brocades and handmade lace. Helen, an American, was married to a Chinese chemist. She travelled frequently to different Asian countries to inspect fabrics and antiquities to add to her stock. On one of these trips she must have met the 'Thai Silk King', the American architect, Jim Thompson, founder of the Thai Silk Company (fifty per cent Thai-owned). Perhaps Helen was a customer for some of Thompson's exquisite materials. A friendship must have formed and blossomed, for it was from 'Moonlight Cottage', the Ling's holiday home in the Cameron Highlands in Malaya that, on 26 March 1967, Thompson went out for a 'constitutional' and disappeared, never to be seen again.[7] In 1974, he was officially declared dead in both the US and Thailand. Six months' later, Thompson's older sister, Katherine, was battered to death in her house in Pennsylvania. Her desk was rifled but her valuables and money were untouched.

I have one permanent memory of Helen Ling and that is a rosewood cupboard of Chinese design, purchased from her in 1953. In its day, this cupboard has suffered from expansion and contraction pains, according to the climate. Contraction in multi-seasonal Burma, expansion in tropical Indonesia, contraction in Britain and Tokyo, expansion in Hawaii and Saudi Arabia, expansion and contraction in Hong Kong, and contraction in Andorra. If furniture could speak the cupboard would no doubt comment acidly on the frequency of its comings and goings. What is a good cupboard to do?

– 17 –

Mount Pleasant

After our return to Singapore in early 1956, we were allocated a spacious house in Mount Pleasant, a verdant part of the Colony, close to the Polo Club. At that time rumour had it that the most senior members of the government preferred to move into new – labour-saving – flats. This meant that some of the larger 'quarters' became available for less senior officers, such as myself.

Number 162, Mount Pleasant is a very large colonial style black and white house with a very sizeable living-cum-dining room and cloakroom on the ground floor, a capacious balcony on the first floor and two massively-sized bedrooms. It is one of a number of such houses still to be found in parts of Singapore. The 'black and whites' as they are called, take their names from the black creosote painted on the woodwork to deter white ants and borer beetles and the white brickwork is daubed with a preservative named 'kapor', made from sea shells. A major feature of each black and white is the double 'jack' roof which allows hot air to rise, creating a cooling breeze. I don't know whether or not the relatively recent introduction of air conditioning has affected this long-established system.

As is the case for all the houses in Mount Pleasant, Number 162 has an extensive garden. This was home – according to my former colleague, Shamus Fraser – for nests of hamadryads (cobras), always poised to strike. Shamus, who invariably talked in poetic sentences, was an alarmist. When we were in occupation we saw no snakes, long or short, poisonous or non-poisonous. If there had been any, they might have 'spooked' the two horses which (for a short time) we agreed to house in our stables, as a favour to the nearby Polo Club.

Mount Pleasant was my son Simon's first home. He joined his sister Karen there after he was born on 28 June 1957 at Kandang Kerbau ('Buffalo Enclosure'!) hospital in Singapore. The delivery was supervised by a Professor Sheares, a gynaecologist who later became the second President of Singapore. Simon was christened at St Andrew's Cathedral which was gazetted as a national monument in 1973.

*****

In my book, *Searching for Frederick*, I describe a visit to the Glenfiddich whisky distillery in Scotland's Dufftown where I bought a copy of Derek Cooper's, *The Little Book of Malt Whiskies.*[1] It was Derek who recruited me in 1956 as a part-time newsreader for Radio Malaya. He and his wife Janet lived next door to me in Mount Pleasant. From time to time we took a 'dram' together, such as the occasion when he hosted a reception for two internationally recognised authors, both visitors to Radio Malaya. Derek's guests revealed quite different public personae. The American, Pulitzer Prize winner James Michener, was well-mannered, outgoing and courteous. The Ulster poet and broadcaster, Louis MacNeice, was monosyllabic, irritable and angular, probably struggling against what he felt to be the psychiatric 'darkness' inherited from his mother.[2]

*****

Although I was fully occupied with teacher training responsibilities, newscasting and other broadcasting activities for Radio Malaya and the BBC, it was impossible to ignore completely the significant political and social changes that were taking place in both Singapore and its neighbour, Malaya. In December 1956, it seemed time for us to take a holiday, away from the political ferment. Attracted by a colourful brochure, we took passage in a Dutch-owned vessel to Hong Kong. The journey from Singapore took three days. Once in Hong Kong, we continued to live on the ship but also enjoyed five days of sight-seeing in various parts of the Colony before we returned on the same ship to Singapore.

Hong Kong is a very different place today. In 1956, the harbour was larger; the much-loved Repulse Bay Hotel had not been demolished and the New Territories consisted mainly of paddy (rice) fields, fishponds and poultry farms. Russian-owned restaurants such as *Tkachenko's* (famous for

154

its liberal servings of caviar and its cakes and pastries) flourished, as did the old Hong Kong Club building. Some tailors not only made three-piece suits and silk dresses in twenty-four hours but also provided a chauffered car to take the customers on trips to the New Territories.

We left after five days, burdened with photographs and laden with Fuji silk monogrammed shirts, ladies' sharkskin skirts and lace tablecloths. Eighteen months after we arrived back in Singapore after this brief holiday, we moved from Mount Pleasant into an easily managed flat in Leonie Hill. From Nassim Hill to Goodwood Hill; from Mount Pleasant to Leonie Hill. Many 'ups' and 'downs'.

The new flat could not accommodate more than one servant and so we helped Mina, Maria and Mousse to find employment elsewhere. We were sad to see them go but were grateful to them for recommending Seni, another hard-working Malay girl.

After a few months in Leonie Hill, Seni married a Malay gentleman. Seni's wedding contract, the *nikah*, was signed on a Thursday evening, as the eve of Friday (*malam Jumaat*). That done, her future husband visited her parents' house where he pronounced the marriage formula, supported by relatives and guests and the *kathi*, an official empowered by the government to register Muslim marriages and divorces. Later, female representatives of the groom entered the house, bringing with them a gold ring, a new suit of clothes and a box containing the *belanja* (wedding expenses). When we attended the climax of the ceremony (the *bêrsanding*) on the Friday, Seni and the groom were sitting together on a splendidly decorated throne (the *pêlamin*). When we departed, we were each presented with a coloured, hard-boiled egg (*bunga telor*), attached to a package of yellow, glutinous rice. On the following day, Seni's husband went back to his own house to sleep. On the day after that, there was another ceremony at which the couple sat together, covered in a *sarong*, and both were bathed by female friends (*mandi mandi*). The groom was now allowed to sleep in his bride's house.

I do not know what marital arrangements Seni had agreed for, after a few days, she returned alone to her small room in our flat. Perhaps she saw her new husband at weekends.

*****

One Saturday afternoon in 1958, I happened to be in the library of The Tanglin Club. I was there to return a book entitled *Casino Royale*, written by a then largely unknown author, Ian Fleming. On the way out, my business done, I picked up a copy of *The Lady*, a magazine that features articles styled on a domestic life that may now have disappeared forever. The magazine's loyal subscribers in former times would have been critical of today's men and women who eat, drink and smoke in the street and who carry on trivial mobile telephone conversations in public for everyone to hear.

The Lady magazine has survived, presumably because of its loyal, middle-class readership and its advertisements, mainly of a classified nature. In the past, many of these advertisements listed vacancies for cooks, parlour-maids and au pairs. Today, the paper is a little glossier, the layout is a little jazzier and full use is made of up-to-date colour processing. But in its fundamentals the magazine remains the same. Many pages continue to be devoted to properties for sale and to let. Nannies, chauffeur/handymen and au pairs are still in demand and the advertisements are charmingly anachronistic. In an issue published in May 2006, for example, Mr Jarvis of Hertfordshire wondered if anyone could advise him on how to clean yellow piano keys and Mrs Jameson of Wiltshire asked the editors if they could recommend a recipe for apple cake.

On the last page of the copy of the magazine which I glanced at in 1958, I spotted the following advertisement:

Cottage in St Agnes, Cornwall. Three beds, living room, dining-room, study. Raised garden. Half mile from cove. Sterling Pounds: 2,000.

We were tempted and after too short a discussion, I sent off a telegram. (Today, it would be an e-mail).

Re your advert in The Lady, will purchase if not yet sold.

Almost immediately, it seemed to us, a reply came:

Thank you. The property is sold to you. You have now entered into a legal obligation to purchase. Details to follow.

I wasn't too sure at the time that the Cornish agent's legal position was valid but – no matter – we *wanted* the cottage. The upshot of the negotiations was that, in November 1958, my wife, Lois, and our two small children, Karen and Simon, took passage for England in the P&O liner, *Chusan*. After a few days spent in the hotel next door they took possession of the cottage.

The property was situated in the village street opposite St Agnes Church. The well-meant efforts of its campanologists were a minor irritation. (The bells clanged twice a week as well as on Sundays.) The description of the property and its facilities in *The Lady* were accurate enough. What the advertisement did *not* say was that for many years the cottage had been the home of two elderly ladies who kept cats... many cats. The cats had gone but, as several letters from Lois testified, their fleas had not. Many applications of a powerful insecticide were necessary to persuade them to leave.

*****

After my family left Singapore I continued to work as usual at the Teachers' Training College as well as at Radio Malaya and the BBC. It must have been in February 1959 that I was introduced to Mr Dick Church, a senior officer in the British Council. He was on the last leg of a tour of Southeast and East Asia. I enjoyed a pleasant lunch with Church and Stuart Smith, the Deputy Representative of the Council in Singapore. Smith and I had a common interest in jazz and we were both delighted when news came of a United Services Organisations (USO) sponsored visit to Singapore of the veteran American trombonist Jack Teagarden and his small, supporting band. We bought tickets, not only for ourselves, but also for the wife of the Council Representative, Dorothy Hardwick. It was a splendid evening marked by a curious incident at the end. After giving a very lively performance, the band played two national anthems, *God Save the Queen* and *Terang Bulan*, the Malayan National Anthem based on the State Anthem of Perak and formerly a popular song. Drums, double bass, guitar, trumpet and trombone together started to play both anthems in an appropriately solemn manner. But, after a tentative beginning it was too much for the band and they began to swing both pieces; something of an improvement, it seemed to me.

At the time of Dick Church's visit, I had begun to give careful thought to my future. In the normal course of events as a 'substantiated' officer in the Colonial Education Service (now re-named the Overseas Civil Service), I would have to retire at the age of fifty-five but could, with permission, retire on pension after reaching the age of fifty. But the old days had passed. Many officers were being replaced by Singaporeans and so at the age of thirty-three I decided to leave the service and commute my very small pension based on my approximately eight years' service. If I resigned now, it would surely be possible to start a new career. If I waited (apparently the last date would have been at some time in 1962), it might possibly be too late. In these circumstances I welcomed the opportunity to meet Dick Church and to explore employment possibilities in the British Council. He encouraged me to make a formal application and I did this before leaving Singapore in May 1959 in the passenger-cargo ship *Benvannoch*, along with eleven other passengers.

The Singapore of 2009 is understandably very different from the Singapore of 1959. The so-called 'cultural desert' has bloomed. A fine new Esplanade theatre complex (the 'Durian')[3] and concert hall provides a home for many different cultural manifestations, including performances by the impressive Singapore Symphony Orchestra, formed in January 1979 under the baton of Choo Hoey.

The orchestra is descended from a group of enthusiastic amateurs formed by the Singapore Musical Society in the 1950s. A good friend of mine, the oboist Paul Mosby, was one of four professional musicians brought from Britain to provide the orchestra with some professional expertise. Apart from playing in several concerts each year, the British musicians were contracted to give a certain number of master classes to local members of the orchestra. Paul was startled and certainly uneasy when he learned shortly after his arrival in Singapore that he was expected to allow his pupils the use of his own instrument. And this at a time when tuberculosis was still rife in Singapore, as elsewhere.

Today, the new theatre and concert hall are complemented by two other venues: the Singapore Arts House which has been sensibly converted from George Coleman's 1827 Parliament House and the Singapore Repertory Theatre which now functions in a new Drama Centre created from a refurbished warehouse.

But these developments were all in the future. My Singapore was different and the thought of leaving it in 1959 was a considerable wrench. Singapore was not my first home in the tropics and at the beginning of my stay I was often reminded of India and Ceylon. The nights were as steamy, the palm trees were as lush and there were the same flamboyant butterflies and multi-coloured birds. Yet Singapore in the 1950s added its own characteristics. Every day (except Sunday), businessmen could be seen in cream-coloured, monogrammed 'Fuji' silk shirts, clutching round tins of cigarettes and heading for offices that still lacked air conditioning. On the pavements and in the 'wet' markets hawkers touted for business. Eating places flourished everywhere: some were indoor restaurants; some were outdoor stalls cluttered with blackened woks bubbling with bean sprouts, prawns, squid and vegetables. In the back streets of Singapore and on buses, the smells of fragrant orchids competed with foul-smelling durians. The scents in libraries and archives were compounded of damp and insecticide and each book had to be coated with a transparent varnish, to ward off cockroaches and mould. A *musang* (a kind of civet cat) chattered in our roof at Goodwood Hill. A 'Shanghai Jar' in our Mount Pleasant outhouse came in useful when piped water failed. Brown fly-spattered boxes, homes for ceiling fan switches, disfigured the walls of bungalows. Persistent carpet salesmen visited homes and unrolled their wares with a flourish. 'A beautiful piece. You pay me next time, sir.' Teck Joo, the grocer in Orchard Road, was invariably persuasive. 'All right, you pay next month, I wait. You want two bottles whisky or three?' Hotels tempted; with pastries at The Adelphi Hotel, rijstaffels at The Cockpit and a variety of curries at the venerable Raffles Hotel. Cheaper, but just as tasty, were the fish, lamb and rice, transported by 'tiffin carrier' from the Islamic Restaurant. People dressed themselves in sarongs, kebayahs, songkoks, dhotis, evening trousers, white sharkskin jackets, cummerbunds. There was dancing at the Prince's Restaurant in Orchard Road. The party was over when the staff turned off the newfangled air conditioning and started to put the chairs on the tables. Street names memorialised colonial civil servants and entrepreneurs: Raffles Place, Sassoon Road, Nichol Highway, Scott's Road, Coleman Street. Travel was by shabby trucks, single-decker buses, rickshaws and Morris Minors with silken cushions obscuring their rear windows (no Mercedes Benzes then).

Outside the home, 'canned' entertainment ranged from plays (mainly Western) at the Victoria Memorial Hall to street puppet shows called *wayangs*. Western epics, 'thrillers' and romances at the Cathay and Pavilion cinemas and Malay films about *pontianaks* (vampires) rang the changes with Cantonese and Mandarin dramas produced in Hong Kong and Taiwan. These films were presented mainly by the Shaw Brothers' unique organisation; its founders alliteratively and tongue-twistingly named Runde, Runme, Runje and Run Run.

There were dying houses, temples, shrines, secret societies, dragon dances and processions associated with Diwali, a major Hindu Festival. It was going to be hard to leave it all.

******

With one mental foot still in Singapore, I arrived in England in May 1959. The voyage had taken a little longer than was usual, since it proved necessary for us to load and unload cargo for two days each in the Maldives and Port Sudan and for four days in Hamburg.

Ten passengers, including me, joined the ship in Singapore. Two men had boarded in London. Theirs was a round-trip except that they were obliged to leave the ship in Hong Kong before it proceeded to China. One of these men was a retired farmer who revealed an encyclopedic knowledge of London night-clubs. The other was a Mr John Bushnell, a Royal Waterman. Royal Watermen had the privilege of rowing the monarch and his/her courtiers up and down the River Thames. The practice is no longer observed but the title still exists, as an honour.

Before joining the *Benvannoch* in London, Bushnell had undergone major surgery and this necessitated the use of a colostomy bag which for some reason, he decided to show me. I expressed interest, weakly. Bushnell spoke proudly of his son (an Olympic Gold Medal winner) and allowed me to see his splendid Waterman's blazer, all the while regaling me with an account of the last occasion when the royal vessel was used for its proper purpose. The passengers were King George V and Queen Mary. King George was the first to get into the barge and after he was safely aboard, he tried to help the Queen. Unfortunately he failed to take a firm enough grip of her hand and she slipped, landing flat on her back in the boat. 'But I was there,' said Bushnell. 'I pulled down her skirts and helped her to her feet. She said, "Thank you, Bushnell" and gave the King hell all down the river.'

Mr Bushnell told me that he came from the town of Wargrave in England where he managed a boat-building business. In August 2004 I thought that it would be interesting to try to contact the present owners. In reply to my e-mailed enquiry, I received the following message from Mr David Bushnell:

> Mr John Henry Bushnell was my great grandfather. He passed away in 1970 aged 86 (I think). He had two sons, Len and Bert. Len was my grandfather and Bert won an Olympic Gold Medal in 1948 in the double sculls, rowing at Henley during the London Games. John Henry was a Royal Waterman like his father before him. His eldest son, Len, became a Royal Waterman. Len had two sons, Nick and Paul; Paul also became a Royal Waterman (my father). My father and I currently run the family business in Wargrave-on-Thames. If you would like any further information I would be more than happy to help.

It was good to have confirmation from Mr David Bushnell that I had not imagined my meeting with his great-grandfather.

*****

The *Benvannoch* docked in London and, after seeing to my baggage and personal effects, I journeyed down to Cornwall and The Corner House. The next four months were occupied mainly by cleaning, painting and decorating, with occasional pleasure jaunts to 'our' cove, and towns such as Truro, St Mawes, Falmouth and St Ives. The climate in Cornwall is in some ways quite benign but it seems to encourage dry rot, wet rot and woodworm. At least The Corner House enjoyed the company of all three of these life forms. On one occasion I painted the kitchen with blue, thixotropic paint. Within two weeks mould began to appear on the walls. Frustrated, I called in a local decorator who inspected the walls with a beady eye. 'This is terrible,' I said. 'I've only just finished painting, and now look at the mould.' 'Oh,' said the expert, in a rich Cornish accent, 'Don't you worry about tha-at. We've all got tha-at. This house is made of good, old Cornish granite and cob. Don't you worry about tha-at.' The mould remained and I had no choice but to think of it as a 'feature'.

Shortly after arriving at St Agnes, I submitted applications for three jobs. The first was for a permanent position in the British Council; the second for the post of Head of the Department of English at the then Cardiff College of Technology and the third for a post as an announcer at the BBC. I was called for interview by all three organisations.

The interview for the British Council in London seemed to go well. The interview for the BBC was not a success. When I arrived at Broadcasting House, I was greeted by a receptionist who directed me to a deserted studio. I was not introduced to a human being but instead found an instruction card placed on a table in front of a microphone. After reading the card I was instructed through a loudspeaker to speak a number of different passages that were set out on the card. I did so and at the end was thanked by the remote voice and told that the interview was over. 'Thank you for coming.' Somewhat dazed by this experience, I began to make my way out of the building when I met David Kennard in the corridor. Kennard had been a Senior Programme Officer in Radio Malaya. 'Hello!' said he. 'What are you doing here?' 'I came for an interview for an "on-mike" job.' 'Oh,' said David, 'You don't do it *that* way! I wish that you had contacted me.' But it was too late. A little bit of cronyism might have helped.

Before driving to Cardiff for my interview there, I received a letter from the British Council offering me a career position as a 'cadet'. Nevertheless I decided to journey to Cardiff before making a decision on the Council's offer.

The interview in Cardiff was satisfactory. Before it concluded, I informed the Interview Panel that I had already been offered a position by the British Council. 'What will you do if *we* offer you a position?' 'That would be very kind of you. I would have to consider it.' 'Thank you. Would you please wait outside?' After about fifteen minutes, I was called back into the room. 'Mr Bickley, we have decided to offer you the post. Could you please let us know your decision within a week?' 'Thank you very much. Yes, I will certainly do so.'

Now here was a conundrum. Accept the offer from Cardiff and settle down in Britain after an absence of eight years or go on our travels again? After considerable heart-searching, we decided that I should accept the British Council's offer and so informed the College in Cardiff. In late August 1959 I journeyed to London for a British Council Induction Course and in early September 1959 we decided to sell The Corner House (*sans* fleas). In late September we found ourselves at sea once again, this time on the Bibby Line ship, *MV Derbyshire*. We were bound for Rangoon, Burma.

Despite the frustrations caused by fleas, mouldy walls, spoilt paint and two kinds of rot, we enjoyed our time in Cornwall with its narrow hedgerows, mysterious lanes (playgrounds for *pixies*) and its dramatic cliff-top views. We were warmed by the friendliness of the people in our village. They gave the lie to those who had warned us that the Cornish Celts might be standoffish and even hostile.

The year 1959 appeared – at least on the surface – to be an excellent year for many people in Britain. Indeed, the Prime Minister, Harold Macmillan told the people in a television broadcast that this was the case. His sentence, 'You've never had it so good,' was to come back to haunt him. If Macmillan were still alive, he would point out that what he actually said was, '*Most of our people* have never had it so good.' He then continued, 'What is beginning to worry some of us is, is it too good to be true? Or perhaps I should say, is it too good to last?'

As we steamed nearer and nearer to Burma, my first British Council posting, we wondered if the remainder of 1959 and the subsequent years in our new life would continue to be good for us. So far we had no cause to complain.

We were on our way to the Land of the Crested Lion.[4]

THE SIXTH STEP

BURMA: LAND OF THE CRESTED LION

– 18 –

Intruders, Snakes and Ruined Dinners

In 1991, thirty-two years after we arrived in Rangoon (now Yangon), Ralph Isaacs, a British Council Officer stationed in the country, undertook to recruit a team of artists and craftsmen for the British Museum. Their task in Mandalay was to construct a *palin* (a platform-throne). This *palin* would form the base for a Buddha image which the former naval officer and successful writer, Captain Frederick Marryat, had acquired during the First Burmese War (1823–26).

In 2005 the British Council Association Newsletter published a shortened version of what it described as 'an excellent and entertaining talk by Ralph Isaacs'. His talk focused largely on the colourful life of Captain Marryat and in particular Marryat's involvement in Burmese affairs.

One quotation from Isaacs' talk deserves to be given in full:

> Marryat thought the Burmese people to be 'the most even-tempered race I ever met with, handsome, industrious and polite' and there is a startlingly modern ring in (Marryat's) assessment: 'The government is despotic, cruel and treacherous but the people are neither cruel nor treacherous; on the contrary, I think they would make most excellent and faithful soldiers... The English sailors... declared they were the best set of chaps they had ever fallen in with.'

Marryat's words would have found favour with us if we had encountered them during our short stay in Burma. We met many 'handsome, industrious and polite' Burmans during our British Council 'tour' in their country.

It is comforting for the new arrival in a strange country to be met at airport or dock. In Rangoon in the autumn of 1959 it was good to be received by the British Council Deputy Representative, David Pritchard. He steered us through Customs and Immigration, displaying admirable patience as various bureaucratic formalities were completed. Someone once libelled Australia (of all places) with the words, 'the British invented bureaucracy but the Australians (of all people) have refined it'. In Rangoon bureaucratic entry procedures were neither inventive nor refined. The screening of new arrivals was tediously lengthy and progress was very slow. At last however, we were clear of officialdom and on our way to a bungalow in Dubern Road, Rangoon.

The house was relatively small, with two bedrooms, a bathroom, a living room, a dining room and a kitchen, but it came with a cook – a Burman of Indian ancestry – and a watchman. The watchman stationed himself every evening in a wicker chair outside the front porch. There on most nights he enjoyed a quiet nap. This was certainly the case a month or so after our arrival. One very early morning, at about two o'clock we were awakened by a soft, scratching sound. Then the bedroom door opened slowly, just loud enough to jerk us awake. Muddled with sleep I shouted something and tried to get out of bed but became entangled in my mosquito net, giving the intruder time to retreat. The Ealing Comedy continued as finally free of my bed I seized an umbrella and with this menacing weapon at the ready advanced into the garden, urging the watchman to wake up as I did so. But our visitor had gone, never to return. Or had he? Did he metamorphose into the snake which a few days later curled itself round the concertina-like metal gate that, when closed, was supposed to prevent access to the front door?

Security at the Dubern Road house was poor. The cooking was worse. The cook produced a succession of tasteless dinners that on most nights featured curiously blackened meat, softened somewhat by a mud-coloured liquid that bore little resemblance to the gravy that it aspired to be. Not that it was easy to obtain the makings of a well-balanced European diet in Rangoon. In the late 1950s the British Council enjoyed diplomatic status in several countries and the duty-free liquors and imported foods that went with it. Not in Burma. From time to time, David Pritchard, a most amiable man, was forced to smile through his teeth when an Embassy colleague thoughtlessly quipped, 'Missing your bacon, David?'

After a few days in Rangoon, we were introduced to a 'wet market' where we bought eggs, poultry and some meat which, although doubtful-looking, had not been subjected to the misguided efforts of our flatteringly named cook. Groceries should have been available at the provision store, *Shwe Mya* (142 Fraser Street, Rangoon) but the stock was very limited and 'Western' food was at a premium. To compensate, occasional tins of ham and 'Spam' were available and there was plenty of rice and an abundance of fruit, including mangoes, strawberries, durians, bananas, custard apples, avocado pears, apples, mulberries and watermelons. We enjoyed excellent tea, grown on plantations in the Shan State, and aromatic coffee cultivated in the Chin Hills.

*****

In the 1950s and 1960s the British Council office in Rangoon was situated in Strand Road, not far from the well-known but sad-looking Strand Hotel, once one of the Grand Hotels of Asia fit to be ranked with Raffles Hotel in Singapore and the Eastern and Oriental in Penang. The Strand, the Raffles and the Eastern and Oriental were established by the enterprising Sarkies brothers, natives of Armenia.[1] Reduced in the 1960s 1970s and 1980s to a fading shadow of its former self, the Strand was taken over by the Burmese government and for some years operated as a shabby resthouse. But some old hotels never die. I'm told that an international hotel chain has refurbished the building and that it now functions as Burma's version of a five-star hotel.

At the Council's office, I was introduced to the Representative, Harry Lawrence, and to members of the local staff, including the Deputy Librarian, Monica Mya Maung and the 'fixer', 'Swami'. If you needed an official document to be stamped, Swami would get it stamped for you. If your car broke down, Swami would find someone to mend it. If your ceiling fan ceased to work, Swami would replace it. Every office in Rangoon needed a Swami.

And every office needed a Monica. She arrived in Rangoon with her Burmese husband, Percy, just before the Second World War. During the War she was persuaded to work as a hospital nurse in difficult conditions. After the War came to an end and after Burma was granted independence, she was appointed to the British Council's library staff.

In an article published in the summer of 2004 in the British Council Association Newsletter, Tom White describes the problems encountered by the Council, following General Ne Win's military coup in 1962. In 1967 the Council was obliged to withdraw from the country. However, almost single-handedly, Monica kept the library going and, despite many vicissitudes, it remains in existence today – as White notes – 'the only uncensored public library in the whole country of 45 million people'.

Monica's persistence paid off, for despite the present military dictatorship's disapproval, it is reported that the library now has approximately seven thousand members. The late Harry Lawrence, the Council's Representative (Director) from 1958 to 1960, would have been delighted.

Harry – a headmaster in a previous existence – was an old hand in the British Council. A bluff, 'down-to-earth' man, he was both kind and supportive to his staff. I have my own experience to quote as testimony to this. Some months after I began work in Rangoon, I sent a report to the Council's Headquarters in London about some aspect of my work. I failed to set out the report in the customary format. This was noted by an Assistant Director, the late Dr Arthur King (later Deputy Director) who pointed this out to Harry Lawrence in somewhat abrasive language. Harry wasn't having any. He wrote a stinging reply along the lines of 'this is no way to treat a new recruit to the service who has not yet had the time to learn the ropes'. Arthur was irascible and impatient but he accepted the rebuke and I learned my lesson. After his retirement from the Council, Arthur became a member of the Church of Latter Day Saints and it was in that capacity that I met him many years later in Honolulu. He was most affable.

*****

After a few 'settling in' days (and after signing the Ambassador's book), I was taken to the State Teachers' Training College in Kanbe (*kan-bay*), a suburb of Rangoon. I had been appointed British Council lecturer in English at the College but I combined my duties there with other British Council work which I chose to carry out in, or from, the Council's head office in Strand Road. For example, I arranged drama evenings, organised two summer schools for teachers, made appointments for a visiting British plastic surgeon and in my second year in Rangoon set up a photographic exhibition of radio isotopes, something to do with a treatment for cancer.

The Burmese word for 'school' is also the word for monastery. For centuries, monasteries were the only centres of education and the Buddhist priests were the teachers. In the middle of the nineteenth century the British authorities tried to include monastic schools in a scheme for secular education and attempts were made to widen the religious curriculum by translating geography, science, arithmetic and literature textbooks into the Burmese language. The monastic schools were not, however, responsible to any central authority. The monks were suspicious, resenting any interference from the foreign intruder. Protestant and Roman Catholic missions were also hostile towards the idea as being too favourable to Buddhism. The solution adopted was to leave the monastic schools to their own devices and to build up a system of lay schools as alternatives.

With the coming of the British, education could not escape the influence of trade. More and more commercial enterprises opened branches in Rangoon, Mandalay and Moulmein. New firms – such as Steel Brothers and the department store, Rowe and Company – were founded and flourished. The English language followed trade and new opportunities opened up for Burmese youths provided that they could demonstrate an adequate knowledge of English. Increasing numbers of students flocked to the lay schools and the monastic schools tended to lose influence. One perhaps unanticipated result of this was what J.S. Furnivall called, 'the all-pervading bookishness and the dissociation of education generally from life and occupation'.[2]

Some of the opposition that existed between secular and monastic education is described in this passage written by Daw Mi Mi Khaing who succeeded a British Council appointee, Timothy Slack, as Principal of Kambawsa College in the Upper Shan State:

> In about 1922 my Uncle Pyant, who was then a serious student at the University, told me that the world was round, 'but,' he added, 'the *pongyis* (monks) don't believe it.' My husband also tells me that when he went home from his government school with the statement that the earth spun around on its axis and took twenty-four hours to do it, the elders were most scornful. 'In that case,' they said, 'if you were to go up into the air and stay there for some time, you could not come down to Kengtung until the same time the next day, but might land in England for your lunch.'
>
> Another difference between old and new ideas of education was that elder people were aghast at the long years which a modern education from primary to university lasted. They felt that, at least, one must have learnt everything there was to be learnt by then, for a few years at a monastery taught a boy all the reading, writing, calculating and literature which any grown man was expected to know.[3]

Until 1957, the staff of the English Department in the College at Kanbe comprised three Burmese nationals, one being the Head of Department. In 1957 this staff was increased by the arrival from the United States of a lecturer recruited under the Fulbright scheme. In 1959, after the departure of one of the local staff to Canada to study educational psychology, I was appointed to the Department.

I worked quite closely with the Fulbright lecturer, Mary Jane Himmel. Together, we practised what became known as 'Anglo-American Cooperation in Language Teaching', supporting each other, but approaching our work from different perspectives and with different teaching materials. In 1960, for example, I gave three talks on English literature at the Burma–America Institute in Rangoon. These were followed by a number of presentations made by American academics on American literature.

Both Mary Jane and I would have been surprised to learn that, by speaking at the Burma–America Institute, we were (as one writer has claimed) 'imposing new mental structures through English',[4] and 'promoting national and Western interests and English linguistic imperialism (that) both facilitated global imperialism and was a consequence of it'.[5] We were mainly concerned to help our Burmese students to improve their English language listening, speaking, reading and writing skills.

Throughout Burma, the Teacher Training Institutes prepared teachers for work in the primary schools and the middle schools. English was not included in the curricula except in the Rangoon and Mandalay Institutes. It was the task of the Faculty of Education at the University of Rangoon to train teachers for work in the high schools.

Three British Council lecturers – namely Raymond Adlam, William Oldfield and John Dent-Young[6] – taught English Literature at the University but had no teacher-training responsibilities. Established in 1878 as an affiliate of the University of Calcutta and named Rangoon College, Rangoon University was organised along Oxbridge lines. Its student body was drawn mainly from schools in which English was the medium of instruction, for example, Kambawsa College in the Shan State, St Michael's Girls' School in Rangoon and the Government English High School in Maymyo. Today, after many politically-motivated closures, the University has been re-named Yangon University.

In the Rangoon Teachers' Training College, a total of twenty-five periods a week was allocated to the Special English Class. Fourteen of these periods were given to the improvement of the trainees' own use of English and the remaining eleven periods were devoted to methods of teaching the language. There was close liaison between the lecturers concerned with teaching English language and those who introduced different methods of teaching it.

The majority of the students at the College were Burmese and all had been born in Burma. A few came from English-speaking home environments; others spoke Burmese, Kachin, Shan, or any other of the country's many languages and dialects.

With memories of my work in Singapore still in mind, I was able to compare teacher-training provision in both Singapore and Burma. There is no doubt that the academic quality of applicants for in-service courses at the Singapore Teachers' Training College was higher than that of the in-service teachers who applied to join the one-year courses in Burma. Neither is there any doubt that when their periods of study were completed, the Singapore trainees were probably better equipped to take charge of classes in primary schools than their opposite numbers in Burma. There were several reasons for this. First, the Singapore student teachers would have attended a full-time course for two years or a part-time ('Normal') course for three years. Second, the young men and women who applied for entry to the Teachers' Training College in Singapore had mostly been educated in secondary schools in which English was the medium of instruction (although students from Chinese-medium schools were enrolled in special courses from 1957 onwards). Students who had

Lunch at the State Teachers' Training College, Rangoon, Burma, 1960. The author facing the camera. Two German guest lecturers, a Burmese female lecturer make up the party, with three college servants in attendance.

received their own education in English-medium schools were regarded as ineligible to appear before a Selection Board unless they possessed the Cambridge Syndicate's School Certificate. Once they had been accepted for the part-time 'Normal' training course (spread over three years),[7] or the 'Certificate' training course (two years, full time), they received stipends which were considerably higher than those paid in Burma.

On the other hand, Burmese trainees came to Rangoon or Mandalay from different parts of Burma, many having served as unqualified teachers in remote rural areas until they were accepted for in-service training. Most of these students had been pupils of Burmese high schools in which Burmese was the medium of instruction and English was taught as a foreign language.

I was fortunate to be in Burma during the premiership of Thakin[8] U Nu, like Aung San and Ne Win, a former wartime collaborator with the Japanese. His reign as premier was very short. In 1962 he was toppled from his throne by his fellow collaborator, Ne Win.

In 1959 certain features of the Rangoon of colonial days had already disappeared. After over one hundred years of business, the shipping agents Scott and Company had closed. Scott's rival, Mackinnon and Mackenzie, had stopped trading. The Rangoon Turf Club in the suburb of Kyaikasan had ceased to function and the finest race-course in Asia lay derelict. The department store, Rowe and Company and Scott Market (Bogyoke Market) had very few goods to sell. The churches were still in place but there were very small congregations at the (Anglican) Cathedral of the Holy Trinity and at the (Catholic) St Mary's Cathedral.

The old ways and the old customs were going, 'giving birth to new'. Unfortunately, the assassinations of Aung San and his six Cabinet colleagues had created a political vacuum. Today, they must lie uneasily in their Mausoleum on Arzani (Martyrs') Hill since Burma has almost reached the stage of being dubbed a 'failed state'.

Despite all these difficulties, the students appeared to accept their lot with equanimity and on the whole, they were a delight to work with. But, politics aside, I enjoyed working with my students in Rangoon. They were polite and enthusiastic despite having to work in conditions of considerable difficulty. When an in-service trainee entered College, payment of his normal teaching salary would stop and he or she would receive a small, monthly stipend in lieu. This financial loss was harder to bear because of the tight discipline imposed on the students – both men and women – after classes had finished for the day. The training colleges were residential and the students lived in hostels attached to each College.

In Rangoon, the living space in the hostels was extremely cramped and students were locked in at 7pm each evening. There were no common rooms and no facilities for private study. Any work done out of the lecture room had to be done on the students' beds which they turned into desks for the purpose. In addition, the administration of the College was woefully slack. There was, for example, no College Calendar. Holidays were often declared on the day that they took place. Staff meetings were arranged at a moment's notice and took up the best part of a College day because there was no systematic agenda. Examinations were held at the traditional times during the year but the results were never analysed or collated.

From time to time, especially on holidays, members of the staff association or the administration would arrange a feast at the College. Whilst appreciating the spirit of hospitality, I was always rather nervous about the food. The custom was to prepare it several hours in advance of being eaten and to lay the different dishes on mats on the floor, where it became a target for all the flies in the district, untroubled by the fans waved by several members of the 'minor' staff. I do not exaggerate when I write that at Western receptions, a frequent – almost an overriding – topic of conversation was the latest treatment for amoebic or bacillary dysentery and other perhaps more exotic intestinal diseases. One treatment which caused considerable comment was popularly known as 'The Magic Flute'. I never found out what it was but, being rather imaginative, it made my toes curl.

The political situation in Burma since the end of the Second World War has been one of upheaval and discontent. Before and during the Japanese occupation, certain prominent Burmese Thakins ('Masters') joined the Japanese side with the slogan 'One Blood, One Voice, One Command'. In their comprehensive review of *The Fall of British Asia 1941–1945*, Christopher Bayly and Timothy Harper refer to the way in which Aung San – perhaps the most prominent of the young nationalists – fled to Japan, there to 'bow to the imperial palace' before returning to Burma.

> A Tokyo dentist fitted Aung San with a set of false teeth to conceal his identity for his clandestine return to Burma... This disguise was enough to put British intelligence off the scent... He reached Rangoon on 3 March 1941. Over the next three months, the Minami Kikan organisation smuggled out thirty young men from Burma. These were to be the famous Thirty Comrades, the Knights of the Round Table of Burmese independence and its evergreen heroes.[9]

During the Japanese occupation, several of these nationalists worked with the Japanese. A few, such as 'General' Aung San, Thakin Ba Maw and

Thakin Nu were rewarded with ministerial-level positions. At a critical stage during the British advance on Rangoon, they changed sides. On 19 July 1947, their leader, Aung San and six other persons were assassinated by followers of U Saw, a former Prime Minister. U Saw was hanged for the offence on 8 May 1948.

In an essay entitled *My Father*, first published in 1984 by the University of Queensland in its 'Leaders of Asia' series, Aung San Suu Kyi, as a loyal daughter, refers to her father in glowing terms:

> '...his innate ability and sense of responsibility came into play' (page thirty-three)
> '...a loving husband and father' (page eleven)
> '...one of the few considered above faction and jealousy' (pages eighteen and nineteen)
> '...had a deep and abiding interest in religion' (page eight)
> '...a soldier of great skill and courage, able to bear much hardship' (page fifteen)
> '...a strong leader and an able statesman'[10] (page twenty-five).

But I have a question. Rangoon fell to the Japanese in March 1942. In 1943 the Japanese gave Aung San the title of Minister of War. On 27 March 1945, the Burmese Army rose against the Japanese. How many Allied soldiers and airmen were killed during the three-year period in which Aung San collaborated with the Japanese?

> The British General Sir William Slim had no doubt about Aung San's guilt. In an interview, conducted after Aung San had changed sides again, he said:
>
> Apart from the fact that you, a British subject, have fought against the British Government, I have here in this headquarters people who tell me that there is a well-substantiated case of civil murder, complete with witnesses, against you. I have been urged to place you on trial for that.[11]

Following Aung San's assassination, Thakin Nu served as Prime Minister and was in and out of office from 1947 until March 1962. From time to time during that period, he would enter a Buddhist monastery to meditate and enjoy spiritual refreshment. During one such sojourn, General Ne Win led a Tatmadaw (Army) coup that dismissed Parliament and scrapped the Constitution. From that time Ne Win took the reins of government and grasped them tightly until he retired in 1988.

Since Ne Win's death, General Than Shwe and his colleagues have operated a corporate dictatorship, opposed in different ways by Aung San's daughter, Aung San Suu Kyi. Whilst one cannot fault Ms Aung San's desire to see the present military-led dictatorship changed in favour of a freely elected government, one cannot help wondering, on a personal level, why she did not make more of an effort to visit and support her husband in England in his last days. This does seem to be a case of placing country before family. The son of a former senior British Council officer, John Aris, Dr Michael Aris died on 27 March 1999 of prostate cancer. A cremation service was held in Oxford on 31 March. His wife was not present.

*****

In March 1961, Thakin Nu published a political play entitled, *The Wages of Sin*. My autographed copy includes an introduction by E.M. Law Yone, then editor of the newspaper, *The Nation*. Law Yone's introduction included the following paragraph:

> In 1956, the AFPFL[12] stood for Democracy as opposed to Communism. The elections that year gave less than one-fifth of the total number of seats to the Communists but in terms of the popular vote the Communists polled 1.4 million ballots to the AFPFL's 1.7 million. The danger signal was up, the warning was clear. Democracy was losing ground and could be swamped at the next election. If today U Nu seems obsessed with the ideals of benignity and rectitude on the part of political leaders, we must at least concede there is method in the obsession. In 1960 not a single Communist candidate was returned to Parliament, one unknown fellow-traveller got in, but only after he had forsworn the National United Front.[13]

It was, perhaps, an excess of benignity that led to General Ne Win's military coup. In a Foreword, U Nu stated that:

> Parliamentary democracy cannot endure, and must sooner or later perish in a country where those entrusted with its governance are:
> (1) Addicted to spirituous liquor;
> (2) Given to over-indulgence in such things as the pleasures of women;
> (3) In the habit of gambling;
> (4) Unable to rise above bribery and corruption; and
> (5) Are guilty of misusing power for the sake of the Party.[14]

These were fine words but, unlike the son of the main character in his play, U Nu was slow to act:

> Po Thoung: I do not come in the capacity of your son. I come in the capacity of a citizen of the country.
> U Po Lone: I don't care in what capacity you come. You are not to see me. Go away, you swine!

Po Thoung: Why have you declared our classes illegal?
U Po Lone: Because it pleases me. Get out. I don't have to answer to you (*to the peon*). Throw him out. (*The peon catches hold of Po Thoung who roughly pulls himself free.*)
Po Thoung: Why have you arrested our teachers unlawfully?
U Po Lone: Because it pleases me. Get out! Look here! Are you getting out or are you not?
(*While talking he walks angrily towards Po Thoung to push him out of the room. Po Thoung whips out a revolver from his hip.*)
Po Thoung: All right. Take this for arresting him. (*He fires one shot. U Po Lone is hit in the chest but continues forward a step.*) All right, take this for stopping our classes! (*Po Thoung fires another shot. U Po Lone collapses onto the floor. The peons run out. As Po Thoung stares down, his face distorted with hate at his father's corpse, the curtain comes down slowly.*)[15]

During the short time that I spent in Burma (September 1959 until August 1961), U Nu's government came under fire for its apparent weakness and incompetence. 'The packs of wild dogs are back,' said somebody. 'Get out the catapults.' This last remark was not made in jest. Packs of wild, perhaps diseased, dogs – eliminated during an earlier short period of military rule – had returned to roam the streets. The catapult salesman stationed outside the British Council office in Strand Road appeared to do good business.

My comments are, of course, based upon a very small sample but many of the diplomats, educationists and men of business, with whom I came into contact, expressed doubts about the solidity of U Nu's regime. During his comparatively short first term in office (1958–59) Ne Win was considered by some to have brought about significant improvements in governance. This was a view held abroad, as well as in Burma itself. The 1967 edition of *Chambers's Encyclopedia*, for example, notes that, 'in seventeen months this government, consisting of General Ne Win and civil servants, did much to improve administration and reduce insurgency. Certainly, the government took effective measures to recover hidden arms, intensify offensives against insurgents, improve the overall administrative machinery and institute weekly cleaning campaigns in Rangoon.'[16]

The February 1960 election returned U Nu to power but in March 1962, Ne Win again felt himself compelled to intervene. Unfortunately, as has often been the melancholy case, the (Burmese) knight was transformed in office. His armour ceased to shine and his administration became increasingly oppressive.

In the last few years, Burma has slowly opened its doors to the outside world, largely in search of the tourist dollar. For the visitor there is much to be seen and much to be experienced that is Buddhist-based. It is comforting to know that despite the present political situation there is still room for dance, whether improvised as in the various kinds of *pwes* (theatrical performances), or in the *yein pwès*, group dancing in balletic style that requires much rehearsal. As far as I know, *Wayangs*, as presented in Singapore, Malaysia and Indonesia, were not practised in Burma when I was there but the *yoke thay* (or marionette show) which I did experience is not dissimilar, featuring themes that are usually derived from the birth stories of Buddha and the Burmese chronicles.

Pagodas abound in Rangoon. One hopes that, one day, the purpose for which the Kaba Aye Pagoda was completed in 1952 will be achieved. It is dedicated to World Peace and Understanding.

The Sule Pagoda and the Chauk Htat Kyi, Koe Dat Kyi and Nga Dat Kyi pagodas have their place but there is no doubt that the city's principal landmark is still the Shwe Dagon Pagoda, believed to have been built in 585 BC. It is claimed that the Shwe Dagon is the only pagoda to contain eight hairs from the head of the Gautama Buddha.

I visited the Pagoda twice, once by myself and once with a visitor. It is mandatory to remove one's shoes but some visitors, including foreigners, are permitted to retain their socks before entering the building. I welcomed this concession. On both occasions (and I mean no disrespect) I trod on thick lumps of spittle.

*****

In 2005 it was reported that General Than Shwe had shifted the country's administrative capital from Rangoon ('Yan Gon': meaning – 'end of strife') to Pyinmana, four hundred kilometres north of Yangon. The name for the new, fortified capital known as Naypyidaw ('the abode of kings'), perhaps reflects the Junta's desire to set up a strategically placed 'command and control centre'. Some people in Rangoon (Yangon) have re-named Pyinmana, 'Escape City', although who is escaping from whom has yet to be determined.

– 19 –

Maymyo, Taunggyi and Miss Gulliver

I was fortunate to be in Rangoon at a time before serious repression began. There were however, problems of insurgency in Upper Burma (although one person's insurgent is another person's 'militant' or 'freedom fighter'). Negotiated agreements have now been reached with many of the ethnic groups except the Karens. Although depleted in numbers and lacking up-to-date arms and equipment, they continue to operate from their base on the banks of the Moei River that separates Burma from Thailand.

Large numbers of Karens were (and are) Christians. In the colonial era many of them served in the British Army in which they were known for their soldierly skills and their mixed choirs. We were fortunate to be supported by a Karen family in our house in Prome Road. The wife took charge of the cleaning and her husband did the cooking. His specialities were *mohinga* (fermented rice noodles in a fish soup) and a wonderful *khaukswe* – a mixture of noodles, lemon grass and 'secret spices'. Every month on pay day and as regular as the best clockwork, he would beat his wife. She did not seem to resent it. Or if she did, she didn't let on.

In the early spring of 1960, the lease of our house in Dubern Road expired and we moved into the 'British Council House' in Windsor Road. This was an extraordinary building, almost mediaeval in design. A large, central hall was flanked by two sets of private rooms; two bedrooms, a bathroom and a living room on the left and two bedrooms, a bathroom and a living room on the right. We occupied the rooms on the left-hand side. Harry Lawrence had the rooms on the right-hand side.

Randolph O'Hara (now a retired senior civil servant of the Hong Kong government) was born and grew up in Burma. In what seems to be a personal account told in the third person, he recalls a visit to the house long after it had been vacated by the Council:

> He had lived there for a while, and had never been happier. He was amazed that it was still there, but it now looked rather neglected and forlorn. The house itself obviously needed a good coat of paint, while the garden needed attending to. For some reason he did not venture further than the open gate, although the guide was keen to go into the garden with him… The guide said to him, 'Uncle, what was the road called before?' In answer he said 'Windsor Road'. 'Oh', said the guide, 'that is why the hotel down the road is called Windsor Hotel'. And sure enough, a few houses down, the 'Windsor Hotel' came into view. Strange, he thought, how governments might wish to erase the past and rename roads, yet, the people needed roots and still cherish the past.[1]

One day, I returned to the Windsor Road house from Kanbe, to be greeted at the entrance by a line of young people who proceeded to douse me in water. Spluttering and dripping, I broke through the cordon and in the safety of the lobby asked the 'butler' for an explanation. The incident was, it seemed, related to *Tagoo*, the first month of the Burman year (a moveable feast). Normally, water-throwing takes place for three days and the feast is also celebrated by parades, dancing and singing.

After several weeks in Windsor Road, we were fortunate to be able to move into a splendid house in Prome Road, not far from Inya Lake. The house was leased by the Council from the *Sawbwa* (Chief) of Kengtung, an important town in the Shan State. Disrespectfully but affectionately known to some as 'Shorty', he was one of the thirty-three *sawbwas* who governed the State until they were deprived of office by the Ne Win regime.

Under the British colonial administration (from 1887) the then Shan States were governed by their hereditary chiefs until they were united as the Federated Shan States in 1922. In 1947, a single Shan State was established by the new Constitution. This arrangement held until the year in which I arrived in Rangoon (1959) when the *sawbwas* relinquished much of their authority to the Burmese government. The State's autonomy was further eroded in 1974 when the amended Constitution promulgated in that year introduced additional centralisation measures.

*****

During my time in Burma, I directed two vacation courses for teachers. The first of these was held in Maymyo, a hill station forty miles east of Mandalay.

Founded in 1887 by a Colonel May of the 5th Bengal Infantry, Maymyo ('May Town') has been re-named Pyin U Lwin by the present government.

During the British era the government spent the months April to June and September to October in Maymyo. The town was not only the temporary seat of government but also a military station, overseen by a Major-General. The regiments stationed there included the King's Own Yorkshire Light Infantry, the King's Royal Rifle Corps, the Burma Rifles and the Cameron Highlanders.

Soldiering was not the only activity in Maymyo. By exercise of one's imagination, one can hear the sighs of the lonely women approached by Captain Williams of the Burma Rifles… 'A notorious playboy type, who would have a quick affair with one young wife and, when she returned, usually after a short stay, to the plains, would switch to another. He was always known as "Temptation Bill."'[2]

Our Maymyo vacation course was held for part of each day in 'Candacraig', a house that served as our temporary lodgings. Built by the British to accommodate staff of the Bombay Burmah Trading Company, the ghosts of young sprigs of commerce still haunt the building, now a six-bedroom hotel supervised by the present regime's Ministry of Hotels and Tourism.

The staff of the vacation course was drawn from the British Council in Rangoon and Mandalay, supplemented by Dr James Noonan, a visiting Senior Lecturer from the University of London's Institute of Education. Overall, the course was very successful, although marred somewhat by the illness that struck John Dent-Young at the beginning of the course and Jimmy Noonan at the end of it. Noonan suffered from an unavoidable, unpleasant attack of influenza but Dent-Young's dysentery could probably have been avoided.

We had been driven up to Maymyo by the late Wilfred Kirkpatrick, a British Council lecturer stationed in Mandalay. Wilfred was a delightful man with an impish sense of humour. He stopped the car about ten miles from Maymyo and suggested that we should take some refreshment at a roadside stall. Glasses and chipped cups were laid out on a rickety table, covered by a tattered oilcloth. The gap-toothed proprietor of this 'restaurant' squatted on a low stool, fanning the flames beneath two bent braziers. Wilfred, the perfect host, asked what we would like to drink. He and I chose hot tea. John seemed uncertain, so Wilfred persuaded him to try what he described as a 'most delicious drink, fit for the gods'. John agreed and downed a glass of mud-coloured liquid, chilled by lumps of floating ice taken from a bucket. In the right circumstances, and in a hygienic setting, the yoghourt-based drink known as 'lassi' can be refreshing. Not by the side of a dusty road in Burma. Bacillary dysentery struck almost as soon as we reached Candacraig.

The consequence of Wilfred's joke was that we were short of a lecturer for most of the refresher course. Wilfred was crestfallen and blamed himself although of course John – a relative newcomer to Asia – could have been laid low anyway.

It was a shock to learn that Wilfred died a year or two later in India. He was found murdered in a hotel room in Calcutta.

*****

My second vacation course took place from 24 April to 13 May 1961. I am certain about the dates, having unearthed a group photograph taken on the last day. I appear in the second row from the front and am flanked on my left by Sau Saimong.[3] The person on his left is Sau Tung Aye, then State Minister for Education and Health. Alton Becker, a lecturer brought to

At the summer school in Maymyo, Burma, 1960. From left: colleague Helen McAlpine, the author, colleagues Mary Clague, Dr James Noonan, John Dent-Young.

Burma under the Fulbright Exchange Scheme, is seated on my right. On his right, in order, are Mrs E. Gaudoin of Rangoon University, Mr Robert Nelson, a volunteer teacher at Kambawsa College, and Miss Mary Clague, a colleague at the State Teachers' Training College.

The course was held in the capital of the Shan States, Taunggyi, on the campus of Kambawsa College, formerly a school for the sons of Shan Chiefs, but democratised after the Second World War.

Sau Tung Aye was a generous host who willingly entertained the staff of the 'refresher' course at its beginning and at its end. Both he and Sau Saimong moved easily and courteously among the guests from Rangoon. One can only hope that both men survived the Burmese government's anti-Shan pogroms and 'ethnic cleansing' campaigns. According to Emma Larkin, the Shan language is no longer taught in schools; Shan names have been Burmanised and all Shan street signs have been pulled down. In 1991, an 'old palace' in Kengtung was destroyed to make way for a government-run hotel.[4] This 'palace' may have been the venue I visited in 1961, for Sau Tung Aye's receptions.

Four thousand feet up in the mountains, Taunggyi was ideal for our academic purposes. No fear that the teachers (or staff) would be tempted to drift off to sleep in the afternoons. No fear that one would be kept awake at night by the heat. Although the sun was sometimes very strong at midday, the temperature dropped sharply in the evenings and we welcomed the layers of blankets on our beds.

*****

In February 1961, I was asked to take a box of books to Kyaukpyu ('Chowpyoo'), an island off the Burmese Arakan coast on the shores of the Bay of Bengal. The books were a gift from the British Council to a teachers' training college on the island. Logically, the college should have been situated in Akyab (now re-named 'Sittwe'), the capital of the Arakan. But (so the rumour went), the parliamentary representative for the Arakan came from Kyaukpyu, so naturally…

The small island town of Kyaukpyu has grown in significance since my visit. It now has a naval base and deep water harbour that is being developed as a terminal for rich oil and gas deposits discovered recently off the coast. Kyaukpyu is to be the starting point for a pipeline which will carry the oil and gas, much of which will be piped to China. Contracts for three offshore blocks were signed in 2007.

But I am jumping ahead. Forty-eight years ago, I flew in a well-worn DC3 aircraft to Kyaukpyu and was met at the airfield by Miss Gulliver, a British medical missionary who had lived on the island since the late 1930s. I was to stay with her for one night before returning to Rangoon. She was a kind hostess but for reasons of propriety I could not spend the night in the main house that she shared with her Bible woman. I was accommodated instead in a garden hut. I hoped, fervently, that I would not have to share it with one or more of the island's many snakes.

The Arakan region was the scene of some of the most savage battles of the Second World War. Abandoned by the Allies in their evacuation of Burma during the period May to October 1942, both Akyab and Kyaukpyu were recaptured in late January 1945 with the help of salvos from the battleship, Queen Elizabeth, 'in her first engagement since the Dardanelles in 1915'.[5] The rusting damaged tanks and savaged armoured cars in Miss Gulliver's garden were stark evidence of the battle.

After a satisfying dinner and an undisturbed sleep in my little hut, I was taken by Miss Gulliver for an early morning stroll around Kyaukpyu's wet market. Rows of Arakanese ladies sat cross-legged on the ground, rolling cheroots between their thighs. They smiled at Miss Gulliver and muttered as we passed. Miss Gulliver said later that they thought I might be her son.

'The rusting, damaged tanks and savaged armoured cars in Miss Gulliver's garden were stark evidence of the battle.' Kyaukypu, the Arakan, Burma, 1960.

Over lunch, Miss Gulliver told me that as a young woman, she had worked as a nurse in a British hospital. Occasionally, during breaks, and out of sight of the Matron, the nurses would 'read' each other's teacups. One day, Miss Gulliver's teacup revealed that in the future, three bad things would happen to her. She would, however (said the tea leaves), survive all three. After she had been in Kyaukpyu a few years, Japanese invaders penetrated the Arakan and approached the capital, Sittwe (formerly Akyab). Miss Gulliver hurried to the city and (unbelievably) asked for her account at the Standard Chartered Bank to be transferred to Calcutta. She then joined a group of people who walked into India, with much suffering on the way. Bad Thing Number One. Arriving in Calcutta, Miss Gulliver was taken straight into hospital, suffering from a life-threatening attack of dysentery. Bad Thing Number Two. After several weeks in hospital, she was discharged, but when she was passing through the hospital gates – or nearly – she was bitten by a rabid dog. She was taken back into the hospital for a course of painful injections in the stomach. Bad Thing Number Three.

Miss Gulliver was a most extraordinary, indomitable woman who had suffered much and had many a rich tale to tell. I am sure that there were more stories and I would like to have heard them but, unfortunately, it was time for me to return to Rangoon.

The facilities at the tiny airport consisted of a white-painted wooden hut and a separate latrine. I was asked to wait in the wooden hut until the aircraft arrived, the only plane scheduled to land at Kyaukpyu on that day. After a long wait, I saw the vapour trails of a plane high in the sky. This had to be my plane. There would be no other until the next day. Suddenly, without warning, dysentery struck. What action could I take? I rushed into the filthy latrine and squatted over a hole in the ground. I could hear the plane land. Could I risk leaving my hole? Yes, I must. What else could I do? My day-old copy of *The Nation* came in useful. Conscious of the risks, I pulled up my trousers and made my way very slowly to the aircraft that waited impatiently for its only passenger from Kyaukpyu. The plane was full. I took the last vacant seat, in which I was trapped because most of the aisle was blocked by hessian-covered kegs of country spirit. The smell added to my misery. Would I be able to make it to Rangoon? If I failed, what would be the consequence?

Yes, I am happy to report that I was able to hold on and survived the journey without further 'incident'. But it had been a dramatic few days, a reality show that was very different to that portrayed in the many plays presented over the years by the Rangoon Theatre Club. My album reveals that on 19 and 20 August 1960 I appeared in the Club's seventy-third presentation, Roland and Michael Pertwee's play, *The Paragon* and, on 15, 16 and 17 December 1960, I directed a production of *Treasure Island*. John Dent-Young played Jim Hawkins and Raymond Adlam took the part of Dr Livesey. General Ne Win, Supreme Commander of the Union of Burma Army, was one of the Patrons, as was the Honourable Prime Minister, U Nu! I must assume that both gentlemen gave permission for their names to be used.

*****

Our days in Burma passed very quickly, perhaps because it was such a busy life. I suppose that we made it so. We must have enjoyed the tension. Our Burmese friends were more relaxed. I once asked a Burmese colleague why Burmans rarely replied to written invitations. He said, 'If we reply and say that we will come and then, perhaps because of illness or some other unanticipated emergency, we are unable to come, you will be offended. If we do not reply, then we can come, or *not* come. Also, in Burma the unexpected guest will always be welcome because it is easy to boil more rice.' I swallowed this information and attributed it to a cultural difference. But it could sometimes be very inconvenient. There was, for example,

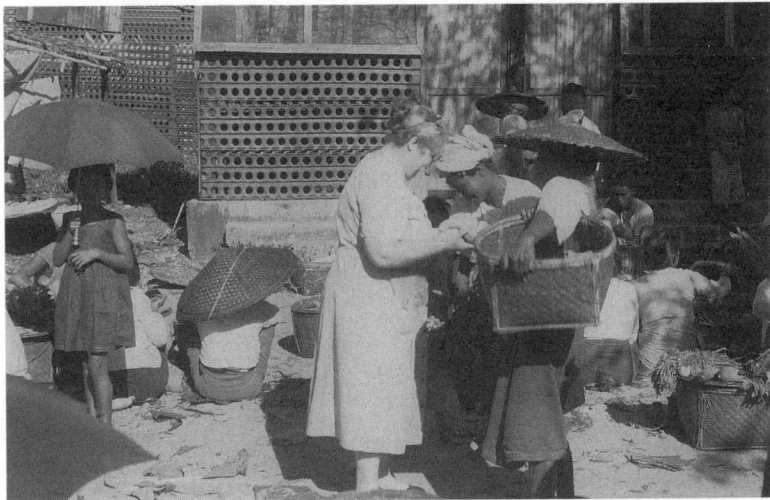

Miss Gulliver at the early morning market, Kyaukypu, the Arakan, Burma, 1960.

185

the occasion when Harry Lawrence's successor as the British Council Representative, Bill McAlpine, sent out about fifty written lunch invitations, some to senior members of the Burmese government, including the Minister of Education. The guest-of-honour was Lord Bridges, son of the poet, Robert Bridges. Lord Bridges was Chairman of the British Council, a role most recently filled by the businessman, Sir Martin Jacomb.

The dining-table at the house in Windsor Road accommodated some twenty-four persons. McAlpine sent out more than twice the number of invitations and, as a precaution, he arranged for his secretary to make follow-up calls. The lunch was delicious. Bill's cook excelled himself. It was enjoyed by Lord Bridges, Bill and Helen McAlpine, my wife and me. We were the only participants...

*****

Burma is a goldmine for those interested in learning about other cultures or it *was* when there was easy access to the country. The name that a person bears is a case in point. In Burmese society, 'Daw', as in 'Daw Htin', applies to persons older or in a higher position than oneself. 'Ma', as in 'Ma Pu', applies to persons younger or the same age as oneself. 'U' as in 'U Kyin', applies to persons much older or in a much higher position than oneself. 'Ko' as in 'Ko Tin' applies to persons of the same age, or slightly older than oneself. 'Maun' as in 'Maun Chit' applies to persons younger than oneself.

But I have oversimplified. Naming in Burma is not a simple matter. In his book, *The Burman: His Life and Notions*,[6] Sir George Scott ('Shway Yoe'), explains that a 'child's name must begin with one of the letters belonging to the day on which it was born... As an immediate consequence it follows that a Burman has a birthday every week, a frequency of recurrence which renders the event monotonous, and precludes the friendly amenities of western nations on such occasions.'

*****

The many tribes that have lived and worked for centuries in Upper Burma have added to the cultural mix. During my visit to Taunggyi, I was able to buy, from an Anglo-Burman painter, a number of small water-colours depicting persons from the following tribal groups:

Karen, Chin, Naga, Padaung, Kachin, Shan, Lisu, Kayah, Shan Tayoka and Ekaw.

The people in these groups and others enjoyed their own languages and dialects and their own customs, all of which were quite different from those of the largest group, the Burmese. I made an effort to learn some Burmese during my short time in Burma but my lecturing-work, and certain administrative duties, impeded my progress. These were excuses and probably not good ones.

Burmese is a tonal language, that is, the intonation given to a word is part of its meaning. There are four tones. According to my primer, 'prepared by Emilie M. Ballard with the Language and Orientation Committee of the Burma Baptist Missionary Fellowship', the First Tone is high but shortened by a slight 'throat-catch'. The Second Tone is low and level but may rise slightly at the end of phrases or when words are pronounced alone. The Third Tone is in relation to other tones, a high tone and is always heavily stressed. The Fourth Tone is high and stressed and is cut off abruptly by a sharp 'throat-catch' (complete closure of the glottis).

In his Memoirs, A.J.S. White noted somewhat ruefully that the word 'taung' can be used to mean six different things, according to whether the voice rises or falls or is clipped short.

> I remember repeating these six meanings – *hill, stiff, basket, prison, bend* and *bound* over and over again as I rolled the lawns (at home in England)... so as to get them by heart. The villagers have no clocks and have their own ways, sometimes rather quaint, of expressing the time. Having no single word for dusk, they call it 'The time when even brothers would not recognise each other.' Periods of time are 'one-pot-boiling of rice' or 'one betel-chew'... similarly with dates... a sample date would be the 'tenth waxing of the moon of Thabaung, 1295 B.E. (Buddhist Era)...' They have no single word for cousin but call him 'brother one belly removed.'[7]

*****

During his service in Burma, Harry Lawrence, the British Council Representative, provided some financial support for a young Burmese boy, an expert swimmer. I was fortunate enough to be invited to the boy's *shinbyu* ceremony. This – a kind of baptism – marks the time when a boy becomes a novitiate and is initiated into the priesthood as a probationer (*shin*). In the ceremony he loses his secular name and receives an honorific title, a *bwe*. He loses this name when he returns to the world at the conclusion of the novitiateship.

At the beginning of the *shinbyu* ceremony, a feast is held and the boy is dressed in elaborately coloured clothing and graced with jewels of different qualities, according to his family's means. In some ceremonies (but not on the occasion that we attended), he is given the opportunity to ride around his village or town on a white horse (the 'dancing pony'), followed by a procession of family members, friends and guests.

Then suddenly, sooner than the boy might secretly wish, the ride is over. He returns to the priests and his family; is divested of his fine clothes and jewels and his head is shaved. On the next day he joins other priests in a procession, eyes lowered and begging bowl in hand, His mother makes obeisance to him, for her son is now a member of a priestly order; a holy person; a *hpongyi* (pronounced, 'pon-ji').

*****

I am not well read in the literature of feminism but I doubt that the relationships between men and women in Burma have been a frequent subject of discussion. Such relationships, as described by Mi Mi Khaing, would surely do more than raise eyebrows in some societies, perhaps even provide a justification for one of the protest marches which are so much a feature of modern life. Mi Mi wrote:

> Although the women of Burma figure as actively and have the same rights as men in the fields of business, property and professions of the modern world, we always keep alive in us the religious feeling that we are 'below' mankind. It is not so much a feeling that women are a lower race as that a man has the nobility of manhood in him. We call it *hpon*, the glory, the holiness of a man, and we respect this not with subservience but with the same feelings as we respect monks and parents. A wife does not throw her *longyi* across her husband's bed; she does not touch any of his possessions with her feet in carelessness. She uses a separate mug for her bathwater. A bad wife who does not respect her husband's manhood does him the greatest harm, for a man cannot prosper if his *hpon* is hampered; indeed, some women who indulge in black magic deliberately *hpon-nein* their husbands, that is lower his *hpon* by carelessly wielding brooms above his head, throwing women's *longyis* on his pillow, thus making him subordinate, and believing that this makes the wife's will prevail over the husband's. But such a man can never make progress in his career.[8]

*****

The British Council is respected for its long-standing visitors' programme. For many years, it has arranged for orchestras, solo musicians, artists, legal experts, academics and others to visit different countries to 'show the flag' in their various ways. Unfortunately, very few visitors found their way to Burma and it may be that this is still the case. During the admittedly short time that I spent in the country, only two sponsored visitors came – first, the plastic surgeon already mentioned (I have forgotten his name) – and second, a cancer specialist named Peter Alexander. Then in his late thirties, Alexander was energetic and fully fit when he arrived in Rangoon. After most of his official duties were completed, he expressed a wish to visit Mandalay. Always willing to please our guests, we arranged for him to fly to the ancient city, there to spend a few days in sightseeing activities. After returning to Rangoon, he was to dine with us in Prome Road before catching a plane to London on the same evening.

But the man who arrived at our house did not seem to be the man who had given a sparkling lecture in Rangoon on the connection between betel-nut chewing and cancer of the mouth. He was pale, bowed and clearly unwell, another victim of Burma's favourite disease, dysentery. Instead of joining the rest of us for dinner, he lay on my bed until the time came for him to catch his flight. This was a sorry end to an otherwise successful visit.

*****

In early 1961 we were happy to entertain an unofficial visitor, Dr G.E.D. Lewis, a geographer and former Director of Education in one of the Malay States. Despite the very difficult time that he had experienced as a prisoner of the Japanese, he had not lost his sense of humour. He told us that before independence came to Malaya he was asked by his Deputy (a Malay) for a letter of reference. He said, 'You write it, Ahmed, and I'll sign it.' The time came after Independence had been achieved when the Deputy became the Director and the Director became the Deputy (in an advisory role). Before leaving Malaya for the last time (at least in an official capacity), the Deputy/Adviser asked for a letter of reference. 'You write it and I'll sign it,' said Ahmed, the new Director.

*****

Shortly after G.E.D. Lewis's visit, a gentleman came to Rangoon whose name would be frequently at the end of my pen (or, rather, keyboard) from 2001, the year that the English-Speaking Union was established in Hong Kong. Sir Evelyn Wrench founded the Union in 1918. Then aged seventy-nine (he was born in 1882), Sir Evelyn was a charming man, who spoke willingly and enthusiastically about the two organisations that he founded, namely the Royal Overseas League (1912) and the English-Speaking Union (1918).

In Hong Kong, as Chairman of the Executive Committee of the English-Speaking Union, I compile a monthly Newsletter for the 'ESU' and have included in each of several issues an extract from one or the other of Sir Evelyn's nine books.

*****

On 11 May 1961, I received some surprising news from the British Council in London. I was to relieve Dr Bernard Lott as Professor of English at the University of Indonesia in Jakarta.

Rather bemused after such a short stay in the Land of the Crested Lion (a mere 18 months), I participated in several quite moving farewell ceremonies. The most affecting of these took place at the State Teachers' Training College. On my last day at the College, the students presented me with what seemed to be an umbrella. I thanked them for this and told them that whenever I was obliged to use it in Indonesian rain, I would think of them. It was only very much later that I realised that the silver-handled object was not an umbrella but an elegant *parasol* that would on no account ever be used to ward off the rain.

With the parasol safely stowed away, we made final preparations to leave for Indonesia, a country made up of 'three thousand islands from Sabang to Merauke' (as its leader, President Sukarno, boasted more than once). 'Three thousand' is a nice, round figure but Sukarno's estimate was rather modest. There seems to be some doubt about how many islands there actually *are* in Indonesia. The Embassy of the Republic of Indonesia asserts that there are 17,508 islands and islets of which about six thousand are habitable. Whatever the truth of the matter, it is clear that Indonesia is a very large country, and in 1961 we were heading for it.

THE SEVENTH STEP

INDONESIA: A MULTITUDE OF ISLANDS

– 20 –

Culture

Disregarding the traumas brought by the Second World War and the pains resulting from its present military dictatorship, Burma holds on to its traditional ways. The festivals of Thingyan (the 'Water Festival'), Thadingyut (the 'Festival of Light') and Waso (the beginning of 'Lent') are celebrated enthusiastically and boys are still initiated in *shinbyu* ceremonies. Despite the political gloom, it is still possible to appreciate and enjoy *pwès* (plays), dancing and music.

Indonesia has its own riches to offer, fashioned from its patriarchal and matriarchal societies and from its mix of cultures: Hindu, Muslim, Christian and animist.

In late 1962 a senior official in the Djakarta Ministry of Education offered to accompany me on a three-day tour of schools in central Java. I was hesitant at first but finally agreed to take advantage of the offer whilst determining (with intestinal experiences in Burma in mind) to drink only bottled water or beer.

The visit included a short excursion to Borobudur, near the city of Yogyakarta. Unfortunately shortage of time did not permit us to visit the nearby Prambanan Temple Complex, a tenth-century survivor of a group of more than two hundred and fifty temples. This was a lost opportunity that cannot now be remedied because the temple complex was damaged severely in a devastating earthquake in 2006. It has been estimated that rebuilding this UNESCO World Heritage site will take at least five years at a cost of at least US$5.8 million.

The schools were disappointing but Borobudur was revelatory. Now also a UNESCO World Heritage site and originally a Hindu temple, it is one of the largest Buddhist *stupas* (hemispheric domes)[1] in the world. Created like Prambanan in the tenth century, the giant squat structure is impressive. Based on Buddhist cosmology, its several levels suggest that man might progress from the world of animals (*Kamadhatu*) to the world of intelligent higher forms (*Rupadhatu*). From there it might be possible to reach the highest sphere of the formless and finally the abstract 'nothingness'. 'Nothing will come of nothing' (as Shakespeare's King Lear said to his daughter, Cordelia) but the reliefs that decorate Borobudur are *something*, elegantly illustrating the main events in the last life of Buddha *Sakyamuni*, and events in his previous lives (*jataka*).

Time (and visits to more schools) did not permit us to do more than gaze at the outer walls of Borobudur. My companion tried hard to explain its deep significance but his command of English and my command of Bahasa Indonesia (the Indonesian lingua franca) were unfortunately unequal to the task. This was a great pity since I have not found another opportunity to revisit the monument.

*****

Borobudur was impressive, but something of a mystery. *Wayang Kulit* (*wayang=shadow, ghost; kulit=leather*) was less so, for I had seen this 'shadow play' in Singapore, years before. I was reminded of it at a performance held in a University of Indonesia building in 1962. Puppets made of leather were manipulated by a *dalang* or story-teller, who crouched before a lighted screen, recalling the myths of the Hindu *Mahabharaata*. His puppets were differentiated by colour. Women were yellow, clowns were white, giants were red and heroes were green, black or blue. The villains had prominent eyes and snub noses whilst the heroes and heroines had narrow eyes and straight, thin noses. Before and during the long performance, the gongs, drums and viols of the *gamelan* were played, softly at first, but reaching a climax towards the end as a mythical battle began.

The *Wayang Orang* differs from the *Wayang Kulit* in several significant ways. First, the puppets are actual human beings, rather than leather cutouts and the clowns have significant symbolic roles to play. *Petruk*, with fixed grin and long nose, stands for intellectual strength, Fat *Seman* represents ambition tempered by wisdom and *Gareng* portrays honesty.

No doubt aware of his nickname, 'The Great Puppet Master', the late former President Sukarno is said to have been fond of *Wayang*. He would have been able to choose among *Wayang Kulit*, *Wayang Orang* and *Wayang*

Golek (using wooden doll puppets). But possibly his favourites were *Wayang Suluh* that used realistic figures extolling government virtues, and *Wayang Pantja Sila* that referred to Indonesia's, 'Guided Democracy', an invention dear to Sukarno's heart.

*****

One of the female students in my literature class at the University of Indonesia excelled in the art of Javanese dance. On a memorable evening in a small hall, 'Tutti' joined three other students to dance the *Serimpi*, illustrating a tale of two princesses in the Javanese court who fall in love with the same prince. The *Serimpi* was followed by a *Bondan*, a colourful mime of a mother bathing her baby in a river.

*****

From time to time, shadow puppet shows and dance performances given at the University and at other venues were preceded, accompanied or followed by Javanese and Balinese *gamelan* recitals. This percussive music found favour in the 1960s with *avant garde* American composers such as Lou Harrison who encouraged his students to focus not only on the hegemonic musical tradition of Europe but to embrace the music of other traditions and cultures.

Gamelan orchestras feature a variety of instruments; gongs and drums of different sizes, psalterys (*tjelempung*) which are plucked and the human voice, male and female. Performers sing in unison, usually with a nasal timbre.

I like particularly the liquid sounds made by the *angklung*, an instrument made by placing several vertical bamboo tubes together. These tubes are of different lengths. Each different *angklung* emits a note of a particular pitch and each player must therefore be alert to when it is his turn to play.

*****

In sharp contrast to the traditional music of Indonesia was melody of a very different sort, performed in a musical written and produced in 1962 by two members of the US Embassy in Jakarta. Charlie Finan (the Cultural Affairs Officer) was responsible for the lyrics. The two lions that guard the doors of the New York City Museum are said to roar when a virgin passes by. Inevitably, Charlie's theme song for the musical began with the words, 'Why don't the lions ever roar any more?'

Charlie told me that he had composed one line of the popular song, *Moonlight in Vermont* by John Blackburn and Karl Suessdorf. Charlie's claim to immortality rested on: 'Telephone cables sing down the highway.' Charlie was a cordial host and on several occasions invited us to spend a day at his bungalow in the Punjak, a kind of hill station outside Jakarta. The air was cool, the coffee was hot and the *margaritas* were stimulating.

*****

Like Malaysia, Indonesia is well known for its textiles, its dyeing techniques and distinctive garments – in particular, *batik* and *ikat* – well described by Jack Lenor Larsen, Alfred Buhler and my former colleagues, Bronwen and Garrett Solyon[2] in their magnificent volume, *The Dyers' Art*.[3] The authors note that since independence, Western-style trousers, shirts and dresses are worn for everyday work more often than *batik*. *Batik* and *ikat* stand out, however, as major contributors to Indonesian and in particular Javanese culture.

*****

Painting as an art form was slow to develop in Java, partly – it has been said – because of Islamic sensitivities concerning the representation of living forms. It has, however, flourished in the last eighty years or so, despite such sensitivities.

Two of the Indonesian studies on the walls of our present home were painted by Van Achen, a Dutchman who lived in Hindu Bali. A third is by the Javanese, Effendi, a sombre study entitled 'Widows'. I was unable to afford paintings made during the Dutch colonial period by Raden Saleh or later by the revolutionary artists, Affandi and Sudjoyono, both of whom flourished at the time of the pre-Second World War agitations for self-rule. They were were later courted by the Japanese for propaganda purposes. After the War, Affandi achieved some fame in Europe and even succeeded in selling a painting to the British art historian, the late Sir Kenneth Clark.

Paintings by Affandi, Effendi, Kusnadi and Surono are still sought after. But according to Sonia Kolesnikov-Jessop,[4] they are now challenged by a new generation of artists who have moved away from the 'protest art' that became fashionable during the final years of the régime of Sukarno's successor, President Suharto. Certainly, there was no lack of visual stimuli in Indonesia. It provided a flamboyant backdrop to my work for the next three years.

*****

Although I was posted directly to Indonesia from Burma, we did enjoy a week's leave in Singapore, staying at a modest hotel (now demolished) in Grange Road, near the now fashionable and expensive Tanglin District. The high spots of the week were a drive to a pleasant beach, organised by Donald and Joanna Moore, and a splendid dinner hosted by my friend and former colleague, Mrs Tai Yu Lin.

Other guests at the hotel included a Dutch family waiting to take passage to the Netherlands in the liner, *William Ruis*. Although the Dutch tricolour was flown for the last time in Indonesia on 27 December 1949, a number of Dutch businessmen stayed on in various capacities. Our neighbours in the hotel were among this group.[5]

*****

I became belatedly aware of the Dutch East Indies in the late 1940s when I studied colonial history at Cardiff under Dr Ivor Powell. I am surprised now that I failed to take more interest in the Indies during my service in Bombay (now Mumbai) for I was slightly touched by events there in 1945. In September of that year a British naval party landed at the port of Tanjong Priok (Jakarta). The Navy's purpose was to begin to disarm the remaining Japanese forces and – in support of the Dutch – to deal with Indonesian nationalists, stirred up by the unilateral declaration of independence (*Proklomasi*) made by the future President Sukarno on 17 August 1945:

Proklomasi
We the people of Indonesia hereby declare the Independence of Indonesia. Matters concerning the transfer of power etc, will be carried out in a conscientious manner as speedily as possible.

In the name of the people of Indonesia.
Sukarno Hatta
Jakarta 17 August 1945

One evening in early October 1945, I received a telephone call at the flat which I shared on the Colaba Causeway in Bombay. The call came from Tony Tubbs. He was aboard a British naval vessel assigned to provide support to a British and Indian task force, engaged in what has become known as the Battle of Sourabaya, now commemorated in Indonesia as 'Heroes' Day'. As already mentioned (Chapter Eight), Tony and I had travelled together from Southampton to Colombo to await further postings – Tony to a frigate and so possibly in harm's way – and me to Bombay to carry out duties ashore. It could very easily have been the other way round.

Tony came through unscathed but when British and Indian troops finally departed from Indonesia in November 1946, they left over five hundred dead and over one thousand wounded. The tragedy for the families of the soldiers who died in the fighting was that the greater War had ended on 15 August 1945 when Japan capitulated. Their deaths must have seemed so unnecessary.

The full story of the Indonesian fight for independence does not belong here and I cannot say that it was at the forefront of my mind as I began my second year at University in October 1948, following my return to Cardiff in October 1947. As I looked forward to Christmas 1948, I learned that an agreement had been signed between the Dutch and the Indonesians. Regrettably, this was terminated on 18 December. The struggle for Indonesian autonomy continued, despite the efforts of officials on both sides and the intervention of the American ambassador, Mr Merle Cochran.

After further negotiations and military actions however, the conflict finally came to an end in the following year, on 27 December 1949. Several issues still needed to be resolved, such as sovereignty over West Irian (New Guinea). But these issues were eventually thrashed out between two nations (Indonesia and the Netherlands) rather than by one nation and its unruly colony.

From the start, independent Indonesia adopted a non-aligned stance in world affairs but attempts were made and (in 2009) continue to be made to draw the country into others' spheres of influence. In the 1950s, under orders from the US State Department, Merle Cochran exerted considerable effort, overtly and covertly, on behalf of the United States.

The historian Dorothy Woodman noted that, on 16 January 1952, Foreign Minister Subardjo signed a secret Mutual Security Aid Agreement

(MSA) with Cochran, an agreement that included military clauses. When this agreement was revealed it was repudiated by the Indonesian Cabinet and a new agreement was signed that excluded the military clauses.[6] His secret diplomacy exposed, Cochran resigned in February 1953. What was not admitted at the time was that in 1952 Cochran told the Defence Minister (the Sultan of Djakarta, Hamengku Buwono IX) and the Prime Minister (Dr Hatta) that the US government could provide clandestine training for an intelligence unit within the Ministry of Defence. Cochran's offer was accepted and the project went ahead. The training of seventeen future operatives was carried out in Saipan in the Northern Mariana Islands. A second group of nineteen 'students' received similar training in Saipan in 1953.

In 1959 lingering American influence was revealed when two of the Saipan 'graduates' attended an inauguration ceremony presided over by President Sukarno for a new agency, the Intelligence Coordination Agency (Badan Koordinasi Intelijen, or BKI). This was re-named the Central Intelligence Agency (Badan Pusat Intelijen, or BPI) in November 1959. It was in the same year that President Sukarno dissolved the National Assembly and re-instituted the 1945 Constitution by presidential decree. 'Demokrasi Terpimpin', or 'Guided Democracy' (an Indonesia brand of dictatorship) was born. In his wisdom, the President considered that parliamentary democracy was unsuitable for Indonesia.

*****

It was the spice trade and its ramifications that attracted my attention to Indonesia when I began to study colonial history at Cardiff. After all, I had been introduced to many different kinds of curries and other spicy dishes during my naval service in India and Ceylon.

In the sixteenth and seventeenth centuries the need for preservatives could not be satisfied in Europe alone. The salt bounty in England, for example, in Northwich (Cheshire), Droitwich (Worcestershire) and elsewhere, was insufficient. There was a growing desire – indeed a desperate need – for the spices of the East: pepper, cinnamon, nutmeg, mace and cloves. All these could be found in abundance in India, Ceylon and the Dutch East Indies. The latter country still bore that name when I began my third year of study at Cardiff in October 1949.

*****

On the way to Indonesia in August 1961, we enjoyed an uneventful voyage from Singapore to Jakarta's Tanjong Priok dock where we were met by Harry Lawrence, the British Council Representative. Harry had held a similar post in Rangoon when I was first posted to the city. We remained at Tanjong Priok until our heavy baggage was unloaded. The air was heavy with dust and the pungent scent of clove-filled cigarettes – kretek – so named because they crackle as they burn.

I found that it helped to be able to communicate with the dock labourers and officials in Malay, although Indonesian Malay differs from the brand of Malay used in Singapore. In the Philippines, Spanish has coloured the pronunciation and vocabulary of Tagalog and other Philippine languages and dialects. In Indonesia, there is still a touch of Dutch in what is now called 'Bahasa Indonesia'. I noticed this first when Harry drove us to our new quarters in Jalan Gresik, in the Menteng District. Situated alongside a noisome canal, the house was fairly new, with two bedrooms, a living room, a bathroom, a kitchen and three servants' rooms. A rather formidable lady named Marwah presided over the house, supported by a maid-of-all-work and a washerwoman. Harry introduced us to Marwah who addressed me – rather rudely, I thought – as 'Mister' (not Mister Bickley, but, simply, 'Mister'). Marwah continued to use the word during the entire period of our stay in Jalan Gresik. It was not until we understood the influence of the Dutch language over the new language of Indonesia that I realised that Marwah was addressing me, quite politely, as 'Meester' ('Boss') rather than with the English, 'Mister'.

In addition to the spoken word, the Dutch language influenced Indonesian spelling. For example, the Dutch consonant clusters *tj* and *dj* were used in words such as 'tjutji' (to wash), now 'chuchi' and 'djalan' (road, path, street), now 'jalan'. For the most part the Dutch versions disappeared after 1972 when Indonesia and Malaysia reached agreement on a revised and uniform system of spelling for Bahasa Malaysia and Bahasa Indonesia. Dutch has however, left an imprint on the language that can be seen and heard in words such as 'kopi' (coffee), 'kantor' (office), 'telepon' (telephone) and 'polisi' (police).

Bahasa Indonesia is today the official language of Indonesia. It has become so because of the need to have a common language of communication in a country which boasts over five hundred languages and dialects.

In Java, as in other parts of the former Netherlands East Indies, the Malay language, originally a lingua franca of the area, spread as a result of Dutch expansion and the nationalist aspirations of Indonesian writers and politicians. Malay was also adopted quite early on (in the seventeenth century) by Protestant Ministers in an effort to oust Portuguese Catholicism.

In 1908, the Dutch colonial government set up a commission with the task of producing reading materials in Malay and distributing them throughout Indonesia. Paradoxically, nationalism in the Indies manifested itself at first in a growing demand for opportunities to learn Dutch because by acquiring this language Indonesians hoped to qualify for better jobs and status in the colonial society. Later, however, following the Indonesian Youth Congress of 28 October 1928 in Batavia (Jakarta), Malay was adopted as the language of the Indonesian nationalist movement and became one of the rallying points of the movement's struggle for independence.

In 1961, Dr Takdir Alisjahbana noted that, in addition to an oath taken at the 1928 Congress (at which the participants bound themselves to 'one fatherland, one nation and one language', Malay), there were six factors chiefly responsible for the development of Malay as the official language of the new Indonesia: the publication of an influential magazine, the *Pudjangga Baru* ('The Young Poet')[7] in 1933; the holding of the first Indonesian language congress in 1937; a ban placed on the use of Dutch during the Japanese occupation of the East Indies; the establishment of a Committee to look into the development of the language in 1942; the publication of a modern Indonesian grammar; and the influence of the *Pembina Bahasa Indonesia*, another magazine that promoted the development of the language.[8] A leading figure in the 'language engineering' efforts which converted coastal Malay into the national language of Indonesia, Dr Alisjahbana re-lived the excitement of the pre-independence years during a visit that I made to his home in Jakarta in 1976.

The several decisions that affected the development of Malay as the official language of Indonesia were not all of the same character. Some – like the publication of the literary magazine, the grammar, and the periodical concerned with the development of the language – were decisions taken on linguistic and cultural grounds. But the most important decisions affecting the choice of language for an independent Indonesia were political in nature. The oath taken at the 1928 Congress; the establishment of the Committee for the Development of the Indonesian Language and the inclusion of the language in the Constitution were all essential steps in the moves to achieve and maintain independence, establish a centralised government and unify a geographically scattered and linguistically complex area through the employment of a lingua franca as a common medium of communication. The agglutinative Malay language became Bahasa Indonesia, one of the symbols of nationalism and – after the Revolution against the Dutch – of the newly independent state.

*****

Before leaving us to take stock of our new home, Harry told us the names of the British Council staff in Indonesia. His deputy in Jakarta, Bob Harrison, was assisted by the voluble Education Officer 'Tommy' Thomas and the patrician accountant Charles Plume, supported by his Spanish wife Concha and a small, white dog, 'Trigger'. I inherited Trigger when Charles was posted back to London on retirement. One day, the dog began to display peculiar symptoms, similar to rabies. This was fortunately a false alarm because he had licked everyone in the house and especially my two children.

John Villiers represented the Council in Bandung. A member of a distinguished British family, John joined the British College in Rome after resigning from the British Council.

Peter Martin had charge of Council affairs in Surabaya. His life, both in Indonesia and out of it, took several quite dramatic twists and turns. After weathering the attacks on British Council property that took place in Indonesia in 1963 (of which more later) and after a spell with the Council in Europe, he was posted to Kyoto to succeed the writer and critic, Francis King. Today, the words *burakumin* or *eta* are 'politically incorrect' in Japan. They refer to 'untouchable' people such as butchers and workers in leather. Because of the nature of the quarter, it was rarely visited by non-*eta* Japanese. With tongue in cheek, Peter suggested that King was perhaps happy with this situation since it gave him the opportunity to write (novels, criticism, etc.) in peace and quiet.

Peter prospered in Kyoto. He supervised the building of a new centre – away from the *burakumin* quarter – and seized the opportunity not only to make friends for the British Council but also to put together a fine collection of antiquarian books on Japan and to write a book on Japanese cooking, in cooperation with Joan, his wife at the time.

'Drunk chicken' (slices of chicken marinated in saké and soy sauce) was a speciality of the Ashiya Restaurant in the Gion District of Kyoto. I understood from Peter that the owner of this restaurant, Robert Strickland, came to Japan to teach English. He married a Japanese lady and decided to risk opening a restaurant, the Ashiya, on a shoe-string budget. After an uneasy start, the restaurant prospered.

I do not know if the restaurant still exists. As I remember it from my several visits, it occupied two floors. The first floor contained the restaurant itself, furnished with a huge, circular bar. There were no tables but a large number of customers could be accommodated around the bar. The menu was restricted to three items, fresh salads, the signature 'drunk chicken' and plates of succulent, tender beef from Kobe's milk-massaged cows. The second floor functioned as a gallery from which paintings, etchings, prints and ceramics were sold.

After further – relatively uneventful – service with the British Council as the Representative (Director) in Tokyo, Peter retired, only to adopt a new guise as a successful crime novelist under the pseudonym, 'James Melville'.

– 21 –

Penasihat

I was posted to the University of Indonesia in Jakarta in 1961. In 1953 a successful textbook writer, Leslie Hill, had been seconded to the University and appointed to the Chair of English. In 1958 after several years of service in Jakarta, Leslie retired to the Channel Islands. He was succeeded by an English literature specialist, the late Dr Bernard Lott, again as Chair Professor in the University's Fakultas Sastra (Faculty of Letters).

I took Bernard Lott's place in 1961 but because of new localisation policies I would not have the title of Professor. Instead I would be dubbed 'Penasihat' or 'Adviser'. I was not too surprised by the apparent downgrading of the British Council post although the work remained the same as that done by Leslie and Bernard. The Department still followed a syllabus compiled by Leslie in the 1950s. I am no longer in possession of a copy of this syllabus but I remember that it included aspects of structural linguistics, phonemics and phonology.

In 1967, in a Japanese journal, I commented on the position of the English language in Indonesia:

> The Indonesian Revolution resulted in the removal of Dutch from the business of administration, from the signs in the streets of the cities, from the day to day life of commerce and from the developing education system. The language which has taken its place is English and this is regarded by the present Indonesian Government as the first foreign language. A growing number of signs and instructions are now written in English, shops are beginning to advertise in the language, the favourite films appear to be those made or dubbed in English and English is one of

the principal means of communication in the commercial world. Each Faculty of Letters in each of Indonesia's Universities stresses the importance of its Department of English. Lectures in these Departments are delivered in the language and examinations are conducted in it. In other Departments lectures are given in Bahasa Indonesia but the majority of textbooks prescribed are in English. An interesting and little known fact is that the English language was first included in a school curriculum in Java in the year 1814. Sir Stamford Raffles, the founder of (modern) Singapore, acting in his capacity of Lieutenant-Governor of Java, provided financial assistance for a Monsieur Pahud, a Swiss teacher who wished to establish a school in what was then called Batavia. Pahud was given five thousand rupees from the General Treasury in the form of an advance and the school opened in 1814 for the benefit of children of both sexes, 'who must be entirely entrusted by their parents or Guardians to the care of the subscriber and his wife'.

Pahud's school was the first in the Indies to offer English as a subject in its curriculum.[1]

In the Dutch East Indies, the curriculum was fairly broad at junior secondary level but it narrowed in the senior secondary schools and the universities. Whilst four or five related subjects might be covered for the *propaedeutisch* examination, the years that took students to *Doctorandus* standard were devoted to one major subject. A *propaedeutisch examen* was taken after the third or fourth year in university and the final examination for the title of *Doctorandus* (or *Meester*) was taken after the fifth or sixth year. This system came under critical scrutiny in newly independent Indonesia.

The vacuum resulting from the sudden removal of the Dutch from the country created an urgent demand for well-trained personnel competent to fill middle-level positions. The length and arrangement of the courses and in particular the system whereby the *candidaats examen* was considered to be an intermediary rather than a final step inhibited the contribution that the universities were making to the qualified manpower of the country. In an effort to improve the position the educational authorities decided to alter the examination structure so that the *candidaats examen* would be regarded as a final examination for many students, providing them with the title *sardjana muda* (young scholar) and qualifying status for middle-rank employment. Students who wished to continue with their university studies could do so for two or three years longer according to individual Faculty requirements and could graduate as *sardjanas* in those Faculties.

Within the Faculties themselves, modifications were carried out following suggestions made by foreign academics and by Indonesians who had returned to their country after study overseas. For example, as a result of Leslie Hill's influence, a detailed syllabus was drawn up to cover the five-year course in the University of Indonesia's *Fakultas Sastra.*

Study groups were organised on the lines of the tutorial systems familiar to most British universities. A departmental library was founded with a stock of texts published in Britain. The *tentamens* were replaced in the English Department by a system of written and oral examinations held once a year, over a fixed period of approximately a fortnight's duration. This examination system was later adopted by other departments in the Faculty and by the English Departments of the Faculties of Letters and Education at Padjadjaran University in Bandung and at the University of North Sumatra in Medan.

The *Fakultas Sastra* was a University Department of language and literature. When I was there, the literature chosen for study seemed to me to be inappropriate for the students, although enjoyable to teach. It included *Sir Orfeo, Sir Gawain and the Green Knight, Piers Plowman* and Chaucer's *The Nun's Priest's Tale.* The class contained only twelve students, all except one being girls of Chinese origin. The twelfth student was a male, probably a native of Sumatra.

The system of marking in the Department followed Dutch practices, and standards were maintained rigorously. All assignments and examination papers were marked out of a total of ten. To achieve a score of ten was unheard of. Most marks that were awarded were in the range four to six.

The Department was headed by Jo ('Yoh') Kurnianingrat, a Javanese lady of good lineage. Whilst keeping a shrewd eye on the administration of the Department, 'Jo' would also occasionally refer wistfully to the country life in Java and wax nostalgic about the oxen, homeward bound from the rice fields (the *sarwah*), their bells 'tolling the knell of parting day'.

Other members of the Department included a Eurasian gentleman of fierce mien, Mr Wachendorff, and Pia Alisjahbana (daughter of the renowned linguist, Dr Takdir Alisjahbana). The staff on the literature side was strengthened by Henry Widdowson, a young teacher contracted to the British Council. Later in his career, Henry studied at Edinburgh University under the auspices of the British Council and then served in Ceylon. After obtaining a doctorate in applied linguistics, he resigned from the Council and joined the University of London where he was eventually appointed Director of the English Department at the University of London's Institute of Education.

In 1961 Henry was at the beginning of his career. His field was originally English literature but he was also beginning to take an interest in language pedagogy. In 1959, he co-authored (with an Indonesian scholar named Pasaribu) an English language textbook course for schools, *The Open Road to Excellent English.*[2] This proved to be very successful, remaining in favour despite the official blessing given by the government to primary and secondary school courses developed by a team of Americans and Indonesians who received logistical and financial support from the Ford Foundation.

*****

After the first month or so, we attuned ourselves to the rhythms of Jakarta, described by one writer as a 'sprawling, over-crowded, sweating, characterless conglomeration of ugly buildings, filthy canals and rowdy traffic'.[3] I can testify to all of these, in particular to the 'filthy canals'. The banks of the waterway that oozed past our house in Jalan Gresik were crowded every morning with lines of earnest trishaw drivers engaged in the absorbing business of defecation.

The Jakarta day begins early. Lectures and meetings at the University started at 7.30am, as did work at most businesses and government offices. To compensate in most cases, the working day ended at 3pm. In other cases, activities such as one-to-one tutorials would begin again at 5pm. The long and heavy Bols Gin-flavoured lunches, served at about 3.30pm on hot and humid afternoons, were one of the less healthy habits of the Dutch, copied (without the Gin) by the Indonesians.

As mentioned earlier, our house in Jalan Gresik had three servants' rooms. Only two were occupied and this gave me the opportunity to use one as a primitive study. It was in this room that I tutored a mature student for his doctorate in Middle English. This was presumptuous since I did not possess a higher degree myself. Something needed to be done about this and so I was impelled to write to the University of Wales to ask permission, as an external student, to submit a thesis for a Master's Degree in Education. Permission was given and I began work on a thesis that eventually occupied 286 foolscap pages. In the Introduction, I declared my intention to '... discuss the problems involved in training teachers of English in (1) Singapore, a part of Southeast Asia where there are still British connections and where progress towards complete self-government will depend upon the combinations emerging after the formation of

"Malaysia," and (2) Burma, a country granted independence from British colonial government in 1948.'

The first part of the Introduction, written at the beginning of 1962, indicates that plans to combine Malaya, North Borneo and Singapore into a Federation were at quite an advanced stage. The Malayan and British governments had floated the idea in May 1961 but there was little reaction from an Indonesian government that was preoccupied with its plans to seize New Guinea (West Irian) from the Dutch.

In early 1962, Indonesian troops carried out a successful invasion of New Guinea. Pressed by the anti-colonial United States, the Dutch signed a final agreement to hand over the territory to Indonesia. In November 1961, Dr Subandrio, the Indonesian Foreign Minister and Chief of the Badan Pusat Intelijen (BPI – Central Intelligence Agency), addressed the United Nations General Assembly and declared:

> We are not only disclaiming the territories outside the former Netherlands East Indies, though they are of the same island, but more than that. When Malaya told us of her intention to merge with the three British Crown Colonies of Sarawak, Brunei and British North Borneo as one Federation, we told them that we have no objections and that we wish them success with this merger so that everyone may live in peace and freedom.[4]

Dr Subandrio's statement cut little ice with the Indonesian Communist Party (PKI) which, according to Bruce Grant,[5] declared its opposition to the merger at a conference held on 31 December 1961. A year later, on 8 December 1962, a rebellion broke out in Brunei led by one Azahari bin Sheikh Mahmud. Its purpose was to expel the British from the Protectorate. The rebellion failed despite Indonesian encouragement. One of its results however, was that Indonesia reversed its diplomatic stance and openly stated its opposition to the proposed Malaysian Federation. On 21 January 1963 Dr Subandrio declared that Indonesia intended to 'confront' Malaysia.

Although diplomatic efforts were made throughout 1963 to ease the tensions that existed between Indonesia and newly independent Malaya, Dr Subandrio and his colleagues worked beneath the surface to forward the 'Konfrontasi' policy. In this it seems they received full support from President Sukarno. Presumably with the President's full knowledge, the BPI formed a special team (Pasukan Gerilya Rakyat Sarawak) that included Communist agents. For three years this team organised armed raids against logging camps, police stations, villages and government forces in Sarawak and Sabah.

*****

The life story of the late President Sukarno has been told many times and need not be repeated at length here. It may be helpful, however, to be reminded that he was born on 6 June 1901 in Surabaya, East Java. His father was a school teacher who died during the Japanese occupation. Sukarno's mother, Bu Sosrodihardjo, was Balinese. Sukarno studied civil engineering in Bandung and graduated in 1925. In 1927 Sukarno helped to found the Indonesian Nationalist Party (PNI). He was imprisoned by the Dutch from 1929 to 1932 for anti-government activities, and again in 1933. During the Second World War, he cooperated with the Japanese during their occupation of Indonesia, but obtained their agreement to fly the new Indonesian flag and to encourage the use of Bahasa Indonesia.

In some ways Sukarno can be compared to Aung San in Burma. Both men sided with the invading enemy against the colonial power. Both men were ambitious and both possessed *charisma* that they were able to exploit for political purposes.

When I first arrived in Jakarta, a few of the Europeans to whom I was introduced referred in somewhat derisive undertones to 'The Bung', an invidious comparison with the round piece of rubber or wood used to close a beer cask. The word was, however, part of the phrase, 'Bung Karno', a nickname that indicated Sukarno's personal popularity among Indonesians of all classes, a popularity that was reinforced by his ability to intellectualise his political message,[6] his penchant for coining telling acronyms and his skilful delivery of mesmeric speeches. Although some of the message may have been lost because of inadequate translation, the following is typical of his emotional and repetitious style:

> Thus the Message of the Sufferings of the Indonesian people is part of the Message of the Sufferings of the whole of mankind. Thus our Message of the Sufferings of the People is not just a national idea or a national ideal. Our Message of the People's Sufferings is interlocked with the Message of the Sufferings of Mankind, the Message of the Sufferings of Mankind is interlocked with our Message of the Sufferings of the People. The Indonesian Revolution is interlocked with the Revolution of Mankind, the Revolution of Mankind is interlocked with the Indonesian Revolution.[7]

I heard Sukarno give some of his speeches on the radio – Radio Republik Indonesia – and was present in November 1963 when he spoke at the opening ceremony of the Games of the Newly Emerging Forces (GANEFO), the first international, large-scale, multi-sport games in which

China had participated fully since the founding of 'the new China'. By design, Sukarno arrived a few minutes late. He was then escorted to a specially-built open box high above the crowd of approximately one hundred thousand people. Dressed in his customary white uniform, with a soldier's swagger stick and *kopiah* (black cap), he waited for silence before beginning to speak – softly at first, loving the microphone – then, as he moved into the body of his speech, he began to vary volume, pitch and pauses so skilfully that he would surely have impressed even the most hard-bitten teacher of Voice and Speech.

Intended to take place, like the Olympic Games, every fourth year, the Games of the Newly Emerging Forces took place only once, largely because of significant political changes in China (the onset of the Cultural Revolution) and Indonesia (where the Indonesian Army organised a coup-d'état in 1965 and Sukarno was replaced by General Suharto).

As to President Sukarno, the inventor of acronyms, I arranged for the publication in 1971 of a *Dictionary of Indonesian Abbreviations*, compiled under the direction of the writer, Elizabeth Wittermans. The book contains over three thousand entries of which quite a number were doubtless created by Sukarno and his advisers. For example, MPPR, Madjelis Pembela Perdzuangan Rakjat – supporting Council for the People's Struggle; NASAKOM – Nasionalisma, Agama, Komunisma (Nationalism, Religion, Communism, three pillars of the Indonesian Revolution represented in party terms by PNP; PNU; and PKI) and NEKAD, *N*egara kita pertahankan, *E*konomi kita sosialiskan, *K*eamanan kita selenggarakan, *A*gama kita muliakan, *D*emokrasi terpimpin kite djalankan: 'We defend the State, we socialize the Economy, we provide Security, we honour Religion, we carry out Guided Democracy.'

Despite the discomforts to come – discomforts that he, and his colleagues, caused – it was difficult to dislike the Bung. He was in no way a Hitler, a Mao or a Stalin. Perhaps he was more of a showman like Mussolini, without quite as much bombast.

– 22 –

The Mob

In early 1962 we began a period of three month's leave in England. This was granted after our two-and-a-half years of service in Burma and Indonesia. After a very pleasant break, we returned to Jakarta, to learn that the administrative officer, Charles Plume, had retired during our absence and left for his home in Spain. I was able to negotiate successfully for Charles's house in Djalan Borobadur.

Situated in the Menteng District, the house faced a Club – 'The Box Club' – founded by Dutch burghers and said to be the oldest cricket club in Asia. It was good to be able to have the opportunity of playing again, and so I did from time to time.

In 1963, Indonesia had been an independent sovereign nation for fourteen years. It was to be a year of high drama and not just on the stage of the *Gedung Kesenian,* one of Jakarta's small theatres. I trod the boards in the role of the General in the Jakarta Little Theatre Group's production of Peter Ustinov's comedy, *Romanoff and Juliet.* Set in the 'smallest country in Europe of the present time', the plot, such as it is, focuses on the General's successful attempts to play off the American and Russian Ambassadors against each other. A cocktail here and vodka there successfully greases the diplomatic wheels.

It is unlikely that cocktails and vodka were on offer at the diplomatic discussions which took place over the Malaysian Merger issue. But the aims (without the alcohol) were similar, to play off opposing sides. At a gathering of the Economic Commission for Asia and the Far East (ECAFE) in March 1963, Indonesia's Foreign Minister Dr Subandrio and the Australian Minister for External Affairs, Sir Garfield Barwick, engaged in private talks. In May 1963, Prime Minister Tengku Abdul Rahman of Malaya and President Sukarno held discussions in Tokyo. It was reported that cordial greetings, handshakes and smiles were exchanged. In June 1963, the foreign ministers of Malaya, the Philippines and Indonesia met in Manila and agreed to 'welcome' Malaysia if the support of the Borneo territories could be guaranteed by the Secretary-General of the UN, or his representative.

Despite these apparently harmonious and constructive meetings, Sukarno reverted to confrontation in July 1963 and on the 10th of that month made a speech claiming that the Malaysia agreement – signed only the day before on 9 July – had not incorporated the wishes of the people. He held firmly to this line despite the United Nations' finding that the majority of the people concerned wished the Malaysian arrangements to proceed.

In July 1963, the Jakarta Little Theatre presented *Twelfth Night*, a production in which I took the part of Malvolio who, as all Shakespeare-lovers know, is gulled by Sir Andrew Aguecheek, Sir Toby Belch and Maria. The part of Sir Toby was played by the second senior diplomat in the British Embassy, the Minister, Peter Oliver. Oliver was later to perform an important contemporary role as British Chargé d'Affaires when 'Konfrontasi' reached its climax.

By September 1963, we had acquired Durwan, a driver able to deal with the eccentricities of my Ford Consul. One of Durwan's important jobs was to deliver my daughter (Karen aged nine years) and my son (Simon aged six years) to school and to bring them back to Jalan Borobadur at about 2.30pm, the end of the school day.

On Wednesday, 16 September, Durwan collected the two children from school as usual. When they arrived at the house they reported that a large crowd of people had gathered in our street. Children's fantasies? No. Sure enough, there *was* such a crowd and it became bigger as we gazed, curious to know what was happening. Truck after truck began to appear, disgorging hundreds of mainly young people, some wearing slogans and headbands; others carrying red and white banners.

The crowd swelled and began, as with one voice, to howl '*Ganjang Malaysia*' (Crush Malaysia). So *that* was what it was all about!

Now the rioters have advanced to the Box Club. What are they doing? Look! They've smashed the windows and torn off the front door. Vandals! They're pushing the Club Secretary's car onto the best cricket pitch. What now? They've set the car on fire! *Ganjang Malaysia! Ganjang Malaysia! Ganjang Malaysia!* Who *are* these people?

Transfixed, we gazed through the windows facing the street. A mistake. We were spotted by someone in the crowd. As if they were one, a thousand heads swivelled. Two thousand eyes stared at us. A movement began. *We've destroyed the Club. Now for another target!* The crowd began to advance towards the house, yelling as it came. I confess that I panicked. I pushed Lois and the children under a bed. Laura Rampen (a British Council secretary who had volunteered to type my MA thesis) appeared from my improvised study. I tried to hide Laura as well. The crowd shouted as it tore off the front gate and advanced down the path. Who was it who said we could take refuge next door? The Danish Ambassador lived there. He was away. Surely, he would not mind?

No time for niceties. I pulled Lois and the children from their temporary refuge. We rushed through the back door. I heaved Simon over the dividing wall; then Karen; then Lois; then Laura; then my typewriter. Then I scrambled over myself. We squatted on the floor of the Ambassador's rather sparse living room hoping not to be noticed by the mob. But of course they knew where we were.

After three or four hours, mainly in crouch position, we heard a friendly voice. It was Charlie Lord, our friend in the US Agency for International Development (AID). As I understand it, Charlie had been alerted to our plight by Alec Shakow, an American graduate student (later

Guests at a function held in the British Council library, Jakarta, 1962. Including Lady Freda Gilchrist, British Council Representative Harry Lawrence, a Consular Official and eight-year-old Karen Bickley.

an AID employee). 'Come,' said Charlie, 'I have the jeep outside. Let's get out of here.' We followed, trying to make ourselves as small as possible. But most of the PKI-backed crowd had dispersed, perhaps following orders from above.

We were driven through the streets to Charlie's house, past burning cars and stragglers from the rabble. After beds had been found for the children, we assembled in the living room. Charlie and his wife Collette were entertaining a guest, a senior Indonesian police officer. As we sipped double whiskies, the policeman apologised for our inconvenience. 'Not at all,' we said, half-heartedly.

Somewhat bewildered, we took our whisky headaches to bed in another of Charlie's rooms. The next morning, Charlie drove me to Jalan Borobadur. The front gate lay in the path and the flower-beds had been trampled on. Otherwise, the house had not been touched. But the servants had disappeared.

After a brief inspection of the house, I drove to the British Council offices, to find little damage there except for some vandalism – thefts of books – in the library. Then I headed for Tommy Thomas's bungalow, not far from Jalan Borobadur. Tommy was away on holiday in Sabah. Unfortunately, whilst he was away, the inside of his house was ransacked; pictures were destroyed, upholstery was shredded and sinks and toilets were smashed. The living room was knee-high in water from shattered plumbing and there was a pervasive, sour smell. Our first house in Jakarta – in Jalan Gresik – was in even worse condition, the same destruction, the same pungent stench.

The Jalan Gresik bungalow had been allocated to Charles Plume's successor after I moved into the Borobadur house in 1962. John was an accountant, certified as such. Many British Council accountants at that time had no formal qualifications for the job except experience. Compiled by a former British Council Representative, the famous 'Idiot's Guide' to official money management was an invaluable aid.

John had an uncomfortable and quite short career in the Council. First, he encountered problems with a financial system that bore little resemblance to the accountancy procedures with which he was familiar. Second, I believe that his wife and two small children suffered from persistent diarrhoea and septic prickly heat. Third and worst of all, his house was attacked whilst he, his wife and his children were *in situ*. Their possessions were destroyed as they watched. They had to flee in only the very casual clothes that they were wearing at the time of the break-in. The same story was true of many homes occupied by British Embassy officials and members of the British business community.

After visiting Jalan Gresik, I drove to the Kebajoran District, to collect Timothy Cock and his wife. I deposited both of them, together with other refugees, in the then fairly new Hotel Indonesia. Timothy had directed *Twelfth Night*, a charmingly buoyant and amusing production. But what happened to Timothy and his (I believe) pregnant wife was no joke. Timothy and his family, and indeed most women and children, were flown out of Indonesia on 17 September. Lois and our two children were taken to Singapore. In that city of refuge they were put up by Donald and Joanna Moore for a few days and then transferred to a hotel where the children promptly contracted chicken pox. My daughter, Karen, remembers (forty-five years after the event):

> Gazing at the burning Embassy as we came home from school.
> Hiding under the beds, frightened.
> Someone [i.e. me, Verner] crawling over to the phone in the (ambassador's) front living room.
> Being collected in a jeep and being stopped for identification.
> Staying at the American home [i.e. Charlie Lord's house] and drinking coca-colas.
> Being interviewed with our mother at the airport [in Singapore].

The damage done to British (and Malaysian) homes was serious enough although, to be fair, I believe that only one person was injured. A man fell whilst trying to escape over a wall. More serious was the destruction of the British Embassy, a relatively new building situated within observation distance of the Hotel Indonesia. Why was this done? One theory is that the huge crowd outside the Embassy walls was driven to frenzy by the antics of an Embassy employee, an ebullient Scot named Rory Walker. As the tale is told, Walker donned his kilt, conveniently kept in the Embassy, seized his bagpipes (also conveniently to hand) and made a slow circuit of the Embassy perimeter, playing a selection of defiant Scottish airs.

What is more certain than Walker's alleged effect on the mob is that secret and confidential documents were exposed to view, According to Ken Conboy, Kartono Kadri (a Badan Pusat Intelijen agent) and Dr Rubijono (Sukarno's personal physician and code officer) 'passed through a police cordon and picked their way through the water-drenched ruins. Gathering up hundreds of pages of documents, they carried them to a nearby police barracks for drying and processing.'[1]

At the time, Embassy staff did not know for sure what documents had been seized. But the most senior diplomats were apprehensive as they peered at the smoking rubble from a window near the top of the Hotel Indonesia. At least they gave me that impression as I – although not so senior, and British Council rather than Foreign Office – peered with them.

Conboy maintains that among the captured papers was a collection of reports from the British Ambassador, Sir Andrew Gilchrist. As the stones clattered against his windows, the Ambassador noted robustly in his own handwriting, 'Sukarno at this time is like a cornered rat.' Sukarno later referred to Sir Andrew's comment in one of his speeches.[2]

Sir Andrew enjoyed a distinguished record of service to the Crown, notably towards the end of the Second World War as a Major in the anti-Japanese clandestine Force 136 and later (1956–59) as Ambassador to Iceland during the so-called 'Cod Wars'. In my opinion he was the man of the hour in Indonesia, firm but resilient. He continued to work in that country under very difficult circumstances until 1966. He served as Ambassador to Ireland from 1966 and – after his retirement in 1970 – became Chairman of the Highlands and Islands Development Board. His official papers were presented to Churchill College Cambridge in 1964.

Sir Andrew was a man of many parts, diplomat, poet and, post-retirement, a writer of lively 'thrillers' all published by Robert Hale, London.

In a letter to the *Daily Telegraph*, published on 8 May 1984, after his retirement from the Foreign Office, Gilchrist referred to the one diplomatic privilege that he regarded as essential, the diplomatic bag. In his own words:

I once served as Ambassador at a post[3] where diplomatic immunity and the immunity of diplomatic premises had for all practical purposes suddenly ceased to operate. With the aid of a small and courageous staff, I carried on the work of this rather important Embassy for about two years, not from the Chancery, which no longer existed, but from a couple of flimsy rooms in the middle of a garden regularly and sometimes aggressively patrolled by soldiers of the host (and hostile) government to which I was accredited. Our only archives were held in a sort of suitcase, guarded night and day by a man who had instructions if any apparent emergency arose, to press the button that would instantly reduce the suitcase to a heap of ashes. Now though I had little claim to be regarded in London as a good Ambassador, I considered myself to be an efficient one, indeed an effective one. How was this managed? It was simply because I enjoyed complete and confidential communications with my own Government. All the other inconveniences and humiliations were well worth enduring.

Author with Harry Lawrence, the British Council Representative in Indonesia, 1963, addressing a group of Indonesian teachers.

Diplomatic relations were well worth maintaining, so long as this essential facility could be retained, thereby giving hope of resolving peacefully a very dangerous situation.

The mechanical side of our communication link was provided by a radio set tuned to London. Such a set, of a relatively unsophisticated pattern, can be bought today for about One Thousand Two Hundred Pounds. The confidentially of the radio traffic was protected by ciphers of a type used by all civilised countries, quite unbreakable. And it is here that we come to the one and only diplomatic privilege which is still absolutely essential, the diplomatic bag. Cypher materials (books, tapes, or whatever) if the cypher is to stay unbreakable, are a perishable commodity; they need to be renewed from time to time like Freya's golden apples in Wagner's Ring. To provide fresh supplies of these golden apples, the diplomatic bag, guarded throughout its transit by a Queen's Messenger, is the unavoidable requirement. Renewal facilities in respect of a moderate-sized Embassy might be taken care of by a large-sized legal envelope, total weight 6lb, delivered twice a month. For a big Embassy, like Washington, double the weight, or the frequency.[4]

Sir Andrew died in March 1993. In 1994 his son-in-law, T. Rayner, edited a book of Sir Andrew's poems, describing him in an affectionate preface as 'distinguished diplomat, administrator, soldier, author and successful family man'. Rayner also mentions the funeral of Sir Andrew's wife Freda, who was obviously a great support during the difficult days in Indonesia: '…when we drove away from Arthur's Crag after the period following Freda's funeral, he (Sir Andrew) gave me an envelope. It contained a poem.'

I have read all the poems in the slim collection. It seems likely that the following composition referred to Sir Andrew's feelings at the loss of Freda:

Untitled
When I creep up these silent stairs
Towards my quiet bed
With single pillow, not a pair,

I think on others in their time
In comparable pain
Who sought the wit of words and rhyme
And found the effort vain.

Old Burns indeed can touch the heart
And yet he surely knew
There is no way for human head

To make one body two.
I envy those whose simple trust
Bears pledge of future joy,
A hope which fear and reason must
For such as me destroy.

After the September tumult abated, we continued to live in the house in Jalan Borobadur. I resumed my teaching in the University, transferring to the 'IKIP' (now 'FKIP'), or Faculty of Education. I had recommended to the British Council earlier in the year that this transfer should take place. It had been a pleasure to lecture on English literature to bright young women of Chinese extraction but there was an urgent need for better-trained teachers of English, now that the language had replaced Dutch as the first foreign language of the country.

When I rejoined my Indonesian colleagues at the University, no mention was made of the startling events of the past few weeks. Perhaps this was because I had ceased to work in the Faculty of Letters so that there was little opportunity for us to meet. Now I was in a different Faculty and in a different building. My students were trainee teachers and vocationally orientated. English literature had given way to classroom methodology.

For two months or so, following the events of 16 September, the United States Embassy allowed their British colleagues to make use of the Embassy's 'PX', a small supermarket that stocked American food and sweetmeats. In addition, we 'fugitives' were invited to attend the feature films that were shown every Sunday evening in the Embassy compound.

It was most kind of our American colleagues to offer us their hospitality but, given our recent experiences, the choice of films for the first two weeks was somewhat depressing. In week one, we were 'entertained' by a garish production of *Sodom and Gomorrah*, a town destroyed by fire from heaven (according to Genesis 19:24–25); in week two, we were shown *Days of Wine and Roses*, a harrowing description of a married couple's descent into alcoholism.

The months went by until Christmas 1963. We celebrated progressively in different houses – mainly American – salad at one house, soup at another, the main course at another. I remember with some delight the last port of call, the home of our good friends, Charlie and Collette Lord. Champagne and cake were served and there was a band. I played the drums and Jack Bresnan (the normally solemn and very proper Representative of the Ford Foundation) stood on a table and sang.

*****

In early 1962, at the invitation of Radio Republik Indonesia (RRI), a small team from the British Council began a series of broadcasts on RRI's special programme, 'Programa Chusus'. I wrote a number of scripts for these programmes, each of which consisted of a short, elementary English language lesson, an interval of British music and, at a more advanced level, a dramatised story. The first programme was transmitted in April 1962 and 122 programmes were broadcast before the Council was forced to suspend its activities in the country in August 1964. I contributed approximately twenty-five scripts to the series.

*****

Before the advent of television on a country-wide scale, the cinema was one of the most popular forms of entertainment in Indonesia. It still has a wide following. Leslie Palmier noted in 1962 that the Indonesia film industry began round about 1927 with very primitive productions, although a few home-grown Indonesian films have been acclaimed internationally since the Second World War.[5]

The upper-class audience in the towns measured Indonesian films against the best foreign imports and this proved to be an obstacle in the way of improving home-grown productions. Undoubtedly the most popular American films were of the 'epic' and 'action' type (I remember *Ben Hur* and *The Guns of Navarone*), and a black market in ticket sales flourished for these in most major towns. Public demand was high but showings were organised on a quota system related to the availability of films produced locally. The purpose of this system was simultaneously to encourage what was considered to be the indigenous film industry and to reduce the influence of so-called 'yellow culture' (i.e. debased 'Western' culture).

The Board of Film Censors in Jakarta was concerned to assess the educational effect of the films submitted to it. It was also conscious that it had to legislate on behalf of a multicultural society in which no uniformity of response to films could be expected because of contrasting value systems. It was well aware of the effect of films on social attitudes and it therefore exercised great care in its selections. The task was not an easy one. First, because a unanimous decision had to be reached by the Board in the case of each film and – following Javanese practice – no majority voting system could be adopted. Second, individual prejudices and loyalties had to be taken into account. Third, some members of the Board functioned better in Bahasa Indonesia than in English.

I attended several meetings of the Censorship Board in Jakarta in 1962 and 1963 and joined in the discussions that followed the showing of films submitted for licensing. Despite the belief among some observers that an open expression of emotion was out of keeping with Javanese traditions, I did not observe this reaction among the members of the Censorship Board. On the contrary, *Room at the Top*, *Saturday Night and Sunday Morning* and *Never on Sunday* were enjoyed as emotional experiences and admired on the grounds of excellent production techniques. The members of the Board were all university graduates, mostly from the Faculty of Letters of the University of Indonesia, familiar with many of the social attitudes and behaviour patterns of people in 'Western' countries (at least those patterns that were current in the early 1960s). The Board's decisions, however, had to be made on behalf of a wider audience and so, after much deliberation, the three films referred to were judged to be unsuitable for display to Indonesian audiences.

Peter Weir's film, *A Year of Living Dangerously*, was not made until 1982. Starring the Australian actor, Mel Gibson, the film recalled the failed PKI coup which took place on 30 September/1 October 1965 and which led to violent reprisals against Communists and alleged Communists throughout the country. The film would certainly have been banned by the Board of Censors if it had appeared in 1964. Indeed, when it was first released it was banned in Indonesia until 1999.

Although I left Indonesia two years before the attempted PKI coup took place, I had the pleasure, in early 1964, of instructing General Abdul Hari Nasution's son in English language teaching methods. The General held government posts which have been described as equivalent to the posts of United States' Secretary of Defence, Head of the FBI and the Chairman of the US Joint Chiefs of Staff, rolled into one. General Nasution survived the PKI-crafted coup by climbing over a wall and hiding out in the garden of the Iraqui Ambassador. His six-year-old daughter, Ade Irma was unfortunately killed in the attack.

In some ways, this attack on the General was a replay of the attacks of 1963, except that, in 1965, they were directed against some of Indonesia's own generals and not British and Malaysian citizens. We were obliged to climb over a wall in September 1964 and so was the General, two years later.

In 1964, the Board of Censors banned *Elmer Gantry* – a film adapted from Sinclair Lewis's novel that focuses on flamboyant American evangelism – on the grounds that it might affect the susceptibilities of certain religious groups. Similar caution, however, was not exercised in the case of *Flame in the Streets* which had racial prejudice and slum landlordism as its theme and presented a somewhat melodramatic – but otherwise balanced – picture of racial conflicts in a particular area of London. The copy under consideration by the Board had an English soundtrack with Indonesian sub-titles. Because of translation inadequacies, these titles did not always strike the balance that was intended and evident in the original dialogue. Nevertheless, the film was released for general distribution.

Flame in the Streets took on an additional meaning in Jakarta on 16 September 1963 with the burning of the British Embassy and the destruction of people's homes. Fiction bowed before reality.

THE EIGHTH STEP

JAPAN: LAND OF THE RISING SUN

– 23 –

Some Surprises

In June 1964 we flew to London via Athens in Greece. A colleague in Jakarta had recommended a serviced apartment in Nikis Street situated near to the Acropolis.

Light breakfasts of toasted bread and milky coffee preceded long lunches which often featured thick, creamy yoghourts, taramasalata, moussaka and other dishes with exotic names that were difficult to remember. It was easier to remember the monuments, Hadrian's Arch, the Theatre of Dionysus, the Acropolis, the City Eleusinion, Agora, the assembly place and the consonant-rich Pnyx Hill.

On the fourth day of our stay in Athens a foreign language cinema offered some relief from the ancient world. Rex Harrison, Stanley Holloway and Audrey Hepburn entertained in *My Fair Lady*, the film adaptation of George Bernard Shaw's play, *Pygmalion*. In my view, Hepburn was miscast as Eliza, despite her charm and elfish looks. Julie Andrews would have been a better choice. Her cockney accent was more authentic and she could sing (a three octave range). If the film was to be seen anywhere, Athens was surely the place. Had not the ancient Greeks introduced the legend of the sculptor Pygmalion, to whom G.B. Shaw referred in his original title?

After an enjoyable interlude in Athens, we flew to London. Our flat in Dulwich had been let first to a New Zealand academic and his wife. Neighbours reported that the Kiwis had been very careful tenants, even covering the carpets and rugs with plastic sheeting to protect them from stains. After this family returned to New Zealand, a physician took possession. Formerly attached to the British Embassy in Jakarta, he and his family mistreated the property, soiled the carpets, broke items of crockery and dirtied the walls. Not only this. This renegade member of the medical profession sub-let the flat illegally to a pop group named The Falcons. This was alarming yet the neighbours said that they preferred the pop group to the doctor. They quite enjoyed the group's music as they rehearsed quietly on our balcony. The Falcons turned out to be a scrupulously honest bunch, leaving an enormous pile of coins in a bowl to pay for their many telephone calls, no doubt related to their negotiations for 'gigs'.

The month of July passed by quickly as we struggled to find a boarding school for Karen. The prospect of returning to an unstable Indonesia indicated that this was the right course of action. I have mentioned earlier that in Burma dysentery was often the principle topic of conversation on social occasions. In Indonesia the main topic was education for the children. There were very few options then for people posted to 'difficult' countries. There were not many international schools except those with military affiliations and, as far as we knew, no such schools existed in Indonesia.

In the opinion of a pessimistic educational consultant, single-sex girls' schools in Britain were in crisis. The latest recession was partly to blame. Changing ideas about education were another factor. Many long-established schools had been forced to raise their fees very substantially. Others – less well endowed – had simply closed down. Did we have any family connections with the 'best' schools, such as Rodean, Badminton, St Paul's, etc? No, we did not. 'Well, I'll see what I can do.'

After several meetings (each with a fee), the consultant recommended a visit to St Leonard's, a town near Hastings in Sussex. He suggested that we should make an appointment to see Miss Amos, the Principal of Hollington Park School. We followed his advice and the result was that we were *all* interviewed as if we were recalcitrant pupils. But Karen was the only one of us accepted for a place.

Then followed several anxious days searching for blouses, jackets, skirts, stockings, hats, shoes, a trunk and the somewhat mysterious, 'Cash's Name Tapes'. Karen was to start her first term in early September.

Early August brought a rare chance to visit Stratford-on-Avon to see the Royal Shakespeare Company's interpretation of Shakespeare's version of history in five of the bard's ten history plays, *Richard II, Henry V, Henry VI, Edward IV* and *Richard III*. It was an excellent opportunity to enjoy the professionalism and artistry of some of Britain's finest actors and actresses among whom were Peggy Ashcroft, Glenda Jackson, Donald Sinden and Dorothy Tutin.

We decided to stay for the whole of our visit at the 'Dirty Duck' Hotel on Stratford's Waterside. On the second morning of our visit, a clerk at the front desk handed me a telegram. It was from the British Council in London, then situated at Davies Street in Mayfair. According to the *Daily Telegraph* of 12 August 1964: 'The British Council confirmed last night that it had been requested by the Indonesian Government to close all its branches in Indonesia by the end of the month. The reasons given for the decision announced in Djakarta were "the present political circumstances."' This was a shock, if only because the news was so unexpected. The Council did not have diplomatic status in Indonesia. This was thought to be sensible because (the reasoning went) if the Embassy was declared *persona non grata* and was obliged to withdraw from the country, the Council could stay, provided that it had no official diplomatic ties.

But the opposite proved to be the case. The Council was to be ejected but the Embassy would remain, even though the Ambassador did have to work in the garden of his burnt-out Embassy building.

After digesting the news of the Council's withdrawal, I telephoned for instructions. 'Just confirm your contact details and we will be in touch shortly.' Sure enough, two days after we had returned to Dulwich I received a letter informing me that I would be granted a year's paid leave in order to study for a diploma in applied linguistics, or some variant of that discipline. I reported that I was already in possession of a Master's Degree. Could we think, instead, about doctoral work?

Some days later, to my surprise and gratification, I was told that if I was accepted by the University of London for a doctoral programme, the Council would be willing to grant me leave. I should submit an application to the University, giving full details of the line of enquiry that I would like to pursue. I followed this up and shortly afterwards received confirmation from the University (and then the Council) that Professor Bruce Patterson, Director of the English Division of the University's Institute of Education, had agreed to be my supervisor. The topic that I had suggested and which had been approved was 'The English language in Java, Malaya and Singapore. A comparative study of its place in the three societies and their education systems.'

So I began a period of research and writing that started in September 1964 and ended in the summer of 1966. I was out of Britain twice during this period. First, for a family holiday in the Netherlands which I combined with some research and second, for a 'duty visit' to Saigon, Hong Kong, and Japan.

*****

The year 1964 was certainly a year to remember. In Athens we had enjoyed visiting the city's monuments and indulging in new gastronomic experiences. In Stratford-upon-Avon we found ourselves reflecting on Shakespeare's view of history as interpreted by some of Britain's finest actors. And it was in Stratford that we learned that we would not be allowed to return to Indonesia.

To round off this memorable year, I had surprising news from the Foreign Office. On Tuesday, 29 December, I received the following letter. It was marked, 'Personal'.

> Sir,
>
> I have much pleasure in informing you that The Queen, on the recommendation of the Secretary of State for Foreign Affairs, has been graciously pleased, on the occasion of the New Year, to direct that you should be appointed a Member of the Most Excellent Order of the British Empire in recognition of your valuable services.
>
> Yours truly,
>
> D.F. Muirhead.

There followed a visit to Buckingham Palace. A small orchestra played light music as the awards were made. I remember in particular the selections from *Oklahoma*.

Our celebratory dinner in the ballroom of the Savoy Hotel was made particularly interesting by the behaviour of Sir Bernard and Lady Docker. Sir Bernard was formerly Chief Executive Officer of the Birmingham Small Arms Company (BSA) motor company from which he had been persuaded to resign (so the rumour went) partly because of his wife's interference with its affairs. It has been said that she was mainly responsible for additions to at least one of the company's new Daimler cars, insisting that it should be finished with gold leaf instead of chrome and that its upholstery should be made of Kenyan zebra skin.

The Dockers lived permanently at the Savoy but, 'on the evening in question', they chose to be on the dance floor rather than in their rooms. They had clearly indulged themselves before and after dinner, to judge by the wavy course that they steered across the floor. During one circumnavigation they began to argue loudly. Sir Bernard tried to persuade his wife to leave the floor. She refused. He tried again. She refused. He tried a third time but she refused again and collapsed to the floor, refusing to move as the other dancers circled round her. Sir Bernard tried persuasion for a fourth time but to no avail. After several more attempts, he walked off, leaving her in the middle of the floor where she remained until she was scooped up by two waiters and carried off, protesting.

Five months later, in May 1965, it seemed that it would be a good idea to combine a short holiday in the Netherlands with research related to my dissertation. To avoid the expense of a hotel, I arranged for us to stay for one week with the widow of a former Dutch East Indies civil servant in Hilversum, a small town situated to the south east of Amsterdam. Each day for seven days I travelled into Amsterdam, making use of a train service that was efficient, clean and swift.

One afternoon I was invited to tea and cakes by Mr Thomas Versteeg, formerly an Inspector of Education (secondary schools) in Indonesia. He favoured me with a first-hand account of the education system in the Dutch East Indies and I found this to be very useful when, a few days later, I consulted various documents in the *Koninklijk Instituut Library*. Founded in Amsterdam in 1851, the library is also known by its acronym KITLV and its English name, the Royal Netherlands Institute of Southeast Asian and Caribbean Studies.

In those days, I used to subscribe to the *Times Educational Supplement*, in which newspaper a Mr Hinloopen was a regular advertiser. Hinloopen was a senior teacher at a Dutch Gymnasium who boosted his income by letting rooms and providing meals for guests in Amsterdam. It seemed that it would be a good idea for us to spend our second week in his large house and so I made a reservation for the four of us.

We were joined at the Hinloopens by four other guests: a rather silent bachelor from the south of England; an elderly woman and her adult daughter from Carlisle and a single woman – a chronic asthmatic – from the south of England. Not only did the Hinloopens provide rooms and three solid meals a day but they also arranged sightseeing tours in their mini-van. Mr Hinloopen described the purpose of each of these trips on the evening before they took place. Sometimes he illustrated his lectures (for that is what they were) with a slide show. His presentations were interesting but they failed to capture the attention of the children present or the older of the two visitors from Carlisle. 'Mother Carlisle' (as we named her) was experiencing her first visit abroad. It seemed that she was not impressed since she was unable to enjoy either a 'good cup of tea' or some fine English cooking. Whatever the sight to be seen, whether building or bridge, Mother Carlisle declared it to be inferior to the same in her own city. This was a pity because she failed to appreciate the Zuiderkerk (south church); the splendid Bodega Keyzer restaurant (founded in 1903) and the Rijksmuseum, with its incomparable collection of Flemish masters.

I missed several of Mr Hinloopen's jaunts, although I am sure that they would have been more stimulating than my work at the library. I returned to the Hinloopen residence every evening at about 6pm, passing rows of similar houses. Front room curtains were very rarely drawn together and it seemed that everyone in the district enjoyed dinner at the same time.

A few days before our visit to Holland came to an end, the Hinloopens took us to Utrecht to visit the thirteenth-century Cathedral of Saint Michael and to enjoy the flower gardens. Heady from the city's floral scents, it was easy to understand the historic episode of 'Tulipmania' when speculation drove up the price of a single tulip bulb so high that it exceeded the cost of a house. Several modern financial journalists have compared this mania of the 1630s with the 'Dot.Com' financial bubble of the 1990s.

During a 'refreshment break', Mrs Hinloopen told us that our fellow guest, the single, asthmatic lady, had taken a turn for the worse and that Mr Hinloopen had driven her back to Amsterdam. He would return for the rest of us in the early evening. This he did. Unusually for him, Mr Hinloopen fell silent as he drove. It was not until dinner was finished that he revealed that the asthmatic lady had died (on the lavatory) shortly after he had taken her back to the house. Aware that children were present, he broke the news very well without euphemisms. He said simply that his guest had passed away and that she had been taken to hospital.

Later that evening, Hinloopen asked me if I would be willing to visit the hospital to identify his late guest. This was a legal requirement. I agreed and the next morning I found myself to be in a Dutch 'Chapel of Rest'. In a long room furnished with several beds occupied by the newly dead, I identified our late fellow guest and signed the necessary documents. This was a peculiar finale to our first and only visit to the Netherlands.

*****

In the summer of 1965, I was asked by the British Council to undertake an official tour of Saigon, Hong Kong and Japan. The tour would entail running a summer course in Saigon for in-service teachers of English, delivering a keynote speech in Hong Kong at a conference organised by the relatively new Chinese University and directing a course for in-service teachers at Unzen, a hot-spring spa in Japan.

Following the murders of the unpopular Prime Minister, Ngo Dinh Diem and his brother, Ngo Dinh Nhu in October 1963, General Nguyen Van Thieu, a skilful manipulator of American patronage, emerged as President of South Vietnam.

Early in 1965, President Lyndon Johnson decided to support Nguyen by confronting the National Liberation Front (the 'Vietcong') directly and ordering the bombing of targets in both North and South Vietnam. The conflict had escalated and the Vietnam War was fully underway. By 1967 the United States was employing as many as 525,000 troops in South Vietnam but without success. The economist John Kenneth Galbraith's prediction proved to be accurate. He told President Kennedy that if two hundred and fifty thousand American troops (soon to more than double) were unable to defeat fifteen to eighteen thousand guerrillas, 'the United States would hardly be safe against the Sioux'.

On 18 July 1965, I flew to Saigon. The city was accustoming itself to periodic bomb blasts, not unlike those that plague Baghdad at the time of writing in 2008. From time to time, a monk would immolate himself, but usually the Viet Cong guerillas were too sensible to blow *themselves* up as well as their victims.

My diary records that, by a happy coincidence, I met the Vietnamese Minister of Education, Mr Ngo Huy Chuong, and also the Head of the Department of Research and Planning, Mr Nguyen-Van-Luong, on the aircraft during my flight from London. Mr Nguyen and I talked throughout the night. He was very ebullient and enthusiastic about the rapid changes that were taking place in the Vietnamese educational system as the result of a National Education Convention that took place in October 1964. A Junior College had been opened recently for the training of junior high school teachers and a scheme for in-service training was to be provided for four thousand public high school teachers working in South Vietnam's 157 secondary schools.

Just before I passed through Saigon Customs, I was asked by a fellow passenger – a BBC correspondent – to carry one of his bags. Foolishly, as it seems to me now, I agreed. I do not know what it contained – drugs? confidential documents? tins of coffee? – I shall never know, for I am unable to ask the man from the BBC. He committed suicide in London a few months later.

When I arrived at my Saigon hotel (blown up a week after I left the city), I opened my suitcase to discover that it contained only a grubby pair of men's trunks and a sweatshirt. I was confident that I had packed more than these unfamiliar personal items of clothing before leaving London. After a quick wash, I changed some money with a furtive gentleman who hovered in a street at the back of the hotel and then I took a taxi back to the regularly strafed airport. Fortunately, I was able to find my own suitcase, a Samsonite replica of the one that had accompanied me to the hotel. I left the other suitcase and the dirty underwear at the airport.

The teachers' course in Saigon seemed to be successful but I often wonder today about the fate of Mr Ngo and Mr Nguyen who opened the proceedings with courteous and enthusiastic speeches. I wonder too if anything unpleasant happened to the two British Council lecturers who helped me with the course. Virginia Greasley was employed in Saigon and Jonathan Trench[1] worked in Hue, the former imperial capital named 'Annam' by the French. It was the centre of a mighty battle during the so-called Tet offensive in 1968.

On 1 May 1975, some ten years after my visit to Vietnam, a headline in the *Singapore Straits Times* read, 'Saigon Surrenders. As conquerors take over, normalcy returns. Communist troops rolled into Saigon today virtually unopposed.' On the same day I was enjoying lunch in Bangkok with the Crown Princess of Thailand, Princess Chumbhot. The other guests were Mr Perry Stiglitz (Public Affairs Officer at the US Embassy in Bangkok), Mrs Boonlua Debuvasan and Mrs Mayuree Sukwiwat. The Princess was an avid collector of ceramics and I had been invited to see an exhibition of these in the family museum which she and her husband had established.[2] It was the day following the surrender of South Vietnam to the combined forces of the Democratic Republic of Vietnam (DRV) and the National Liberation Front (NLF). The talk at the lunch focused entirely on the possibility of 'escalation'. Would the successful Communist forces now turn their attention to Thailand? Fortunately, this did not happen.

In the evening before I left Saigon in July 1965, I was invited, together with some Vietnamese dignitaries, to dinner and a film-showing at the home of Mr Lancashire, a First Secretary (Information) at the British Embassy in Saigon. Mr Nguyen offered to collect me from my hotel and to deliver me to the diplomat's house. As I stepped out of his large American car, Mr Nguyen leaned across to close the door. Ouch! Of course he could not be blamed for trapping my right-hand thumb. Indeed, I remember smiling politely and thanking him for his kindness as I was welcomed by my host and took my damaged hand into the house.

*****

I left Saigon for Hong Kong on the morning after Mr Lancashire's party. I was to be a keynote speaker at a conference jointly organised by the Hong Kong government's Department of Education and Chung Chi College, the latter a component of the then new Chinese University of Hong Kong. The conference was organised by Dr Bertha Hensman, head of the University's Department of English. I was quite prepared to stay in a hotel on the 'Hong Kong side', even though this would have meant a daily ferry and train journey to the University – the cross-harbour tunnel from Hong Kong Island to Kowloon had not yet been built – but Dr Hensman insisted that I stay with her.

A former missionary in China – as dedicated as Miss Gulliver, my host in the Arakan – Dr Hensman lived in a brand-new concrete house on the University campus, not yet equipped with air conditioning. It was August. In Hong Kong, humidity was in the nineties and temperatures in the mid-thirties Celsius. I was hot and itchy and my thumb throbbed. Dr Hensman noticed my swollen digit and suggested that I should consult the University doctor 'down the hill'. I accepted her suggestion and prepared to walk to the doctor's surgery. 'I'll come with you,' said Dr Hensman. I protested that this was unnecessary but Dr Hensman insisted. We met the doctor at the outer door of his surgery. He was about to leave for home but gave way to Dr Hensman's pleas and, somewhat reluctantly, opened up again. 'Ah, yes,' he said, inspecting my damaged body part and seizing a scalpel. 'I'll just ventilate it a little.' 'Let me help,' said Dr Hensman, briskly. 'I got used to this sort of thing in China.' 'No, no,' said the doctor. 'I think that I can manage. This is very minor. Do sit over there, Dr Hensman.' She reluctantly sat down on a hard-backed chair and the 'ventilating' began.

The first incision had been made when suddenly there was a crashing sound and a cry. Dr Hensman had slumped to the floor. The doctor thrust my bleeding thumb into a kidney dish and rushed over to Dr Hensman. The patient could wait. It was more important to save the distinguished scholar's face than to bother about some piddling little injury suffered by an unknown patient. 'Dr Hensman,' said the doctor (aware that face did indeed need to be saved) 'I have many times asked the Senate to install air conditioning in this room. And now you see that it is too hot for you.' She smiled, weakly. I shifted in my seat. 'Excuse me,' I said, as the water reddened in the dish, 'do I need to do anything else?' 'Oh,' said the doctor, noticing that I was still there, bloody but unbowed. 'Alright, I'll put a bandage on it. Don't worry.' The bandage was enormous and it surely impressed the conference audience as I gave my speech, punctuated by occasional waves of my right hand to drive home a point.

*****

Although the pain had subsided somewhat, my bandaged thumb continued to give trouble, necessitating a visit to another doctor in another country, Japan. In the spa town of Unzen on the island of Kyushu, the doctor looked disparagingly at the rather grubby dressing, unwrapped it, inspected the – by now fiery – wound and then said, 'If you were a Japanese I would cut it open, but since you are not I will give you some antibiotic tablets.' Clearly I lacked the samurai spirit.

Deflated (but relieved), I returned to my hotel in Unzen. I had flown there after receiving a briefing in Tokyo from the British Council Deputy Director, Alan Baker, and the British Council Representative (Director), Frederick Tomlin.

The late Frederick Tomlin was a man of academic distinction. A kind and thoughtful person and a considerable scholar, he published six full-length books on philosophy and metaphysics, as well as numerous essays on a variety of subjects.[3] He was elected a Fellow of the Royal Society of Literature in 1963 and was made CBE in 1965. I believe that Frederick probably did much to improve the reputation of the British Council in Japan after the unhappy reign of his predecessor, Ronald Bottrall, who was – according to his former Deputy, Bill McAlpine – a moody, irascible character who on several occasions locked himself in his office and brooded like Achilles in his tent.

Frederick succeeded in engaging a charming and efficient group of Japanese ladies for his staff. Recruited from families of distinction, they worked efficiently under the watchful eyes of Miss Shizuko Eguchi and Mr Takahashi, the British Council 'Adviser', who had, so I understood, familial connections with descendants of the Shogunate Tokugawas. The Tokugawas were the most important Shoguns, the Japanese generals who ruled Japan as military dictators from 1603 for the following 264 years. During that period the Emperor remained a figurehead until the 'Meiji' restoration in 1868. Meiji was the title of the Emperor Mutsuhito who ruled until 1912.

'Tomlin's Young Ladies' invariably married well, for example Miss Kosugi married a British Embassy Third Secretary who eventually achieved

Ambassadorial rank and my secretary, Miss Mori, charmed and married the Director of an English language tutorial centre in Tokyo.

Following my short stay in Tokyo, the British Council Deputy Representative, Alan Baker, and I travelled by train to Nagasaki where we met a very tall and thin academic who was contracted by the British Council to a university in the city. Ironically, his name is David *Short*.[4] David was one of the four lecturers engaged to assist me at the Summer School. The other three were also tertiary-level teachers of English on temporary British Council contracts. This arrangement followed a tradition established in the nineteenth century and still continuing, despite the hiatus caused by the Second World War. Both before and after that War, Japan welcomed British poets, novelists, linguists and teachers, appointing them on non-tenurable terms to schools, language learning centres and universities. These included literary men such as Lafcadio Hearn (1850–1904), William Plomer (1903–73), Edmund Blunden (1896–1974), Sir William Empson (1906–84), Ralph Hodgson (1871–1962), Ronald Bottrall (1907–89), Francis King (1923–), Anthony Thwaite (1930–), George Barker (1913–91) and Denis Joseph Enright (1920–2002), as well as linguists such as Edward Vivian Gatenby (1892–1955), Arundel Del Re (1892–1974), Harold Palmer (1877–1949) and Albert Hornby (1898–1978).

The names Palmer and Hornby may not be well known to the general reader but they will be familiar to applied linguists as pedagogical giants of the past. In the 1920s Palmer was appointed as the first Director of the Institute of Research in English Teaching in Tokyo. His Japanese colleagues and friends included the veteran Japanese linguists, Sanki Ichikawa and Takeshi Saito, the latter responsible for inviting the poet and academic, Edmund Blunden, to Japan after the First World War. Wherever Blunden went in Japan, he was persuaded to compose a poem. As far as I know the linguist, A.S. Hornby ('Ash') was never asked to write poetry but he *was* urged to give innumerable lectures. It was in Tokyo that, as a colleague of Harold Palmer, he compiled his famous *Advanced Learners' Dictionary*, published by the Oxford University Press.

In 1969, the Oxford University Press invited Hornby to Japan to work on the latest edition of the *Dictionary*. The idea was that he would meet with former students and colleagues at two receptions that I organised in Tokyo. Following the receptions, it was arranged that he should go into seclusion in a small hotel outside the city. There he would be able to carry out his assignment for the Press without interruption. Unfortunately, his hideaway was discovered and troops of students, former colleagues and well-wishers visited the hotel. The intruders urged him to give lectures but he said that he no longer gave lectures. They asked him to write articles but he said that he no longer wrote articles. They asked permission to record their conversations on tape and to this he reluctantly agreed. Remorseless, they then asked him to edit their transcriptions. In the end he gave up and made himself available to anyone who wished to meet him. I took advantage of this and had the pleasure of showing him and his wife around Tokyo and its environs, much changed since his first post-war visit. We even found time to participate together in a tea ceremony.

In 1961 Hornby set up the A.S. Hornby Educational Trust to provide grants that would enable English teachers from overseas to go to Britain for professional training. Since the Trust was established, hundreds of teachers have been able to develop their expertise at post-graduate courses and through Summer Schools organised by the British Council.

Founded in May 1923, the Institute of Research in English Teaching is still in existence. In the 1960s it complemented the work of newer organisations such as Zen Ei Ren, with over fifty thousand members, the English Language Education Council (ELEC), the Council On Language Teaching Development (COLTD) and the Monbusho's (Ministry of Education's) own Council for the Improvement of English Language Teaching (CIELT).

A similar organisation that has flourished since the 1960s is the Japan Association of College English Teachers (JACET). During the four years that I spent in Japan, I gave talks on linguistics and pedagogical subjects to members of each of these organisations, except JACET.

In 1968, as a 'Visiting Scholar', I had the privilege of delivering a series of lectures on British Life and Institutions to students at 'Todai' (Tokyo University). It was a strange year in which to give such lectures, for students in many Western universities – described by some as 'revolting' students – were neglecting their studies to conduct campus and street protests. Japan was no exception. Each week, the chauffered car provided for me by the British Council had to thread its way through noisy (though mostly harmless) groups of protestors. Despite the hubbub outside and in the corridors, the students in the lecture room were quietly attentive. However, some of them were hostile to their own professors. An academic with whom I became quite friendly – a Shakespearean scholar named Ozu – suffered quite badly at the hands of his students, and was kept awake for several successive nights by their threats and taunts.

I thought that the students' attitude towards me reflected their courtesy to a guest. And who knows? It is just possible that their teachers or grandparents remembered the gift of books and manuscripts, 'Illustrative of the History of Printing and Book Production' made by the British government to the Imperial University of Tokyo (modern Tokyo University) in 1929. Presented as a contribution towards the replenishment of the University's English Library as a result of a fire that followed the great earthquake of 1 September 1923, the books focused primarily on Law, Literature and Economics. By the end of 1928, about thirty-one thousand volumes had been presented to the University.

*****

August in Japan is a steamy month and it is a good idea to desert the exciting cities and take one's prickly heat to a resort. We stayed in Unzen, nestling among the azaleas and maple trees in Amakusa National Park in the hills of Kyushu. Unzen gives its name to the volcanic region of Mount Unzen-dake and it is said to be particularly popular because of its cool summer weather. Certainly it was cool enough for all of us – lecturers and students – to look forward to the five o'clock communal bath at the end of each working day. In Tunbridge Wells at such a time one might prefer

A tea ceremony with Mr and Mrs A.S. ('Ash') Hornby, Tokyo, Japan, 1969.

tea. In Unzen, the bath seemed more appropriate. Besides, as I soon discovered, my student teachers wanted to practice their English-speaking skills. What better place to do this than in the bath?

The bath held about twenty medium-sized people. It was made of natural rock and tiled at the bottom. A pipe which curved its way down from the hills brought steaming water from the sulphur springs. Almost fully immersed, you relaxed and devoted yourself to conversation and banter with your companions. Smaller baths were available in which the members of a family could meet together to relax and talk of family and other affairs.

It was a busy time, so much so that we tended to ignore our surroundings. I have to confess that I did not realise then that we were in close proximity to one of Japan's seventy-five active volcanoes. Another twenty-eight years were to pass before in 1993 it produced a pyroclastic flow that killed one resident.

– 24 –

Tokyo Perspectives

After the Summer School in Kyushu was over, I took the train to Tokyo to give a keynote speech at a conference organised by the Japan Association of Phoneticians. On the day following the conference, I flew to Bangkok for a discussion with my co-author, Kenneth Methold. Three days later I boarded a plane at Haneda Airport, heading for home. Once back in London I was tempted to dally but realised that I could not escape. The time had come for me to write my doctoral dissertation.

Before I began to type (on my Olivetti portable), I bought a cheap whitewood desk at one of the fashionable Habitat stores. On the day that I finished the work, the desk collapsed, its duties complete. I nearly collapsed with it. At over six hundred pages the study was far too long and I feared that it would be rejected on the grounds of its prolixity. Fortunately the assessors who questioned me at the *viva voce* agreed that it was not repetitious and I was awarded my PhD in August 1966.

I had done most of my writing in the flat at Hitherwood Court but in the late spring of 1966 we moved into a house in the pleasant town of Beckenham in Kent.

We were still accustoming ourselves to our new surroundings when news came about my next British Council posting. It was to be Tokyo, Japan. After 'positive vetting' by an official at the Foreign Office, and after I had been examined by a Foreign Office doctor, we flew there in late September 1966. I would have two titles: English Language Officer and First Secretary (Cultural).

We were met on arrival at Haneda Airport by Alan Baker who accompanied us to the San Bancho Hotel, close to the British Embassy.

We stayed there for two weeks before moving to a flat in Harajuku near to the Shinjuku District. The Japanese name for our block of flats translated bizarrely as 'Green Fantasia', an odd name but appropriate since we did find some experiences during our four-year stay in Japan to be quite extraordinary.[1]

*****

To take but one example of the unusual, there was the occasion when I received a letter from the British Council in London, passing on a request from the composer, Benjamin Britten. It had been suggested to Britten that the original score of Henry Purcell's opera, *Dido and Aeneas*, might be in Japan. One theory was that no such score was extant and that the only source was a libretto by Nahum Tate. Nevertheless – in my role as First Secretary (Cultural), rather than British Council English Language Officer – I made a number of enquiries, eventually being referred to a certain Mr Kyubei Ohki. He was said to possess a large collection of books about music as well as original music manuscripts.

I contacted Mr Ohki through his secretary and was invited to meet him at his house in Odewara, a small town not too far from Tokyo. After I had presented him with a bottle of malt whisky and the formalities had been concluded, he told me that he owned a collection of books and music manuscripts. At that time he was not much interested in this collection, much of which had been put together in London by Marquis Yorisade Tokugawa, a member of the distinguished Japanese family. All the items were stored in a Tokyo warehouse.

After we had chatted for some time it became clear that his interest had now been aroused and our meeting ended by his agreeing to open his collection to the public. He thought that one of the music academies in Tokyo would be willing to mount an exhibition.

Some weeks after my meeting with Mr Ohki he was able to arrange for his exhibition to take place. It was organised by the Kunitachi Music Academy (Kunitachi Academia Musicae) and, for the first time, his amazing collection was put on show for the public to see. The exhibition proved to be of particular interest to Tokyo's musicologists. Never before had they had the opportunity to view some of the items on display including (I believe) not only the *Dido* score but other original scores by well-known and respected composers.

Pleased by the success of the exhibition, Mr Ohki declared it to be his intention to house all the items in some kind of cultural centre where they could be seen by musicologists and other interested persons. He kept his promise and the items may now be viewed in the *Ohki Collection* maintained by the Nanki Music Library in Tokyo. I missed the opportunity to congratulate Mr Ohki then but was able to do so when – by coincidence – we met again in 1975 in Honolulu. At that time I was living in leafy Kahala Avenue, just opposite a street named Black Point. Early one evening, I emerged from my garden and, to my surprise, met Mr Ohki in the street. He had either rented or bought a house in the district. We exchanged warm greetings and I invited him to join me for tea. Unfortunately, he had a prior engagement that afternoon and was unable to accept. He had to leave for Japan on the next day and, regrettably, I have not had the opportunity to meet him since.

The investigations carried out in the 'Ohki Case' led to my being invited to visit other collections of rare documents and objects. For example, a telephone message from Mr Yoshio Ito, Librarian of the Musashino Music Academy, led to an invitation to tea and an opportunity to see some of the Academy's treasures. Amazingly some of these were kept in an old cupboard in Mr Ito's office, although they included original copies of music by composers such as Jules Massenet, Antonio Salieri and Franz Schubert.

After a tea-time visit to a traditional Japanese house situated outside Tokyo, I was startled when the owner (a Mr Matsudaira) invited me to see his collection of sword hilts. We walked along a corridor at the rear of the house. My host slid aside an ordinary looking *shoji* screen to reveal a steel door. The room beyond the door was crowded with antique sword hilts, taken out only once or twice a year to be exhibited in Tokyo.

On another occasion, in a small private museum in Tokyo I was shown a large collection of original letters from luminaries such as George Bernard Shaw, T.S. Eliot, W.B. Yeats and others. Perhaps the most interesting item in the collection was a letter from Nelson to Lady Hamilton about a prize cow.

*****

Tokyo is a vibrant city. Certainly I found it to be so, given my dual role as English Language Officer and temporary diplomat. As the British Council's first English Language Officer in Japan it was part of my duty to make contact with senior university professors of literature and linguistics, the latter including such academic offshoots as sociolinguistics, psycholinguistics, applied linguistics and semantics. At that time it was against British Council policy to engage in the direct teaching of English. although such teaching had been offered in the 1940s and 1950s in a number of Latin American countries. Direct English language teaching by Council personnel was revived successfully in the 1970s in Hong Kong and profitable British Council English language teaching centres are now flourishing in many parts of the world.

My brief in Tokyo included exchanging ideas with Japanese scholars and teachers about recent developments in language pedagogy. For this purpose I was allocated space for a small 'Language Centre' in the British Council office. After the customary round of introductions, meetings, telephone calls and despatch of informative leaflets, I was able to establish a regular programme for senior and junior high school teachers of English. This included founding and nurturing a 'Society for Teachers of English in Tokyo' ('STET'); stocking and opening an English Language Teaching Information Section and organising an annual Summer School. Two years later it was possible to offer a 'seven point programme' that included, in addition to the Summer School, a weekly 'English by Television' programme on the Nippon Hōsō Kyókai (NHK) (equivalent to the BBC) and the publication of a monthly journal *Journal of English Teaching* ('JET'), published by the Oxford University Press.

I arrived in Japan for the second time twenty-one years after the surrender to Allied Forces. It was one of the unstated but important roles of the British Council to mend the metaphorical fences that had been severely damaged by an over-ambitious military régime. The Foreword to the exhibition of books presented by the British government to Tokyo University, to which I have already referred, states that a

> fine specimen of the Kelmscott Chaucer will be presented personally by the Secretary of State for Foreign Affairs to His Excellency the Japanese Ambassador, as representing the gift offered by His Majesty's Government to the Tokyo Imperial University, as a contribution to the cause of knowledge and as a symbol of friendship which has so long flourished between the peoples of Japan and Britain.[2]

Twelve years after this presentation was made, Japan attacked Pearl Harbour and occupied the British colonies of Hong Kong, Singapore, Malaya, North Borneo and Sarawak as well as the Dutch East Indies (Indonesia). Yet Japan had allied itself with Britain in the First World War, capturing with a small British force the German-leased territory of

Shantung (returned to China in 1921) and helping to clear the Pacific Ocean of German ships.

A discussion of the reasons for Japan's changed political stance and the circumstances that led to its military adventures in the 1930s and the 1940s has no place here. But the history of the 1930s and the 1940s could not be entirely forgotten in the 1960s. In some ways, one antidote was to think of the past, to remember the Japan that existed at the time of the Perry Expedition at Shimoda in 1854;[3] to consider the reminiscences of Isabella Bird who visited Japan in 1878 in order to 'recruit her health'[4] or the tales of old Japan that were recalled by diplomats such as A.B. Mitford.[5]

Certainly, whilst they were aware of their roles as diplomatic representatives and conscious of their own national loyalties, the British officials whom I met during my stay in Japan had formed affections for the country and its culture. The two tallest and perhaps most dignified persons with British Embassy connections were Frederick Tomlin (already mentioned) and John, later Sir John Figgess. Figgess's connections with Japan reached back to his pre-war days as a man of business. During the Second World War, he served with the rank of Colonel in the British Army and shortly after the end of the war he was appointed Military Attaché to the British Embassy. Later, he was made Information Counsellor and it was in that capacity that I met him when I first arrived in Tokyo. Figgess was respected for his fluency in Japanese and also for his interest in many different aspects of Japanese culture. In particular he had formed a passion for Japanese pottery and was, I believe, a competent potter himself. He was a force in the Oriental Ceramic Society and served for a term as its President.

Hugh – later Sir Hugh – Cortazzi, the Embassy's Commercial Counsellor, was an irascible man. At least he gave that impression to some newcomers and was sometimes thought to be unnecessarily brusque. Cortazzi had acquired excellent Japanese language skills during his first appointment to the country. In the 1960s he was very active in the organisation of a 'British Week' in Tokyo and of the British participation in the 'Expo' held in Osaka in 1970. As was the case for a number of diplomats appointed to Japan, he was posted to the country several times (1951–54, 1961–65, 1966–70), and in the twilight of his career served as British Ambassador from 1980 to 1984.

It is perhaps a characteristic of diplomats who become adepts in the languages of the countries in which they serve that they become 'culture learners'. That was undoubtedly the case for Cortazzi who at the time of writing still maintains an interest in 'ways of living' in the country in which he spent much of his working life. His fascination with antique Japanese maps, his short history of Japan and Japanese culture (*The Japanese Achievement*)[6] and his informative book on Japan during the time of A.B. Mitford (*Mitford's Japan: Memories and Recollections*)[7] provide strong evidence of this.

*****

On first appointment, a young man or young woman appointed to the British Foreign Service and to Japan would be given the rank of Third Secretary. His or her duties with that title would be nominal since the main task would be to study the Japanese language and its culture. For two years the newcomer would study in Japan for several hours a day with a Japanese teacher and also enjoy a period of one month each year as the guest of a Japanese family.

Some years ago, for reasons of cost, the period of study in Japan was reduced to one year. The second year was spent at Sheffield University under the guiding hand of Professor Geoffrey Bownas. In a recently published memoir, Bownas describes Japan's post-war economic development, beginning from the time in the 1950s when an electric iron was a status symbol up to the long period of growth that came to an end in the late 1990s.[8]

In some cases Japanese language instruction was also provided by tutors in Britain, the best known of these tutors in the 1960s being Dr Carmen Blacker of Cambridge University and Major-General Francis Piggott, son of Sir Francis Piggott, formerly Chief Justice of Hong Kong. Major-General Piggott was attached to the British Embassy in Tokyo from 1910 to 1918 and served as Military Attaché to the Embassy from 1921 to 1926. After leaving Japan, he was appointed senior lecturer in Japanese at the School of Oriental and African Studies in London.

I understand that the wheel has now turned again and that tuition in Japanese for new recruits to the Foreign Service has reverted to Japan, in the town of Kamakura.

*****

The late Sir Francis Rundall was British Ambassador to Japan when I arrived in Tokyo in the autumn of 1966. I met Sir Francis on only three occasions. First, shortly after I had 'signed the book' and attended a welcome lunch at the Embassy residence. Second, when I gave him a cheque as payment for his car that he sold to me before departing Japan. Third, at a reception arranged by the Japan–British Society at which the late Princess Chichibu was the guest of honour. Sir Francis was a tall man, firm but kindly. In contrast to Sir Francis, his successor, Sir John Pilcher, was short and rotund. His stature was made obvious when contrasted with that of his wife, Delia, who was quite lengthy and stately of demeanour. On 31 December 2002, the British government declassified (under the thirty-year rule) a number of papers written by Sir John during his tenure as Ambassador. In one paper he declared that the Japanese are deficient of a proper moral code. 'The bad man restrained in Japan by form with a sense of shame but no inkling of sin, behaves abroad unabashedly badly.' Later in the same despatch he applied the same conclusions to the behaviour of Japan's military during the Second World War. 'I submit that the evil behaviour of the Japanese during the last war was basically due to these factors and of course to traditional contempt for the prisoners of war aided by a deliberate policy to humiliate the former colonial rulers in front of their erstwhile Asian subjects.'

The thirty-year-old despatches have been issued with a linking commentary, by the Japanese Institute of Global Communications (GLOCOM). One contributor, J. Sean Curtin of the Japanese Red Cross University, is critical of Sir John's view and claims that British soldiers have also committed terrible atrocities against unarmed civilians in many countries. In support of his argument, he quotes the killing of thirteen unarmed Irish civilians by British soldiers on 30 January 1972. This surely cannot be compared with Japanese behaviour in the fields of battle, or the prolonged and extraordinarily brutal treatment of prisoners of war in Japanese-administered camps in Malaya, Singapore, Hong Kong, Indonesia and Borneo.

In the GLOCOM commentary, Curtin ignores the Widgery Tribunal which found that the accused British soldiers were not guilty of shooting thirteen Irish civilians in cold blood.

Against a background of changing 'Western' life styles in the 'swinging sixties', characterised by drug use, hippies, sit-ins and caftans, Sir John ventured to write a despatch about the position of women in Japan. He concluded:

> Not being subjected to arduous infantile disciplines, because she is not considered sufficiently important, the Japanese female is more naturally spontaneous, more flexible and more free-moving than the male. She is, so

to speak, quicker on the draw all round and is increasingly gaining the nerve to demonstrate it.

This despatch referred to the feminist movement that was beginning to receive considerable publicity in Japan. Interestingly, Sir John made no reference to the differences between Japanese men's speech and Japanese women's speech, differences that are also governed by three main politeness levels in spoken Japanese; namely the plain form, the simple polite form and the advanced polite form. Since relationships – even today – are not equal, one person usually has a higher position in a conversation. The person in the lower position is expected to use a polite form of speech. Women usually speak one level higher up the politeness scale. The newcomer to Japan notices this almost immediately but as time goes on the differences become less apparent as one becomes used to them.

*****

During the entire period in which I served in Japan, the economy went from strength to strength and in the financial year 1965–66, its Gross National Product (GNP) became the third largest in the world. It seemed then that the phrase, 'ever onward and upward', could be applied appropriately to Japan's financial state. I recall however, the warnings given by John Hill, a British Council economist appointed to Japan in 1968. 'This won't last forever,' he would say to Japanese counterparts. And then he would use a British saying which they may well have found confusing – 'make hay while the sun shines'. Unfortunately for Japan, Hill's warning was correct and, although in recent years it seemed as if Japan had begun to emerge from a long period of economic stagnation, it has now begun to feel the deleterious effect of the financial 'downturn' that began in the summer of 2008.

Although a five-year trade agreement was concluded between Japan and China in 1962, the countries were wary of each other and both Japanese politicians and British Embassy officials were deeply conscious of the threat posed by Communism. In 2009 it is not so much the ideology of Communism that affects relations between Japan and China but rather arguments over the content of school textbooks and the regular symbolic visits made by Japanese Prime Ministers to the Yasakuni Shrine. It is at this shrine in the Ichigaya District, the Minister pays his respects to 2.5 million Japanese servicemen and women who died during the Second World War, including fourteen Class A war criminals.

From 'Green Fantasia' in Tokyo it was only a five-minute walk to another Shrine, this one dedicated to the souls of Emperor Meiji (1852–1912) and his Empress. The Meiji Shrine was constructed in 1920 but destroyed during the Second World War. It was rebuilt in 1958. We took the opportunity to visit it on several occasions.

– 25 –

Culture Learning

During our four years of residence in Tokyo, culture learning for us meant culture with a small 'c' – ways of behaving – as well as culture with a big 'C' – cultural manifestations.

For 'small c' culture in Japan, we relied on our own observations, our involvements with Japanese academics and artists and the ministrations of our friend, Professor Susumu Suzuki of Keio University who seemed to regard it as his duty to ensure that we were exposed to interesting corners of Japan and to its unique culture and cuisine.

It was also possible to journey to other parts of Japan on British Council business. For example, on several occasions we were able to visit Kyoto's temples and gardens. The Council representative in Kyoto, Peter Martin, compiled his own booklet containing unique and valuable information about the city's historical sites, including tourist traps to avoid. He was kind enough to present me with a copy of his manuscript but I made the mistake of lending it to a colleague at the East–West Center in Honolulu. It was never returned.

Professor Suzuki arranged visits for us to several different parts of Japan. Some of these visits were on the tourist route and some of them were rarely visited by foreigners. On one occasion, he accompanied us to the town of Gifu-Hashima to view the cormorant fishing that takes place along the river. To get to Gifu we travelled by the Shinkanzen ('Bullet Train'). On arrival we walked out of the station and stopped to examine a plinthed statue placed in the middle of the forecourt. The statue was surrounded by Japanese schoolchildren in their uniforms. A man (obviously their teacher) was speaking to them and they were listening attentively. I remarked to Professor Suzuki that the statue must be that of a great man since the children appeared to be very interested in him. The Professor corrected me. 'Oh, no,' he said. 'The statue is that of a man who represented this area in the National Diet. Because of his influence it was arranged for the Shinkanzen to stop here, although there is really no reason why it should do so. The man is telling the children that the statue is that of a very corrupt person.'

To be enjoyed to the full, a visit to Gifu-Hashima must be taken slowly. First, it is sensible to relax in one's hotel room and sip fragrant tea prior to a nap on the *tatami* (dried grass floor mat). It is time to walk down the corridor to the communal bathroom, there to sit on a little wooden stool and wash oneself thoroughly *before* entering the water in which one can enjoy the warmth and the banter of one's fellow bathers. Following the bath and wrapped in a capacious *yukata* (dressing robe), it is only a short walk to the river bank where one may join one's companions aboard a long, thin boat, decorated with red lanterns. This boat is pulled up the shallows of the river by four men, each waist-deep in the water. As they pull they are encouraged by the sounds of a *shamisen*, played by a colourfully-robed young woman sitting in the boat beneath the lanterns. At a certain point in the river the men release their ropes and the boat begins to float slowly downstream, providing an opportunity for spectators to observe a group of cormorants on the opposite side of the river. The birds are at work catching fish but they are unable to swallow them because their throats are blocked by thin, silken cords. It is said that each cormorant is aware of its place in a hierarchy and that each must accord respect to the senior bird.

*****

In a book chapter written and published some forty years ago,[1] Professor Kishimoto Hideo advanced the (in my view doubtful) thesis that the Japanese language was more closely connected with man's *immediate experience* than the English language and that this was also reflected in the way Japanese people thought. He went on to note that as a matter of social custom it was regarded as a great virtue to be able to keep the mind tranquil and calm (although, as I observed myself on several occasions, there could be violent, unexpressed emotions below the surface).

Professor Kishimoto might have added to his list of traits those of *persistence and endurance*, for these are certainly of high value in Japan (as, indeed, they are in China and Korea). In Japan, training in them begins when a child is at school, attempting to memorise *kanji* (ideographs) by copying them again and again. Two thousand of these are needed in order to read a daily newspaper. Persistence and endurance also pervade many other aspects of life, for example, *ikebana* (flower arrangement), painting, the entrance tests for Zen Buddhist temples and the *seishin kyoiku* (spiritual education) that is offered by many Japanese companies to their employees to encourage them to observe (what the management considers to be) proper forms of social interaction.

Persistence and endurance are admired traits in Japan, associated with the notion of *gambari*, meaning (according to a dictionary published in 1989)[2] (1) to work hard and patiently, (2) to insist on having one's way and (3) to occupy one place and never leave it. There is a life-sized statue of a dog outside Tokyo's Shiubuya railway station. The dog, 'Hachikosan', used to wait there for his master to come home from work every evening. When his master died the dog continued to come to the same spot and stayed there until the last passengers had emerged from the station in the late evening. This could be a folk tale similar to the story of faithful 'Greyfriars Bobby' in Scotland, but it is sometimes quoted as an example of *persistence* and *loyalty*. Such traits are expected of men, women and children at all age levels but in particular of business-persons, whether 'salarymen' or executives.

*****

Two years after I first arrived in Tokyo, I became entangled in a gift-giving and receiving situation which, if I had not left Japan, might have continued to this day. It began with a visit to my office of a Japanese Professor of Education. He had brought with him a tape-recording of a lecture that he had attended and that had been delivered in English. Would I be kind enough to listen to the tape, summarise it and prepare a list of what I considered to be the key points? I agreed (although rather reluctantly since I had more than enough to do at the time). Two weeks later, I delivered the tape and a list to the Professor. He expressed his grateful thanks. But that was not the end of the story. A few days after I had returned the tape, a messenger brought me a large bottle of malt whisky, a gift from the Professor. I returned the compliment by inviting him to join me at a performance of Shakespeare's, *The Merchant of Venice*. He reciprocated with two (almost unobtainable) tickets for a sumo performance. I invited him to a reception at my home. He sent my wife a basket of flowers. I asked him if he would be good enough to speak at a summer school. He did so and brought with him some books for distribution to the students. I returned the compliment in some way and he responded. So it went on and on and it only came to an end when I left Japan.

How did this come about? Well, largely because the Japanese themselves are always exchanging gifts. Seasonal gifts are exchanged in July and in December and gifts are given and received to mark life's significant phases such as birth, graduating from school and university, weddings and celebrating old age. One Japanese observer has listed eighty-five occasions on which gifts are given and it seems that there are at least forty-three kinds of ceremonial and seasonal gifts, covering all significant events in Japanese life.

*****

It is likely that most business-persons who visit Japan for the first time will be male, although visits by female business-persons are, no doubt, beginning to increase. Assuming that this is correct and that a first visit has been arranged for a businessman, what might he expect? The purpose of his visit – for example, the negotiation of a joint venture relating to electronics – might fit very well into a modern context. But it will be surprising if he is able to conclude an agreement on this first visit. He will certainly be wined and dined and he might even be introduced to more exotic pleasures. From a business point of view, however, he will probably leave empty-handed. A second or third visit might be necessary if there is to be a satisfactory outcome.

After several visits, our businessman may feel that he is getting to know Japan. He has learned something of the etiquette of the bow and of gift exchanges. (They should never be opened on receipt.) He has learned to dress formally, always with a tie. He has accustomed himself to dinners that begin at 6pm and end at 9pm. If he is accompanied by his wife, he may be surprised when an invitation to dinner is not extended to her. And if she is invited then he is shocked (and she is chagrined) if a Japanese colleague tells her that he did not realise that she was so *old*, an intended compliment not always fully appreciated.

At a certain time each year during my four-year stay in Tokyo I was invited with colleagues to a dinner hosted by the Director of the Ministry of International Trade and Industry (MITI). The procedures were always the same. We would meet at an expensive Geisha house (an *okiya*), situated in a side street off the Ginza (a main shopping and business street). No women except the Geisha would be present. After name cards (*meishi*) had been exchanged, we would settle, cross-legged in the *seiza* position on *tatami* mats. Hostesses would make sure that we were well fed with tid-bits, saké and beer. Sometimes we would all play silly games with matchsticks. Later, after a good deal of saké had been drunk and more substantial food had been consumed, the Director of MITI would take off his jacket and urge us to sing. We would all oblige with 'Annie Laurie' and similar songs. Our Japanese hosts would quickly become sweaty and beetroot-red of complexion (perhaps because they were unused to spirituous liquors). All was gaiety, noise and frolic. But then at about 9pm precisely the Director would put on his jacket. We would follow suit. His red face and those of his colleagues would resume their customary pallor. Our red faces remained. Bows would be exchanged and we guests would leave. Our Japanese hosts stayed behind and we never did find out what they did after we had left.

*****

Our involvement in 'big C' culture sprang from the fairly frequent opportunities that came our way to attend concerts of classical music performed by the excellent NHK Symphony Orchestra in Tokyo. There was also music with a different flavour presented by visiting groups such as the Alfred Deller Consort, Barry Tuckwell (a virtuoso of the French horn), Stanley Black and his Orchestra, Lionel Hampton and Duke Ellington and his Band. We also enjoyed Western drama, plays performed by visiting and local groups and traditional Japanese Kabuki, Bunraku and Noh performances.

As a cultural attaché, I would from time to time receive invitations to attend performances at Tokyo's splendid National Theatre and at the popular 'Kabuki-za'. According to a leaflet distributed at the latter theatre, the Kabuki-za opened for business in 1889. In October 1921, the theatre was unfortunately burned to the ground by a fire caused by an electrical short circuit. Restoration was under way when the still unfinished new structure was damaged by the great earthquake that struck the Kanto area of Japan on 1 September, 1923. Re-construction was finally completed in 1924. The new theatre was said to be fire-proof and earthquake proof but it could not withstand a massive air raid by American bombers on 25 May 1945. For a third time the theatre rose from the ashes and was again rebuilt.

Many *kabuki* plays focus on domestic issues but some address larger themes. The well-known *Kandehon Chusingura* (*The Treasury of Loyal Retainers*), for example, recounts the story of the forty-seven *ronin* who revenge their master's killer before honorably committing *seppuku* (a form of ritual suicide).

In Tokyo in October 2007 we were fortunate enough to see Bando Tamasaburo, a distinguished *onnagata* (an actor specialising in female roles), in the play *Kaidan Botan Doro*, a ghost story which draws upon a real-life incident involving a shogun vassal who lived in Ushigome (Tokyo). This was not tragedy on the scale of *Kandehon Chusingura* but it was a gory enough tale of deceit and betrayal.

My impression of the Kabuki-za theatre in 2007 was that it had become more refined since my visits in the late 1960s. The padded seats were much more comfortable, the lighting seemed to be more subtle and the behaviour of the audience was certainly more orderly. The physical features of the theatre had improved. Coin lockers are provided for outdoor clothing. There is a dining room in the basement serving such Japanese-style dishes as Tempura, Sushi and Unagi. There is a 'tea parlour' on the main floor and a variety of drinks and sandwiches can be bought at a cafeteria on the third floor. Programmes are available in different languages 'to further your appreciation and understanding of Kabuki'.

While the Kabuki-za and its linked Shingbashi Enbujo theatres are part of the Shochiku Company in Tokyo, the National Theatre is subsidised by the Japanese government. In the 1960s, the National Theatre devoted nine of the twelve months of the year to *kabuki* performances; one month to a *bunraku* programme and one month to a festival for young Kabuki actors. I do not know if this arrangement still exists.

The *kabuki* performances were puzzling at first but became less so as their origins became clearer. The first appearance of this theatrical form is often attributed to the 'renegade' princess *Okumi*, dating back to the beginning of the Tokugawa era (1603–1867). It originally had associations with prostitution and 'cross-dressing' but eventually developed a wide repertoire of history plays, domestic tragedies and plays that dwelt on social indignities and scandals. The *kabuki* was reformed in the nineteenth century and the link with overt prostitution was broken.

In the 1960s a boost was given to *kabuki* by television performances starring actors such as Shinnosuke, Kikunosuke, Tatsunosuke and, a little later, Kankuro Nakamura and Mitsuteru Nakamura.

In some ways, the *kabuki* at the beginning of the seventeenth century resembled early Shakespearean theatre. Both types of play drew their plots from historical events and favoured elaborate costuming. Each performance featured boy actors who played the roles of women and each provided opportunities for intimacy between actor and audience. Performances took place in the daytime and scenery was minimal, much being left to the imagination:

> Can this Cock Pit hold
> The vastie fields of France? Or may we cramme
> Within this woodden O, the very Caskes
> That did Affright the Ayre at Agincourt?[3]

Joruri (or puppet) kabuki 'plays' can be enjoyed either at the National Theatre or at the Kabuki-za. When they were originally presented, the performances did not allow for improvisation – dialogues could not be altered because the spoken lines had to mesh with the movements of the puppets. Eventually, these restrictions were modified when *joruri* pantomimic movements were introduced, based on gestures made by the puppets and focusing on everyday habits such as drinking tea, combing hair, opening doors, etc.

I was fortunate to arrive in Tokyo during the year when the National Theatre opened and when the two linked seventeenth-century arts – *kabuki* and *bunraku* – were revived and presented regularly in the new venue. In 1985 *kabuki* and *bunraku* were provided with a second regular venue when the National Bunraku Theatre opened in Osaka.

At one of my visits to the National Theatre in Tokyo, I was invited backstage to meet some of the puppeteers. I was told (and I have no reason to believe that my informant was incorrect) that many years of apprenticeship were necessary before a person could be regarded as an experienced *bunraku* performer. An apprentice would begin by being given the responsibility of manipulating the left leg. After some months, and in some cases years, he would be promoted to the right leg. Then again, after a further period of years, he would be given the left arm; then the right arm. His final achievement would be when he was given the honour of manipulating the head.

*****

At some time in 1968 or 1969, I went to a supermarket in Tokyo to buy some butter. The store happened to be next door to a small shop which

254

sold artists' brushes, paints, scrolls and woodblock prints (*ukyo-e*). In spite of a conscious anxiety that I was risking a mess of melted butter (it didn't happen), I walked into the shop simply to 'have a look'. I came out half-an-hour later with a very thin wallet. In exchange for 'x' number of yen I had become the proud owner of four antique woodblock prints, two of these attributed to Toyokuni (portraits of *kabuki* actors in action), one to Eishi, 'Selecting Fans' (1790) and one to Utamoro, 'Famed Beauties in Chusingura' (1785).

One of several styles of traditional painting, *Ukiyo-e* ('floating world') had its roots in *Yamato-e*, a form of painting and printing that depicted the interests and activities of the military classes and the nobility. After the power struggle that took place following the unification of Japan by Toyotomi Hideyoshi circa 1590, Ieayasu Tokugawa was made shogun and moved the nation's capital to Edo (present-day Tokyo). Society now found itself to be bound by rigid rules. One result of this was the gradual development of a plebian culture. Many Edo people within that culture were attracted to the brothels of Yoshiwara but also to a form of art which included the puppet theatre, *kabuki*, music, popular literature and poetry. *Ukiyo-e* paintings during the period 1660 to 1740 reflect this world of individualist pleasures within a rather rigid class structure. *Ukiyo-e* art reached its peak during the eighteenth century and the first half of the nineteenth century. Contributors to the artistic league tables generally agree that the most significant artists were Harunobu (1724–79), Shunsho (1726–92) Utamoro (1752–1806) Toyokuni (1768–1824) and Hiroshige (1799–1858). I was happy to have secured a Toyokuni and an Utamoro.

In 1969, after several months of negotiation and a lapse of many years, the British Council Representative in Hong Kong (Robin Duke) was able, with the help of colleagues in London, to arrange for the first visit of a Noh troupe to Britain. Such a visit had not taken place since before the Second World War, when a number of performances were given under the benevolent eye of the stage designer, Gordon Craig.

I do not have a copy of the 1969 London programme but I understand that several of the Zen-influenced plays took place against traditional backdrops of single, painted pines. They were made acceptable to London audiences by adding short, farcical 'kyogen' (wild words), customarily used to relieve the strain of the Noh performances which probably featured almost static *Shite* (principal actor) dances consisting of five movements.

For those interested, Tokyo provides an ideal opportunity to learn and practise one or more of the martial arts. At least three of the lecturers appointed by the British Council to Japanese universities on contractual terms made full use of this opportunity and I know that two of them achieved 'black belt' standard in Japan. I was able to visit the 'kodokan' in Tokyo on several occasions, observing athletes at work, practising 'kendo' (the way of the sword), 'kenjutsu' (swordsmanship), 'jujutsu' and other arts.

'Sumo' was a sport that was quite new to us when we arrived in Japan. We were introduced to it one evening by Professor Susumu Suzuki. It was Tokyo's turn for a tournament. Three of these are held each year in Tokyo and one in each of Osaka, Nagoya and Fukuoka. Each tournament lasts for fifteen days. I found the rules of sumo to be as confusing as those of baseball. In a small, square, open box – reserved, no doubt, by the Professor at considerable expense – and nourished by pickles and saké, we struggled to learn the rules and regulations of this ancient form of wrestling. It seems that sumo was introduced in ancient times to entertain the Shinto gods. It is still very popular today and has benefited – as have cricket, tennis, golf, soccer, horse and car racing – from regular television coverage.

The sumo wrestlers themselves are impressive, huge, fleshy men nourished on large quantities of milk, rice and other fattening foods, some of which they stuff into themselves before sleeping so as to gain body mass. I do not know of any studies that have been carried out to determine the life expectancy of a professional sumo wrestler but if obesity is a factor in longevity then such a life must be relatively short.

Kabuki, bunraku and Noh performances were enjoyable and interesting. The same must be said about the Western professional and amateur theatrical manifestations that I was fortunate enough to experience during my all-too-short period of residence in Japan. Following initiatives taken by the British Council in London, I was responsible for making the *in situ* arrangements for three of these entertainments myself. These were a visit by the actor Max Adrian and two visits by the 'London Shakespeare Group'.

Max's real name was Maximilian Bor. He had made a name for himself over many years as a gifted player in intimate London revues such as 'Sweet and Low' and 'Penny Plain and Tuppence Coloured'. His versatility was such that he appeared, for at least one season, at what was then known as the Shakespeare Memorial Theatre (now the Royal Shakespeare Company). It is rare for a revue artist to appear in 'legitimate' theatre but Max enjoyed excellent reviews for his performance as Puck in a well-received production of *A Midsummer Night's Dream*.

Max came to Tokyo to present a one-man show about the life of George Bernard Shaw. I met him at Haneda Airport in 1967. He had travelled first class from London but his manager, who accompanied him, had travelled economy class. Either before the flight left London or during the flight, the two had an argument and during their entire stay in Tokyo refused to speak to each other. From time to time this caused some difficulty! That problem aside, Max gave several 'bravura' performances to full houses and the University literary establishment turned out in full force. I have a taped recording made of a conversation between Max and my friend, Professor Ozu of Tokyo University. The conversation took place at the old Imperial Hotel in Tokyo where Max was staying. Max began by revealing that he knew Shaw personally and perhaps to colour his account a little, reminisced about the time when as a little boy he met the great man at the seaside. Said Max (in a rich, but exaggerated, fake Irish accent): 'There he was, Professor – that great-bearded man – and there was I. He took me up in his arms and perched me on his shoulder and we both gazed out to sea. Oh, it was a wonderful sight!'

I have a letter from Max written at the Cyprus Hilton and dated 28 June 1967, thanking us for entertaining him to lunch in Tokyo and continuing:

And about time too, you will say! I'm ashamed to have taken so long to write. It's just that one puts off now what one should do today. Hong Kong was frantically social and so was Tehran and Dr Shwa really materialised there but I did not enjoy the performance, nor the arrangements. However, all is past, but the memory of your unfailing kindness and warm friendliness to me will never fade. I cannot thank you enough for everything. You were perfectly splendid from the moment when we met at Haneda, right through those interminable waits you had in the little ante-room, to your very kind watching of the plane departing, Verner. What splendid hosts you were. Thank you and thank you for my little Saké flask and cups with which I shall have so much fun. I flew from Hong Kong with JAL to Tehran and whiled away a tedious and horribly bumpy flight with a flask or two...

I gave a final performance here in the Ballroom, very grand. I had intended staying in Limasol. We took one look and came straight back here where I live in luxury and happiness. The Managing Director is charmingly kind, his wife and family likewise and I have my friend, Lister, here to share the fun, the sun and the far-above-my-station comforts.

I hope your small family return safely to England and that you spend a lovely summer together. I shall often think of you and your warm kindness. With all good wishes and thanks for everything,
Very sincerely,
Max

– 26 –

How English Works

In 1967, a performing ensemble named the London Shakespeare Group (LSG) was formed in London by a disabled actor named Peter Potter, with the assistance of the British Council. The group – obviously with a changed cast – was still performing in different parts of the world in the 1980s. During its tour of Japan, its only purpose was to visit Japanese universities, perform extracts from the Shakespeare canon and then discuss meanings, language and characterisation from the professional actors' perspective.

Led by Peter Potter, the first group featured June Jago, Kate Binchy, Bill Corduroy and Tom Criddle. Criddle achieved a certain amount of fame in the early 1940s as 'The Boy Soprano, Master Thomas Criddle'. When his voice broke, he took (successfully) to acting.

The members of the group were a talented and courteous quartet who certainly enhanced the reputation of Shakespeare in Japan. The formula worked very well and the group proved to be very popular, more popular perhaps than the Royal Shakespeare Company which gave superb performances in Tokyo and Osaka in 1969, but only in those cities. The London Shakespeare Group was able to visit the smaller cities and perform in relatively small halls at universities. They were able to reach more people.

In 1968, I was fortunate enough to have the opportunity to direct, for a second time, Sir John Vanbrugh's play, *The Relapse, or Virtue in Danger*. I was lucky, also, to be able to cast a former member of the Shakespeare Memorial Theatre, Terence Knapp, in the role of Lord Foppington.

Terence was the first actor to be given a Churchill Memorial Fellowship. This enabled him to spend a year in Japan as a British Council Scholar studying the Japanese classical theatre and also working as a voice teacher. I remember Terry very well because, after leaving Japan, he joined the University of Hawaii Drama Department where I met him several years later. It was whilst he was in Hawaii that he wrote and performed for American Public Television his own one-man show about Father Damien. As is well known, Damien lived with and ministered to lepers on the Hawaiian island of Molokai and died after catching the disease himself.

During his relatively short stay in Tokyo, Terence busied himself outside the theatre by recording the reminiscences of 'Queenie' Day-Mason. A charming Englishwoman then (1968) in her early eighties, Queenie had suffered during the devastating earthquake that struck Yokohama on 1 September 1923, destroying ninety per cent of Yokohama and sixty per cent of Tokyo and killing over a hundred and ten thousand citizens.

Queenie Day was a pillar of the Tokyo Amateur Dramatic Society and took part in numerous productions for over sixty years. Many tales were told about this indomitable lady. One of the best is about the time in 1966 when, at the age of eighty, she was given a small part in the farce, *Charley's Aunt*. George Furness, another veteran (only seventy years old) played alongside Queenie but inadvertently cut one of her lines. In a dignified way, she turned to George and said, 'I haven't quite finished, George.' 'I'm sorry, Queenie,' he replied. The audience loved it.[1] Queenie was ninety-eight when she died in 1981.

At the age of twelve, Linda Purl appeared as a page in *The Relapse*. Linda is the daughter of Ray and Marshie Purl, friends in Tokyo who were heavily involved in various dramatic activities. After a spell studying theatre in England, Linda settled in the United States. She continued to perform and eventually became much in demand on TV, stage and film. She is still very active in the theatre. Linda's sister, Mara, is an author (of some four novels and three non-fiction books) and a script writer. She created 'Milford-Haven USA', a big hit on BBC radio with approximately 4.5 million listeners.

A second London Shakespeare Group came to Tokyo in 1969. This time it was directed by Tom Criddle and included Maria Aitken, the granddaughter of the late Lord Beaverbrook.

The London Festival Ballet arrived in Japan in October 1969 with two productions, *The Sleeping Beauty* and *Coppelia*, both directed by Beryl Grey, formerly primary ballerina with England's Royal Ballet. Under Grey's direction, the Principal Artists included John Gilpin, Galina

Samtsov, Seraphina Landsown, Terry Hayworth, Jorge Salavisa and Lynn Seymour, one of Nureyev's favourite ballerinas.

As mentioned above, performances by the Royal Shakespeare Company (RSC) in 1969 proved to be a major attraction in Tokyo and Osaka. For the RSC it was the first leg of a foreign tour that would continue into 1970 with productions of *Twelfth Night* and *The Merry Wives of Windsor*. I was given courtesy tickets for the third production, *The Winter's Tale*, directed by Trevor Nunn. The strong cast included the future Oscar winner Judi Dench and the well-known television (and stage) actor, Patrick Stewart.

In 1975, I was to bring Patrick Stewart and three other RSC actors to the East–West Center in Honolulu to perform and to conduct seminars similar to those offered by the London Shakespeare Group. It was later in his very successful career that Stewart began to play the leading role in the television series, *Star Trek*. Stewart is a Yorkshireman and is now a well-respected Chancellor of the University of Huddersfield. He has recently returned to the 'legitimate' theatre and in 2006 and early 2007 gave much admired performances in productions of *Much Ado About Nothing* at the Swan Theatre in Stratford and *Antony and Cleopatra* at the Novello Theatre in London.

Actors are sentimental people. The RSC cast on tour had invented a walk-on role for a small boy, named Sam Rich. Sam's father, Roy Rich – a well-known broadcaster[2] – had died just before the Company left for its tour overseas. Sam was brought along, not for any acting ability that he might possess, but rather to help him through the family tragedy.

The RSC had a tragedy of its own to deal with at its next stop. A young, hard-drinking actor named Charles Thomas (Orsino in *Twelfth Night*) was found dead in his hotel room in Melbourne. Richard Pasco stepped into the breach on condition that he did not have to wear Thomas's costume, perhaps because of a theatrical superstition.

*****

When we lived in Indonesia, we were, from time to time, able to enjoy the company of diplomats from other countries. As mentioned earlier, one such person was Charlie Finan who enriched his day job in the US Embassy's Information Section by composing for the musical theatre. He encouraged me to play the drums and was polite enough not to wince when I tried to do so.

I received similar encouragement in Tokyo from the Cultural Affairs Officer at the US Embassy. I have forgotten the officer's name, but not his kindness. It was he who presented me with tickets for a concert by Duke Ellington and his Band and gave me the opportunity to meet the jazz pianist, Teddy Wilson and the vibraphone player, Lionel Hampton.

Teddy Wilson was well known and respected by jazz enthusiasts as a brilliant accompanist to the jazz singer, Billie Holiday. He was also a superb soloist, although he did not perform during his short visit to Japan. He impressed me as a gentle man, slightly bewildered by the warm reception that he received from Japanese musicians and record producers at a reception that I attended one evening, courtesy of the Cultural Affairs Officer.

In 1969, Lionel Hampton's visit was sponsored by the USO which, I believe, had arranged for him to give only one public concert. It was thus a rare opportunity for me when I was invited to meet Hampton at a private function held in the US Ambassador's house. The Ambassador was away and the Chargé d'Affaires acted as host. Being a jazz fan himself, he took the opportunity of Hampton's visit to invite a number of Japanese musicians to tea and canapés at about 4.30pm. The idea was that Hampton and his band (vibraphone, string bass, drums, trumpet, trombone, alto saxophone, tenor saxophone) would play for an hour during the munching and slurping. Then everybody would go home.

All went according to plan until the end of the first 'set' when someone suggested that the Japanese musicians present might like to take part in a 'jam session'. Mild pandemonium followed. Some of the Japanese musicians had had the foresight to bring their instruments. Others rushed away to fetch them and arrived back at the residence, sweating and anxious but delighted at the opportunity that they had been given. After a short interval the jam session began, involving Hampton and his band and a dozen or so eager Japanese players, enjoying a lifetime's thrill. Tea was abandoned. The Chargé d'Affaires called for whisky. Afternoon became evening and the last excited guests left at midnight.

There was only one slightly sour note and that was heard during the tea break (and before the whisky). One of the Japanese musicians enquired about Hampton's age. It was intended to be a perfectly polite enquiry but it was not at all well received. Hampton was then sixty-one and his playing was as crisp as ever. He lived until he was ninety-four.

By 1969 the popular music scene in Britain had changed completely. Dancing had changed too. No longer did couples hold each other; rather they performed individual gyrations in front of (and sometimes behind) each other. A 'band' meant a group of three to four guitarists, plus a drummer who relied heavily on his (or her) bass drum and cymbals. One of the guitarists functioned as the lead singer but to fulfil this role, it was unnecessary to have a sweet voice. Raucousness was acceptable and some 'songs' were heavily laced with sexual innuendos.

The Stanley Black Orchestra was perhaps one of the last well-known 'big bands' of the post Second World War era. In those days a 'band' meant a complete rhythm section of drums, guitar, double bass and piano supporting three to four trumpets, four or five reed players (saxophones and clarinet) and two or three trombones.

Although the Beatles had descended upon the country in 1966 and other small groups such as The Rolling Stones were beginning to gain a reputation (for bizarre, substance-fuelled behaviour, as well as for their talents on stage), the 'big band sound' was still acceptable in Japan. Stanley Black and his Orchestra fitted perfectly into that mould, playing tunes that were written, most likely, in the years between the 1920s and the 1960s as well as up-to-date versions of melodies written by such composers as Irving Berlin, Jerome Kern and Cole Porter.

The Stanley Black Orchestra was brought to Japan by an independent impresario, rather than by the British Council, but I was interested in the Orchestra for two reasons. First, because I knew something of Stanley Black's musical background. He and another musician, named White, were a piano-playing duo in a band led by the well-known Harry Roy, a favourite of England's debutantes. 'Black and White' on two pianos had been very popular. Second, because the guitarist with the Stanley Black Orchestra happened to be a certain Dick Abell (Ah-Bell) who played regularly with dance bands in Singapore and in particular for an orchestra contracted to Radio Malaya, led by a man with the odd name of *Cor Ryf*. I had met Dick a number of times during my part-time broadcasting days in Singapore, most often in the canteen.

*****

The musician Barry Tuckwell retired in 1996. He is a virtuoso with wind instruments, in particular, the French horn. He holds the record for being the most recorded horn player in the world, having made more than forty-five recordings. In 1969 he was sponsored by the British Council for an overseas tour, including Japan. During the tour, he would play with leading orchestras and give lectures to students at universities and conservatoires in Tokyo and Osaka.

I remember Barry well because of an incident involving one of Japan's high-speed 'bullet' trains, the *Shinkanzen*. Barry had given two very successful performances in Tokyo as a guest artist with the Japan Philharmonic Orchestra. His next stop was Osaka where he was to play with that city's excellent symphony orchestra and repeat his Tokyo lectures.

I accompanied Barry to the railway station in Tokyo. He had brought with him a long, wooden box that he had made himself and of which he was very proud. It contained a collection of modern and antique wind instruments that he described and played during his lectures.

We arrived at the station in good time to catch the train. Having completed the usual farewells, Barry got into the carriage. But then – suddenly – the automatic doors closed, firmly. Barry was in the train but his instruments were *outside* it on the platform. He was swept off to Osaka, deprived of the tools of his trade. We were obliged to take emergency action and, I believe, ferried his case to him in Osaka by helicopter. Fortunately, all was well. The precious box arrived in time for Barry's performance. A narrow squeak but not from one of Barry's horns.

*****

I believe that I had been in Japan for about a year when I was interviewed for a television programme broadcast by NHK, Japan's equivalent of the BBC. After that first (successful) interview I made regular radio broadcasts and TV appearances, most often for NHK but also for other – commercial – TV and radio stations. Mostly, the programmes focused on aspects of the English language (a favourite topic was the difference between British and American English) but as time went by I was involved in broadcasts of a different kind. For example, I was asked to do 'voice overs' for a number of NHK programmes that were compiled from that station's archives. I remember three in particular.

The first broadcast was based on an incident that took place during the Second World War. Tokyo suffered from heavy American bombing raids and this bombing intensified as the Americans island-hopped closer and closer to Japan. Eventually, the attacks from the air became so intense that the authorities decided to evacuate large numbers of children to the countryside. The evacuation of one such school and the subsequent return of the pupils and their teachers to Tokyo were photographed and recorded on film by the school doctor. His films were placed in several steel canisters and locked away in a school cupboard. Subsequently the school was bombed and razed to the ground but the canisters survived. I do not know how.

After the war was over, the canisters reappeared. They were given to the rebuilt school and a janitor placed them in a cupboard. Many years later – 1968 to be precise – they were discovered during a 'spring clean'. The principal of the school took the canisters to a producer at the NHK who had the films re-processed and a documentary made out of them, with my narration in English. The nice twist was that the NHK invited the evacuees – now adults – to a party at which they were accompanied by *their* children who all appeared in the programme.

The circumstances surrounding the second broadcast seem rather unbelievable but the incident upon which it was based rang true. The programme focused on the role played by a Japanese submarine during the Second World War. Returning to port after a long period at sea, the captain learned of Japan's surrender through a broadcast of the Emperor's speech. This was too hard a disgrace to bear. When his vessel was almost alongside, he committed 'seppuku' (hara-kiri, from 'hara' the belly and 'kiru' to cut) in the traditional manner.

The third broadcast featured a Japanese family in Kyoto whose son was born without arms. He was a victim of the drug, 'thalidomide'. At the time of his son's birth, the father was in lucrative employment with a well-known company in Kyoto. It was tempting to put the boy aside, as sometimes happened when Japanese babies were born with 'oddities'. But both the mother and father decided to stick with the boy. In consequence, they suffered many hardships. The father resigned from his company and the family moved to Tokyo where the father took a fairly humble job as a shoe salesman and found a special school for his son. The film ended with the boy triumphant, having won a major karate competition for handicapped persons. Here was an example of the quality of persistence so admired in Japan.

*****

In a Press interview reported in *The Independent* newspaper on 9 September 2006, Ms Jean L. Kekedo, the High Commissioner for Papua New Guinea in London, stated (in answer to an assertion made by the journalist – now Mayor of London – Boris Johnson) that cannibalism was stamped out in Papua New Guinea two hundred years ago. This statement, whilst diplomatically sensible, can hardly be correct since in 1969 I narrated a film in Tokyo that included scenes in which slices of human flesh were passed around a circle of tribal members. I remember the filming very well for we did not finish work until 4.30 in the morning, having started at 12 noon. In partial mitigation, I should say that the human meat came from a person who had died from natural causes.

*****

After negotiating with the Correspondence Education Division of the NHK for over a year, I was able to secure agreement for a new television programme. This was to be called *How English Works*. It would be written and presented by British Council staff every Saturday, but directed by an officer of the NHK.

The British Council had introduced a new employment category, that of Television Officer. We now had a vacancy for such a person. In 1968 I was on leave in England and took the opportunity to meet Dr Ian Calder, recently returned from Ghana and now appointed to fill the new post in Japan. Calder had had an interesting and many-sided career, first as a teacher and then as an actor in repertory. His doctoral dissertation was an analysis of the work of the computer pioneer Charles Babbage, rather far removed from his theatrical interests.

Ian is mentioned as a promising young writer in Margaret Drabble's biography of the writer, Angus Wilson. Calder told me that he managed to persuade Wilson to leave his job in the British Library to become a full-time novelist. But that was some time before Ian joined the British Council.

In due course, Ian came to Japan and was given a section of my office in which to write the first two or three programmes in the *How English Works* series. He was, I am sorry to write, painfully slow off the mark. But after causing the NHK director (and me) some considerable anxiety (for the programmes had been 'trailed' and booklets issued and printed), he produced the finished version of the first programme and some notes for the second and third. The formula was (1) an introduction by a Japanese speaker, usually a Professor of English, (2) a sketch (or as the Americans say a 'skit') in English, (3) comments by the Japanese Professor about the language of the sketch and (in the booklets) explanations in English of the idioms used in the sketch.

At the end of the programme that was aired on 4 April 1969, Ian gave what proved to be a valedictory message when describing the format for the following year. He became ill and had to be repatriated to Britain, accompanied by the Council Librarian. Writing the programmes and performing in the sketches would now be my responsibility until a new Television Officer could be appointed.

In the first year of the *How English Works* programmes, two fictitious British families, the Bradleys and the Lydgates, were featured. In contrast, I introduced 'Max Hunter', a British businessman (Hunter Associates) and his secretary 'Jane Portugal'. (I became rather proud of the latter's surname. I thought that it had an interesting 'ring'.) I continued to write, 'anchor' and appear in the programmes until a new Television Officer named Gillate was appointed towards the end of 1969. I had known Don Gillate many years before in Singapore. He taught in an Army school and worked occasionally for the Teachers' Training College as a part-time lecturer. After a 'settling in' period, Don took over the writing chores but I continued to take part in the sketches that he wrote until I left Japan in the late autumn of 1970.

*****

Japan is rightly praised for its many well-stocked museums and I was able to visit many of them during my time in the country. Two were of particular interest, one in the city of Niigata in Northern Honshu on the Sea of Japan and the other situated in the countryside, some miles from the city.

In late 1969, I was invited to give a lecture at Niigata University. After a pleasant journey by fast train, I was met at the Niigata Railway Station by an excited professor of English who took me straight to the hotel where I was to be lodged for the night. I was greeted in the lobby by some of the professor's colleagues and also by the curator of the Niigata Museum. After an exchange of greetings and cards (*meishi*), the curator invited me to stay with him, insisting that I should first visit his museum in the city. I explained that a room had been reserved for me at the hotel but he waived that aside and said that he would drive me to his house. Perhaps a little put out and certainly disappointed, my host, the professor, reluctantly agreed to this new arrangement and after my lecture I was whisked away in the curator's car, first to gaze at the artifacts in his city museum and then to enjoy a thirty-mile journey to his home. We were about five miles or so from the house when the curator pointed to the land on either side of the road. 'This was ours,' he said. 'All of it.' I nodded politely, humouring him. But he meant what he had said. I found out later that he came from a prominent 'daimyo' family whose lands had been confiscated after Japan's defeat in the War. I was still mumbling some sort of commiseration when we arrived at his house, or rather mansion. Oddly, I thought, we had to pass through a turnstile and submit to a guard's scrutiny before we could enter the house. It turned out to be a museum. The curator managed the city museum but he also lived in his *own* museum.

After a welcome drink (a large scotch and soda), I was taken along a corridor to my room. It had, the curator explained, been occupied once by the Emperor. It was not only a great honour to receive the Emperor in one's home but it was also most welcome since the surrounding roads had to be repaired and cleaned before his Imperial Highness arrived.

After a wash and brush up in my imperial bedroom, I was invited to dinner by my host, his American wife and a married couple visiting from the United States. The dinner was served by two men, clearly old family retainers. These were the men who manned the turnstiles during the day. I was impressed. First, at how they both slipped easily into their new roles. Second, because their party tricks included plunging their hands into bowls of boiling fat. These bowls contained some of the largest and juiciest prawns that I have ever seen or tasted.

I can only suppose that the reason why the men did not injure themselves seriously was because of the speed with which they acted.

I cannot say that I remember much of the dinner conversation since very large quantities of saké were served at regular intervals. I do vaguely remember being escorted to my room at the conclusion of the dinner and taking advantage of the large stone *o-furo* (bath) with which my bathroom was equipped.

In the morning, feeling somewhat disturbed after the previous evening's revelry, I enjoyed a conversation with my hostess whilst forcing down a fairly large Western breakfast. She told me that, although Niigata had its points, she was nevertheless quite lonely. Most of all she missed Tokyo's social life. Could I arrange for her to be invited to a cocktail party? I said that I would try. She also spoke about her daughter, a child of about six or seven. She feared that the child had been unduly influenced by certain aspects of Japanese culture, or at least Niigata's version of it. As an example, she spoke of a time when the countryside was snowbound. Despite the weather, her daughter still managed to go to school but failed to return home at the usual time. Her mother watched anxiously from the balcony of the old house. Suddenly the child appeared. She started to walk towards the house and then suddenly knelt down in the snow and refused to enter the house despite her mother's pleading. I asked if there was an explanation for this and my hostess said that the child had been punishing herself for some transgression at school.

The sad sequel to my extraordinary visit (as I learned several years later) was that the parents divorced and the mother took the child away, to live in a less demanding culture.

*****

In his book, *In Pursuit of Publishing*,[3] Alan Hill describes an 'ice-breaking' visit to Japan in 1968 by the heads of eleven British publishing houses. The visit was led by Mr John Brown, then Chief Executive of the Oxford University Press. All twelve of the publishing houses represented were members of the British Book Development Council, a body set up to try to establish close relationships between Britain and representatives of the book trade in other countries.

Apart from attending several receptions I had little to do with the mission myself. Given the seniority of members of the party, this was handled by the Representative, Robin Duke. I mention the mission in order to indicate the attitudes taken by some of the visitors to aspects of Japanese culture that were unfamiliar to them. Hill himself refers to the 'bowing and scraping' which was done to the welcoming party. A little later on in his description he refers to 'the usual bowing and scraping' that preceded a meeting with the Vice Minister of Education. Hill goes on to describe as follows, 'the first of many geisha dinner parties given by the President of Maruzen, the biggest bookseller in Japan'.

> Dear old Bob Lusty, head of Hutchinson's and Vice-Chairman of the BBC, was opposite me, seated uncomfortably on the floor in his stockinged feet, with a geisha girl kneeling beside him wiping his brow with a wet towel; Bob was trying to drink a bowl of seaweed soup, and saying:
> 'Oh dear! Oh dear! Whatever would they say to this in the Hampstead Garden Suburb!'

It took members of the mission some time to adjust to a very different cultural milieu but they rectified this to some extent in Kyoto, when all members of the party – except John Brown – indulged themselves with hot baths and massages. Hill clearly enjoyed reporting this:

She conducted me through a series of hot baths, in one of which I caught up with Max Reinhardt (Chairman of Bodley Head) and his masseuse, looking attractive in her lemon-coloured shorts. Max himself resembled a happily-boiled lobster. Eventually we arrived at the massage room, and I lay on a bed, face downwards. The massage involved wrenches on the limbs and chops on muscles and nerve centres of whose existence I had hitherto been unaware. Eventually the masseuse walked all over me, massaging me with her bare feet; then she knelt on my back, using her knees. This went on for an hour, front and back. I emerged feeling twenty years younger. Henceforward for the rest of the tour, Bruno (John Brown) – who would have none of it – had the bar all to himself at 6.00pm.

The exquisite nature of certain elements of traditional Japanese culture was made clear on the two occasions when I was invited – together with other consular and diplomatic representatives – to pay respects to Emperor Hirohito (Showa Tenno), the one hundred and twenty-fourth Emperor of Japan. In former times, guests at the Imperial Palace in Akasaka were expected to leave the Emperor's presence backwards. This custom was abandoned after the Second World War and it became necessary only to bow appropriately when in the Imperial presence. On both occasions that I attended, an elaborate buffet was laid out for the guests but no time was allowed to eat it. Instead, each guest was presented with Imperial tid-bits wrapped in a silken 'furoshike' (scarf). It was an honour to receive such a scarf and the sweetmeats inside it.

There is some controversy about whether or not Emperor Hirohito approved of the military aggressiveness of his generals and admirals at the beginning of and during the Second World War. He is, however, reported as saying to General Douglas MacArthur on 27 September 1945, 'I wanted very much to avoid war and I feel it is very regrettable that circumstances led to war.' He did indicate his determination to surrender to the Allies on 5 August 1945, to 'endure the unendurable'. In January 1946, he came down to earth and issued a statement denying his divinity.

Hirohito died on 7 January 1989, a respected marine biologist, if not a god.

– 27 –

Celebrities

The years 1969 and 1970 found us busier than ever in Tokyo. In September 1969 we moved from 'Green Fantasia' to a very pleasant house in the Yoyogi-Nishihara district. Built by a developer named 'Homat Homes', the house combined features of Japanese design with modern comforts. It was from this house that I continued to write scripts for NHK, made regular recordings for different educational organisations, lectured in Kyoto, Nagoya and Sendai, ran summer schools in 1969 and 1970 in Chiba (a town quite near to Tokyo) and assisted when required at various functions arranged for a number of distinguished visitors to Japan. Among these were Sir John Pope-Hennessy, Lord George-Brown, HRH The Princess Margaret, The Earl of Snowdon and His Royal Highness the Prince of Wales.

SIR JOHN POPE-HENNESSY

The Pope-Hennessys are a gifted but odd family. I became aware of them first at University when I came across (but cannot claim to have read) Una Pope-Hennessy's biographies of Dickens and Edgar Allan Poe. Her son, James Pope-Hennessy wrote extremely well and cemented his reputation as an author with his well-received biography of Queen Mary (then the Queen Mother), published in 1960. Unfortunately, his homosexuality may have led to his death. He was murdered by three young men in 1974, in his London flat.

Five years before James's death, I entertained his brother John at dinner in one of 'Green Fantasia's' basement restaurants. He was a courteous guest who displayed no sign of his reputation for abrasiveness and impatience. Sir John was then Director of the Victoria and Albert Museum and the well-respected author of such authoritative guides as *An Introduction to Italian Sculpture, Cellini* and *Donatello*. It is reasonable to suppose that he inherited his interest in art from Una who, in addition to her literary biographies, published two books on Chinese jade. John had a particular interest in small bronze statuettes and took the opportunity to search for examples of these in Tokyo and Kyoto. I do not know whether or not the search was successful.

John spent his last years with his partner Michael Mallon in Florence where he died in 1994. I did not know then that twenty-nine years later, Gillian and I would find it necessary to comment on the policies and behaviour of John's grandfather, the bumptious eighth Governor of Hong Kong.[1]

LORD GEORGE-BROWN

On several separate occasions, we joined diplomats and senior members of the business community at receptions held for British and foreign guests in the ballroom of the British Embassy. On one of these occasions the guest of honour was the MP for Belper, British Foreign Secretary, Mr George Brown, later Lord George-Brown. Before his promotion to the Foreign Office, Brown served as Deputy Secretary of the Labour Party and Minister of Economic Affairs. An able Parliamentarian, he also had a reputation for being rude, aggressive and a heavy drinker.

Shifting our legs, one to the other, we waited patiently for the great man to appear. Eventually he arrived, more than half-an-hour late and clearly 'tired and emotional'. Lurching through the double doors, he staggered to a central position in the room in the general direction of the Ambassador, making uncoordinated movements with his hands. Acknowledging the Ambassador with an uncertain wriggle, he started to speak, mangled a few sentences and then called thickly for a drink. I believe that it may have been the Minister himself (second only in rank to the Ambassador) who walked in stately fashion across the floor, took a glass of whisky from a waiter's tray, returned across the room and with false dignity bowed and gave the drink to the honoured guest. It was a carefully studied piece of insolence that completely passed over Brown's head.

It is only fair to note that some of the many stories about Brown's social behaviour have been said to be without substance, whilst his erratic behaviour has been put down to a chronic medical condition, rather than to over-indulgence in alcohol. The claim has also been made that he was one of the best Secretaries of State that Britain has had in relatively recent times.

PRINCESS MARGARET AND THE EARL OF SNOWDON

In 1969, Japan was honoured by a visit from HRH The Princess Margaret and the man who was then her husband, The Earl of Snowdon (Anthony Armstrong-Jones). The Princess and the Earl were visiting Japan in connection with a 'British Week' that turned out to be a very successful way of interesting a cross-section of Japanese people in British technology and British products.

The royal couple and their retinue arrived in Tokyo on 20 September 1969 on a British Airways aircraft. They were met at Haneda Airport by Her Imperial Highness The Princess Chichibu, together with representatives of the government of Japan and the British Ambassador.

I give below details of the royal couple's itinerary to indicate how hard such distinguished visitors must work when engaged on an official visit.

On the morning of 22 September, the royal couple visited the British Embassy to meet staff assembled in the garden of the Ambassador's residence. It was quite a chilly morning for September and in the line-up I remember wishing that I had worn a warmer suit.

The 22 September was a testing day for both the Princess and her consort. According to my diary, the brief meeting in the grounds of the Embassy was followed by an audience with Emperor Hirohito and the Empress at the Imperial Palace. Then followed a Court luncheon and in the late afternoon the visitors joined The Princess Chichibu for tea at the Akasaka Detached Palace. At 6.45pm they attended an informal cocktail party in the embassy, given largely for the benefit of invited members of the Press. At 7.30pm they dined at the Official Residence of the then Prime Minister of Japan, Mr Eisaku Sato. At 10.05pm, they returned to the Embassy, no doubt looking forward to nightcaps and a good night's sleep.

On 23 September, accompanied by the Ambassador and Lady Pilcher, the couple enjoyed their first experience of travel by 'Bullet Train'. Their destination was Kyoto, for two days of sight-seeing which included participating in a 'Tea Ceremony', attending a garden party, shooting the Hozu rapids, visiting Nijo-jo (the Shogun's Castle) and watching a demonstration of *kemari* football, an ancient game that dates back to the

Heian period (794–1185). The game is unique in that it is non-competitive, without losers or winners. The simple objective is to throw a deerskin ball into the air and keep it there. This was metaphorically the duty of the British Embassy, to keep a number of different balls in the air for the royal tour.

Thursday, 25 September was another busy day for the royal couple. First, a visit to the British Pavilion at the Osaka 'Expo' site and then back in Tokyo, to attend a reception at the Okura Hotel and to relax somewhat at the premiere of the film, *The Battle of Britain* at the Hibiya Theatre. Despite the stirring background music and the roar of the planes, I found it difficult to keep awake.

There was little opportunity for the Princess and the Earl (or their hosts) to rest on Friday, 26 September. Their itinerary included a ceremony at the National Theatre to launch 'British Week'. This was immediately followed by visits to the department stores Seibu, Tobu and Mitsukoshi, the Sony Building and the Science Museum. The long day ended with a reception at the Embassy.

On Saturday, 27 September there were more visits to department stores, followed by attendance first at a Gala Fashion Show, 'Fashion Happens in London', and then at a 'Loyal Societies Ball'. The Ball is probably still remembered by its survivors because it was so exhausting. Clearly, the Princess was blessed by extraordinary stamina despite her various unfortunate illnesses. She would not leave and we could not leave until she did, close to midnight.

The programme continued on Sunday, 28 September which included yet more visits to department stores (Isetan, Odakyu, Keio), and also to the Dunhill Shop and the Marubeni-Iida Gallery. Quite late in the evening, the Princess and her husband attended a reception given for the London Philharmonic Orchestra at the Ambassador's house. I remember that evening, in particular, because I was able to talk to one of the musicians about the bassoonist who twenty-five years earlier in 1944 had refused to be hypnotised at Aberdare Hall, Cardiff (see Chapter Six above).

This was not the end. Monday, 29 September began with a visit to a 'Hi-Fi' and Home Appliances Show. There were more visits to shops (Hankyu Department Store, the Pringle Shop, Meidi-ya Store, Maruzen, Sogo) and a drink at the Foreign Correspondents' Club.

Before the royal couple departed for London on 29 September, they attended at a lunch given by the Minister of Foreign Affairs and Mrs Aichi. Duty had been done, without complaint. I do hope that the royal pair were able to sleep on the plane.

PRINCE WILLIAM OF GLOUCESTER

In 1969 the main responsibility for planning British Week was placed in the hands of an experienced events organiser named Thorne. He was supported by a small team of six persons that included Prince William of Gloucester, ninth in succession to the British throne, but then holding the rank of Second Secretary (Commercial). The Prince was a pleasant man, quite free of 'side', and very easy to talk to. He had an eye for maturing ladies of elegance and who can blame him?

Only two years after serving as a member of the team that planned British participation in the 1970 Osaka Expo, the Prince was killed in a light plane crash near Halfpenny Green Airport in England. He was only thirty years old.

AMBASSADOR HOWARD CHERNOFF

Barely recovered from the excitement of British Week in September 1969, British diplomats continued to work with commercial representatives in planning for the Exposition to be held in Osaka in April 1970. This turned out to be an international competition waged

The British Ambassador, Sir Francis Rundall, Lady Rundall and Princess Chichibu at a Japan–British Society reception, 1966.

among different nations, each hoping for strengthened (and lucrative) commercial ties with Japan.

The national pavilions differed markedly in their external and internal designs. The British Pavilion was furnished in modern 1960s style, featuring developments in applied science, education, sport and entertainment.

The USA pavilion took the form of an innovative geodesic dome in which were exhibited up-to-the-minute technological advances of the kind made by commercial companies in Silicon Valley and supported by universities such as the Massachusetts Institute of Technology. The American effort was directed by Ambassador Howard Chernoff, a former Deputy Director of the United States Information Service. Early in his career, Howard served as General Manager of WCHS-AM Radio in West Virginia. From 1938 to 1948 Howard's wife, Melva served as host of the 'Miss 580 Club', a phone-in show.

I was to meet Howard fairly frequently when, at Henry Kissinger's request, he was appointed a Governor of the East–West Center in Hawaii. On one occasion, I stayed with Howard and Melva in their comfortable San Diego apartment.

HRH THE PRINCE OF WALES

HRH The Prince of Wales's visit to Japan in the spring of 1970 was timed to coincide with the Exposition. His programme was as tiring as that arranged for his aunt and her husband a year before.

On 9 April, the Ambassador and Lady Pilcher found themselves, once again, at Haneda Airport to greet their most honoured guest. At 6pm the same evening, Mr Shigenobu Shima, Grand Master of the Ceremonies at the Imperial Household, visited the British Embassy to convey Imperial Greetings to His Royal Highness. He brought with him from the Emperor an invitation to dinner that night. The dinner was preceded at the Embassy by a reception for Commonwealth Representatives.

On 10 April the young Prince left Tokyo Station for Kyoto by 'Bullet Train'. The Ambassador and Lady Pilcher were his hosts at a 'tempura' Japanese luncheon taken at the Miyako Hotel. Lunch was followed by short visits to the Imperial Palace (Gosho), the Nijo-jo (Shogun's Castle) and the Ryoanji (sand garden). In the evening, His Royal Highness joined a reception given by the Japan–British Society at the Miyako Hotel.

HRH Prince Charles at a Japan–British Society reception (with the British Ambassador, Sir John Pilcher), Tokyo, Japan, 1970.

On Saturday, 11 April the real business of the visit began, with a breakfast served at the New Zealand Pavilion on the 'Expo' site in Osaka. Still digesting breakfast, for which only half-an-hour was allowed, the Prince walked through the British, Japanese, India, Netherlands, Belgium and USSR pavilions and the 'Symbol Area'.

Following what must have been a welcome lunch at the British Pavilion, the Prince and his party visited thirteen other pavilions, ending up (with some relief no doubt) at the Amusement Area.

On Sunday, 12 April the Prince paid a pre-breakfast private visit to the Sambo-in Garden and later attended a luncheon hosted by the Imperial Household Agency. In the evening, back in Tokyo, he attended another reception given by the Ambassador at the Embassy.

On Monday, 13 April the Prince began his day by meeting members of the Embassy staff at the Embassy. He then lunched at the Togu Palace with the Crown Prince and the Crown Princess, before proceeding through the gardens of the Palace to meet HRH The Princess Chichibu.

In the early evening, the Prince and some members of his entourage attended a reception given by the Japan–British Society at the Nihon Kogyo Club in the Marunouchi District. My photograph of this affair shows a very young Prince, talking to Princess Chichibu. The Ambassador, Sir John Pilcher is in serious mood. Another photograph in my collection shows his predecessor, Sir Francis Rundall seemingly in a much happier mood at a reception given by the same organisation in 1947.

Tuesday, 14 April was the Prince's last day in Japan. In the morning, he was accompanied by his cousin Prince William on a tour of the Ishikawajima-Harima Industries Shipyard in Yokohama. After enjoying a free afternoon, he and his entourage left Haneda by the BOAC Polar Flight BA 851 for London.

No doubt the Prince was exhausted. We certainly were.

THE NINTH STEP
HAWAII TO HONG KONG

– 28 –

Return to the Service

After Prince Charles's visit to Japan had ended, I travelled to Osaka in the company of Dr Floyd Cammack, an American linguist with whom I had attended various meetings on educational topics. Cammack took part on a regular basis in a TV language learning programme that ran parallel to the British Council programme, *How English Works*.

At first, we went our separate ways at the 'Expo'. I had been charged by the NHK with the task of recording interviews with a few of the Exposition's 'hostesses', most of whom had been recruited from some of Tokyo's best girls' schools. Later, Floyd and I met up again and travelled back to Tokyo in each other's company. During the journey, Floyd mentioned that Dr Everett Kleinjans, Chancellor (later President) of the East–West Center in Hawaii, might be interested to receive an application from me for a senior post in a new Research Institute in Honolulu. The newly established Institute was to focus on language and cultural issues as well as to conduct training programmes, largely for countries in the Pacific Region.

I was intrigued by the thought of working in Hawaii and, in particular, by the *modus operandi* of the Center. Classified as a tertiary, academic institution, it conducted research along problem-focused rather than disciplinary lines, bringing together scholars from different countries, cultures and disciplines to work together on significant problems.

The upshot was that I was interviewed by Dr Kleinjans and his deputy, John (Jack) Brownell after I returned to Tokyo. At the end of the interview it was agreed that we would visit the Center in the later autumn of 1970.

After a relaxing week in Hawaii, punctuated by meetings with Dr Kleinjans and Jack Brownell, we flew to Vancouver, Banff and Toronto for a short visit before flying to London to open up our house in Kent and begin a period of home leave. Two or three weeks went by without a word. Winter set in but no word came from Hawaii and it seemed that the East–West Center had decided not to make an offer. Then, one afternoon, we received a telephone call from Heathrow Airport. The caller, Jack Brownell, asked if we had decided not to reply to their cable of 12 February 1971. I replied, 'What cable?'

For some reason known only to the British Post Office the cable had not been delivered and Jack was obliged to bring it to us himself. The upshot was that, after very careful deliberation, I resigned from the British Council and accepted the offer of a full Professorship in English as a Second Language at the University of Hawaii (subject to approval of tenure). This appointment was to run concurrent with a senior associate position at the East–West Center.

A year later, I was appointed Director of the Center's Culture (and Language) Learning Institute. In that capacity, and starting more or less from scratch, I developed a tertiary level, multi-disciplinary Institute, staffed eventually by linguists, anthropologists, cross-cultural psychologists and literature specialists. The Institute focused on policy-focused culture learning issues that were pertinent across national and disciplinary boundaries.

I had enjoyed my years with the British Council but now, in Hawaii, there were new challenges to face in an apparently similar but really quite different culture.

*****

I stayed in Hawaii for a stimulating period of ten years until October 1981 when I took up a short-term post in Jeddah as Head of Language Training for Saudi Arabian Airlines. Then, in the early autumn of 1983, I came 'home', at least in one way. I was appointed Director of the Hong Kong government's Institute of Language in Education with the rank of Assistant Director of Education. I had returned to the Overseas Civil Service, although that name was no longer used. My new appointment made it possible for me to claim a period of seventeen years of employment with the Colonial/Overseas Civil Service.

I spent nine fruitful years with the Service until I retired in 1992, five years before Hong Kong was returned to China.

– 29 –

Reflections

This has been the story of a long and continuing adventure in four of my seven plus decades, beginning in the year 1926. So far, I have spent twenty-four years in the country of my birth and fifty-eight years in Asian and Pacific countries, three of which have changed their names (Ceylon, Burma and Hong Kong). It would be fanciful to claim that I left England in a search for self-definition, or a fortune, or because I was unhappy. Rather, like many other people, my first spell abroad was determined by wartime exigencies and my second time overseas by career obligations. These experiences were so interesting and absorbing that, on the whole, Asian affairs for me took precedence over developments elsewhere, including in my own country.

Of course, in my subsequent life it was not possible to ignore completely the significance and consequences of the colonial retreat from Africa, the savage conflict in Biafra, the Bay of Pigs and Cuban Missile Crisis, the Prague Spring, the Suez debacle, Civil Rights marches, the self-indulgent hippy movement, the slaughter in Rwanda and Darfur and the wars in Iraq. But, in so far as I shifted at all outside my box as Institute director, departmental head, broadcaster and temporary diplomat, I thought much more about social and political developments in the countries in which I served, rather than those in far away Africa, the Caribbean, the Middle East, Europe or the United States.

At the time of my first visits to Ceylon and India in 1945 and 1946, both countries were on the verge of political independence. Two months had passed since the Second World War had come to a sudden end. Elsewhere, the Japanese occupation of Indo-China had successfully upset the *status quo*, leading to an intensified struggle for 'freedom' from what had become regarded as the colonial yoke. Malaya (and, to some extent, Singapore) was involved in an armed struggle against Chinese insurgents. This was characterised as an 'Emergency'. Later, when terrorism was in retreat in Malaya, frequent cries of 'Merdeka' (independence) could be heard as neighbouring Singapore edged more slowly but surely towards its transition from a Colony to an independent State. A newly freed Burma began its unhappy search for a new role. Indonesia, under Sukarno, set its sights on Borneo and engaged in a policy of 'confrontation' with Britain, Singapore, Malaya and Sarawak. Japan began to emerge as a major economic power.

Four questions proved to be of common interest and were discussed vigorously in 1978, at a conference organised by my Institute at the East–West Center. In my Foreword to a book reporting the proceedings of this conference, I referred to these.[1] Who uses the English language today? In what circumstances is it used? What varieties of the language are used for what purposes by individuals within a country, that is, *intranationally*, and what varieties of the language are used by individuals for purposes of *international* communication? These questions laid the groundwork for a vigorous discussion of the roles of emergent forms of English in countries such as India where English was in frequent use, but in a de-anglicised way.

Speakers at the Hawaii conference noted that these emergent forms were creating a *distance* between native varieties of English on the one hand and non-native varieties on the other. This distinction raised questions of intelligibility and the need to ensure that persons using different varieties of English can communicate successfully with each other. These questions continue to be raised and discussed with equal interest, passion and urgency.

I mention the present position of English in the world to draw attention to the significance of Britain's legacy to the countries that she once ruled. That the English language is still valued is something of a bonus for Britain, although it does not necessarily ensure the maintenance of amicable relations with her former colonial possessions. Neither does it guarantee positive results when one former colony negotiates with another through the medium of English.

My first visit to Asia took place when I was nineteen-and-a-half, a young (very young) naval officer. It was in India and Ceylon that I first learned something about managing people. Years later, this stood me in good stead as an Education Officer and broadcaster in the Colonial

Education Service in Singapore; as a British Council Officer, broadcaster and temporary cultural diplomat in Burma, Indonesia and Japan; as the head of a policy-orientated research and training Institute in Hawaii and (returning to the Overseas Civil Service) as Director of a Government Language Institute in Hong Kong.

What did it all amount to? What did I achieve? I have been fortunate to have been able to serve for over fifty years outside my own country in a fascinating variety of positions in both the public and corporate sectors. I have learned a great deal over the many years. But what impact, if any, did I have on other people's lives?

How did the nervous Singaporean student teacher to whom I gave a leading part in an opera benefit from the experience? In what ways did my students in Singapore, Burma and Indonesia gain from my teachings and broadcasts? Were my lectures, radio and TV scripts in Rangoon, Jakarta and Tokyo of value to the listeners and viewers? As a part-time diplomat in Japan, did I represent Britain's interests successfully? Do the hundreds of graduate students, scholars and researchers in my Hong Kong and Hawaiian Institutes remember their experiences with satisfaction? Only they would be able to tell.

Now, in (so-called) retirement, I find myself to be busier than ever as the Chairman of the Executive Committee of the English-Speaking Union (Hong Kong), a registered non-profit educational charity which has set itself the task of providing opportunities for Hong Kong people to broaden their social contacts through the English language and to advance their knowledge of English as the language of the 'global village'.

I still maintain my British connections and am grateful for the opportunities given to me by the Colonial Education Service and the Overseas Civil Service, both now, sadly, defunct. It would be remiss of me not to acknowledge my debt to the British Council, an organisation which is still very much alive and is certainly a power for good.

NOTES

PREFACE

1   Lee Kuan Yew, *The Singapore Story*, Simon and Schuster (Asia) Pte Ltd under the Prentice Hall imprint, 1998.
2   R.K. Narayan, *My Days*, Picador, 2001.
3   Michael Ondaatje, *Running in the Family*, Picador, 1982.
4   Simon Baker in *The Spectator* Magazine, vol. 302, no. 9305, 9 December 2006.

CHAPTER ONE

1   L. P. Hartley, *The Go-Between* (1953), prologue, Penguin Books, 1958.
2   Rafael Núñez and Eve Sweetser, 'With the Future Behind Them: Convergent Evidence From Aymara Language and Gesture in the Cross-Linguistic Comparison of Spatial Construals of Time', *Cognitive Science*, vol. 30, 2006.
3   Norman Ellison ('Nomad'), *The Wirral Peninsula*, Robert Hale Limited, February 1967, p. 202.
4   In particular at the Baldernock Parish Church in Scotland.
5   Mrs Henry Wood, *Verner's Pride*, Richard Bentley and Son, 1898, p. 3.
6   Leslie G. Matthews, *Antiques of the Pharmacy*, Book Two, Pharmaceuticals Limited, Meadowbank, Hounslow, Middlesex, 1983.
7   The Charron-Laycock was a high quality 'light' car. Its design earned it the reputation of a miniature Rolls Royce. William Samuel Laycock ran a railway and steamship fittings company. Charron was a French motor manufacturer who held a majority holding in Laycock's company. Laycock and Charron made between five hundred to seven hundred cars between 1919 and 1926. See http://projects.lowtech.org/words-n-wheelscharron-laycock1921.html

CHAPTER TWO

1   Children's magazines such *Wizard, Adventure, Hotspur* and others, published either by Alfred Harmsworth's, Amalgamated Press or D.C. Thomson and Company.

2   J.B. Priestley, *English Journey*, William Heinemann in association with Victor Gollancz, 1934.
3   'Joey' – the slang word for a small coin worth three pence.

CHAPTER THREE

1   Clement Vavasor Durell, *General Arithmetic*, G. Bell & Sons, 1936.

CHAPTER FOUR

1   Ofsted (the Office for Standards in Education) is a government department responsible for inspecting schools throughout England.
2   Ralph Reader died in 1982 but his work lives on in the Gang Shows that are still performed in different parts of Britain. Such well-known performers as Dick Emery, Tony Hancock and Peter Sellers earned their spurs in Ralph Reader Gang Shows.
3   A Telemark is a swing turn used to change direction or stop short. The term is used by skiers.
4   A gliding step.

CHAPTER FIVE

1   Melody and text by Jimmy Kennedy and Michael Carr, 1939.
2   Ted Waite, 'If a Grey-Haired Lady Says, "How's Your Father"', Warner/ Chappell Music.
3   After I was demobilised from the Navy in early 1947, I visited the Grammar School and met 'Pug' who had just returned from War Service. I had quite a long chat with him and found him to be most amiable.
4   The Japanese Air Fleet lost four aircraft carriers in this crucial battle. It was the turning point in the war against Japan.
5   *Forces Françaises Libres*. French fighters in World War Two. They continued to fight against Axis forces after France surrendered and much of the country was occupied by the Germans.

CHAPTER SIX

1   Women's Royal Naval Service.
2   Auxiliary Territorial Service.
3   Women's Auxiliary Airforce.

– Notes –

CHAPTER SEVEN

1   Born in 1840, Miss (later Dame) Aggie Weston founded Sailor's Rest Hostels in Devonport, Portsmouth and Chatham. She died in 1918 and was accorded full naval honours.

CHAPTER EIGHT

1   Quoted in Raymond Lamont-Brown, *Kamikaze, Japan's Suicidal Samurai*, Cassell, 2000, p. 160.
2   John Pudney, 'For Johnny', in the anthology, *Dispersal Point*, John Lane the Bodley Head, 1942, p. 24.
3   The other two Presidencies were Calcutta and Bombay.
4   *Dabbawallas* are men who, every working day, deliver approximately two hundred thousand tiffin (food) boxes (*dabbas*) from the suburbs of Bombay to offices in the commercial centre. This occupation is said to have flourished for well over one hundred years.

CHAPTER NINE

1   *Kamikaze* – 'Divine Wind'. Usually taken to mean a Japanese aircraft loaded with explosives and deliberately crashed by its pilot on a selected target. The word is also used to mean 'potentially self-destructive, reckless'.
2   See Raymond Lamont-Brown, *Kamikazi, Japan's Suicidal Samauri*, pp. 112 and 114.
3   Dr S. Paranavitana, *Sigiri Graffiti*, Oxford University Press, 1956.
4   See http://en.wikipedia.org/wiki/Angela_Thirkell
5   I understand that the night-club has now been re-named. No longer 'The Silver Faun', it is now 'The Blue Leopard'.

CHAPTER TEN

1   The weather was so unpleasant that the author, James Lee-Milne, gave the title *Caves of Ice* to one volume of his diary. See James Lee-Milne, *Caves of Ice*, Faber and Faber, 1984.
2   According to the 27 May 2006 issue of *The Spectator*, the Audit Commission suggested that postmen, along with dustmen and street cleaners should help fight crime by devoting part of their time to reporting antisocial behaviour and low-level offences.
3   Peter Wright with Paul Greengrass, *Spy Catcher*, Dell Publishing, 1987, p. 193.

CHAPTER ELEVEN

1 Stephen Inwood, *City of Cities*, Macmillan, 2005.
2 Wm. Shakespeare. Ulysses in *Troilus and Cressida*, Act 1, Scene 3.
3 Lionel Charles Knights, *How Many Children Had Lady Macbeth?* The Minority Press, Cambridge, 1933.
4 Wm. Shakespeare. Lady Macbeth in *Macbeth*, Act 1, Scene 7.
5 W. Moberly, *The Ethics of Punishment*, Faber and Faber, 1948.
6 Sir Walter Moberly, *Crisis in the University*, SCM Press, 1949.
7 I have told the story of the incident at Cumberland Lodge in my book, *Searching for Frederick*, published by Asia 2000 in 2001.

CHAPTER TWELVE

1 At the Annual General Meeting of the Overseas Service Pensioners Association held in 2005, it was, 'decided that a Working Party should study the question of many members not being entitled to full or larger State Retirement Pensions because they had not known of the option to pay voluntary National Insurance contributions during their colonial service.' *The Overseas Pensioner*, no. 91, April 2006, p. 4.
2 The several nutmeg plantations in the Orchard Road area were decimated by a plant disease in the 1840s. When his nutmeg plantation failed, Cuppage substituted fruit trees.
3 Verner Bickley, *Searching for Frederick*, Asia 2000, 2001, p. 164.
4 At the time of writing (2009) 85-year-old Chin Peng was still alive and living in Thailand.
5 Letter to *The Sun*, Friday, 19 May 2006, p. 13.
6 Letter to *The Sun*, Friday, 19 May 2006, p. 13.
7 G.E.D. Lewis, *Out East in the Malay Peninsula*, Penerbit Fajar Bakti Sdn. Bhd., 1991, pp. 164–65.
8 Verner Bickley, *Searching for Frederick*, op. cit., p. 164.
9 Lee Kuan Yew, *The Singapore Story*, Prentice Hall, 1998, pp. 238–39.
10 Ilsa Sharp, *There Is Only One Raffles*, Souvenir Press, 1986.
11 Gillian Bickley, *The Golden Needle*, David C. Lam Institute for East–West Studies, Hong Kong, 1997.
12 E.Wijeysingha, *The Eagle Breeds a Gryphon*, Pioneer Book Centre, Singapore, 1962.

CHAPTER THIRTEEN

1 As Alec Peterson remembered it, Churchill's orders were given in a private room and not at the dinner table.
2 *The Straits Times*, 17 January, 1952.

3   John Attenborough, *A Living Memory*, Hodder and Stoughton, 1975.
4   John Attenborough, ibid.
5   John Attenborough, ibid.

CHAPTER FOURTEEN

1   Andrew Biswell, *The Real Life of Anthony Burgess*, Picador, 2005.
2   Imre Nagy was the unfortunate Prime Minister of Hungary who, in 1956, led an unsuccessful revolution against the USSR. He was hanged after the revolution failed.

CHAPTER FIFTEEN

1   G.E.D Lewis, *Out East in the Malay Peninsula*, 1991.
2   Francis Thomas, *Memoirs of a Migrant*, University Education Press, 1972.
3   Malcolm Macdonald, *People and Places*, Collins, 1969.
4   The oldest part of the Memorial Hall was completed in 1862 and functioned as the Town Hall. In 1905, the Victoria Memorial Hall was erected next to the Town Hall which was then converted into a theatre. The gap between the two buildings was later filled with a central tower. The People's Action Party was formed at an inaugural meeting held in the Victoria Memorial Hall on 21 November 1954. See Edwin Lee, *Historic Buildings of Singapore*, Preservation of Monuments Board, 1990.

CHAPTER SIXTEEN

1   'Rose, Rose, I Love You.' Popular Chinese song of the 1950s.
2   Felix's reputation as the 'world's most famous cat' was heightened with the publication (and popularity) of the song, 'Felix Kept on Walking', published in 1923 with music written by Hubert David and lyrics by Ed. E. Bryant.
3   Greta Colson, *Voice Production and Speech*, Museum Press Limited, 1963.
4   Government White Paper, *Communism in the Nanyang University*, Kuala Lumpur, 1964, p. 3.
5   Lee Kuan Yew, *The Singapore Story*, 1998, p. 512.
6   Ground next to the Pavilion Cinema in Orchard Road was converted into a car park for the cinema's patrons. It was available as such only during the day. At night it was converted into a space where food stalls could be set up.
7   In his book, *Jim Thompson: The Legendary American of Thailand* (Jim Thompson Thai Silk Co., 1983), William Warren summarises the various theories associated with Thompson's disappearance. The most likely reason is

simply that Thompson lost his way, stumbled down a slope and was consumed by the rain forest.

CHAPTER SEVENTEEN

1 Derek Cooper, *The Little Book of Malt Whiskies*, Illustrated by Jane Dodds, Appletree, Belfast, 1992.
2 See Derek Mahon's review of *Spice of Life, Collected Poems by Louis MacNeice*, ed. Peter McDonald, *Literary Review*, May 2007, p. 18. 'The darkness derived from a psychiatric disorder in his mother which proved incurable; from a sheltered childhood in "darkest Ulster", and an ambiguous fear of solitude: at school in England his fellows "could never breathe my darkness."'
3 Named after the pungent local fruit, its gracefully curved exterior resembles the shape of that fruit.
4 The Crested Lion is the *chinthe*, the mythical beast which guards pagodas in Burma.

CHAPTER EIGHTEEN

1 Martin Tigram and Arschak Sarkies. Arschak took a particular interest in Raffles Hotel and the Eastern and Oriental. Alas, the original 'E & O' has been demolished and replaced by a less interesting modern version.
2 J.S. Furnivall, *Educational Progress in Southeast Asia*, Institute of Pacific Relations, New York, 1963, p. 61.
3 Mi Mi Khaing, *Burmese Family*, Orient Languages, Calcutta, 2nd Edition, 1956, p. 44.
4 Robert Phillipson, *Linguistic Imperialism*, Oxford University Press, 1992, p. 166.
5 Phillipson, ibid., p. 169.
6 Shortly after I arrived in Hong Kong in 1983, I discovered that John Dent-Young was a lecturer at the Chinese University of Hong Kong Language Centre.
7 In Singapore in the 1950s, some primary schools operated for five hours only in the mornings and other schools operated for five hours only in the afternoons. Student teachers working in 'Morning Schools' would attend 'Normal' teacher training classes in the afternoons. Student teachers working in 'Afternoon Schools' would attend 'Normal' training classes in the mornings.
8 British officials in Burma were usually addressed as 'Thakin' (Master). In India 'Sahib'; in Malaya, 'Tuan'. Young nationalists in Burma adopted the name, 'Thakin', as an ironic act of defiance against British rule.
9 Christopher Bayly and Tim Harper, *Forgotten Armies: The Fall of British Asia, 1941–1945*, Allen Lane, 2004, p. 13.
10 Aung San Suu Kyi, *My Father*, University of Queensland, Leaders of Asia Series, 1984, pp. 8, 11, 15, 18, 19, 25, 33.

11 Sir William Slim, *Defeat into Victory*, Cassell & Co, 1955, p. 515. Pragmatically, Slim did eventually agree that he could work with Aung San.
12 The Anti-Fascist Peoples' Freedom League, a confederation of parties, including the All Burma Peasants' Association and (the most powerful) the Socialist Party.
13 E.M. Law Yone, 'Introduction' in U Nu, *The Wages of Sin*, privately published, Rangoon, 1961.
14 U Nu, *The Wages of Sin*, ibid.
15 U Nu, *The Wages of Sin*, ibid.
15 U Nu, *The Wages of Sin*, ibid.
16 *Chambers's Encyclopedia*, Pergamon Press, 1967, Volume 2, p. 689.

CHAPTER NINETEEN

1 Randolph O'Hara, *The Homecoming*, Mingun Books, Box 252, General Post Office, Hong Kong, 2004, p. 69.
2 A.J.S. White, *The Burma of 'AJ'*, BACSA, 1991, p. 102.
3 Sau Saimong is the author of *The Shan States and the British Annexation*, Cornell University, Cornell, 1969.
4 Emma Larkin, *Secret Histories: Finding George Orwell in a Burmese Teashop*, John Murray, 2004, p. 173.
5 John Latimer, *Burma: The Forgotten War*, John Murray, 2004, p. 369.
6 Sir George Scott ('Shway Yoe'), *The Burman: His Life and Notions*, Macmillan and Co. Limited, London 1927, First Edition 1882, op. cit.
7 A.J.S. White, p. 46, op. cit.
8 Mi Mi Khaing, *Burmese Family*, Orient Languages, 2nd Edition, 1956, p. 40.

CHAPTER TWENTY

1 A *stupa* is a dome-shaped monument which may or may not house Buddhist relics.
2 At the East–West Center in Hawaii.
3 Published by Van Nostrand Reinhold in 1976.
4 Sonia Kolesnikov-Jessop, 'Indonesian Inspiration', *Sunday Morning Post* (Hong Kong), 19 February 2006.
5 All Dutch enterprises were formally nationalised in 1959.
6 See D. Woodman, *The Republic of Indonesia*, The Cresset Press, 1955, p. 410.
7 Edited by Takdir Alisjahbana and Armyn Pane.
8 Takdir Alisjahbana, 'Language Engineering Molds Indonesian Language', *The Linguistic Reporter*, June 1961.

CHAPTER TWENTY-ONE

1   Verner Bickley, 'English Language Teaching in the World Today', *The Zen Ei Ren Magazine*, Tokyo, 1967.
2   G.B. Pasaribu and H. Widdowson, *The Open Road to Excellent English*, Djakarta, Penerbit and Toko Buku, n.d.
3   H. Forster, *Flowering Lotus*, Longman, Green and Co, 1958, p. 274.
4   Quoted in Bruce Grant, *Indonesia*, Melbourne University Press, 1964, p. 141.
5   Grant, ibid., p. 141.
6   E.g. his notion of the Five Principles or Pillars of the Constitution, the Pantja Sila: belief in God, respect for all humanity; national unity; democracy and social justice.
7   Reproduced in B. Grant op. cit., pp. 35–6.

CHAPTER TWENTY-TWO

1   Ken Conboy, *Inside Indonesia's Intelligence Service*, Equinox Publications, 2004, p. 40.
2   Conboy, ibid, p. 40.
3   Here, Sir Andrew was obviously referring to Indonesia.
4   *Daily Telegraph*, 8 May 1984.
5   Leslie H. Palmier, *Indonesia and the Dutch*, Oxford University Press, 1962.

CHAPTER TWENTY-THREE

1   Jonathan was the son of the then Governor of Hong Kong, Sir David Trench.
2   At that time I was the Director of the East–West Center's Culture Learning Institute in Honolulu. We were sponsoring a museum management project which provided training for the managers of small museums.
3   For example, *The Western Philosophers: An Introduction*, Radius Books/ Hutchinson, 1950. Reprinted 1954 and 1968.
4   David could be delightfully entertaining. He gave the funniest (if just a little disrespectful) imitation of a Japanese Noh performer that I have ever seen. It was made funnier, as he rose from a very low bow, because of his considerable height.

CHAPTER TWENTY-FOUR

1   In 2007, we visited Tokyo to attend a meeting organised by the Japan Branch of the English-Speaking Union. Amazingly, 'Green Fantasia' still appears on street maps and tourist brochures. We found it without too much difficulty and enjoyed a curry lunch in one of its basement restaurants. It was heartening

to find that one of our favourite shops in the area still existed (our last visit probably took place at some time in 1968). The 'Oriental Bazaar' still sells kimonos, *yukata* (dressing gowns), Chinaware, silk screens, antiques and oriental furniture.

2   This edition of Chaucer's works was printed with 'Chaucer' in black and red, with 87 woodcuts designed by Sir E. Burne-Jones and numerous woodcut borders and initials specially designed for this work by William Morris. Bound in pigskin by C. J. Cobden-Sanderson at the Doves Bindery, it was blind tooled to a design by William Morris. Only 48 copies were bound in this manner. The Kelmscott Chaucer is generally considered the finest work, with woodcut illustrations, ever printed.

3   Commodore Matthew Perry's Expedition at Shimoda in 1854 was largely responsible for opening up Japan to the 'West,' i.e. the United States. On 31 March 1854, a Treaty of Friendship and Amity was concluded at Kanagawa. Its most important clauses covered the opening of the ports of Shimoda and Hakodate to American ships; establishing an American consultate in Shimoda and exchanging consular officials between Japan and the United States.

4   Isabella L. Bird, *Unbeaten Tracks in Japan*, John Murray, London, 1905.

5   A. B. Mitford, *Tales of Old Japan*, Macmillan and Co, 1894. Algernon Mitford served as Second Secretary to the British Legation in Japan. Later he became MP for Stratford-Upon-Avon and was made a Baron in 1904 as Lord Redesdale. He was grandfather to the notorious Mitford sisters.

6   H. Cortazzi, *The Japanese Achievement*, Sidgwick and Jackson, 1990.

7   H. Cortazzi, *Mitford's Japan: Memories and Recollections, 1866–1906*, Athlone Press, 1985.

8   Geoffrey Bownas, *Japanese Journeys: Writings and Recollections*, Global Oriental, 2005.

CHAPTER TWENTY-FIVE

1   Hideo Kishimoto, 'Some Japanese Cultural Traits and Religions', in Charles A. Moore, *Philosophy and Culture East and West*, University of Hawaii Press, 1962, pp. 245–54.

2   *Sanshodo Japanese Dictionary*, Kenbo, 1989, p. 218.

3   William Shakespeare, *Henry the Fifth* (Prologue).

CHAPTER TWENTY-SIX

1   Quoted in Miranda Kenrick, *Tokyo Weekender*, n.d.

2   Rich was particularly well-known as the 'anchor man' in the programme, 'Desert Island Disks'.

3   Alan Hill, *In Pursuit of Publishing*, John Murray in association with Heinemann Educational Books, 1988.

CHAPTER TWENTY-SEVEN

1   See Gillian Bickley, *The Golden Needle*, The David C. Lam Institute for East–West Studies, Hong Kong, 1997 and Verner Bickley, *Searching for Frederick and Adventures Along the Way*, Hong Kong, Asia 2000, 2001.

CHAPTER TWENTY-NINE

1   See Larry Smith, *English for Cross-Cultural Communication*, The Macmillan Press Limited, 1981.

REFERENCES

Alisjahbana, Takdir. 1961. 'Language Engineering Molds Indonesian Language'. *The Linguistic Reporter*, June.

Anderson, Patrick. 1955. *Snake Wine*. Chatto and Windus.

Attenborough, John. 1975. *A Living Memory*. Hodder and Stoughton.

Baker, Simon. 2006. *The Spectator*, vol. 302, no. 9305, 9 December.

Barnard, H.C. 1947. *A History of English Education From 1760*. University of London Press.

Bayly, Christopher and Harper, Tim. 2004. *Forgotten Armies: The Fall of British Asia, 1941–1945*. Allen Lane.

BBC War Report Tape. 1985. *The Second World War*. BBC Worldwide Limited.

Bickley, Gillian B. 1997. *The Golden Needle*. David C. Lam Institute for East–West Studies, Hong Kong.

Bickley, Verner. 1967. 'English Language Teaching in the World Today'. *The Zen Ei Ren Magazine*, Tokyo.

Bickley, Verner. 2001. *Searching for Frederick*. Asia 2000, Hong Kong.

Bird, Isabella. 1905. *Unbeaten Tracks in Japan*. John Murray, London.

Biswell, Andrew. 2005. *The Real Life of Anthony Burgess*. Picador.

Booth, Cherie and Haste, Cate. 2004. *The Goldfish Bowl: Married to the Prime Minister*. Chatto.

Bownas, Geoffrey. 2005. Japanese Journeys: *Writings and Recollections*. Global Oriental.

Buccianti, Natasha. 2006. 'Revealing Rangoon'. *British Council News*, February–March.

Chapman, Frederick Spencer. 1948. *The Jungle is Neutral*. Chatto and Windus.

Cheng, Irene. 1997. *Intercultural Reminiscences*. Davis C. Lam Institute for East–West Studies, Baptist University, Hong Kong.

Colson, Greta. 1963. *Voice Production and Speech*, Museum Press Limited.

Conboy, Ken. 2004. *Inside Indonesia's Intelligence Service*. Equinox Publications.

Cortazzi, H. (ed). 1985. *Mitford's Japan: Memories and Recollections, 1866–1906*. Athlone Press.

Cortazzi, H. 1990. *The Japanese Achievement*. Sidgwick and Jackson.

Farrell, J.G. 1978. *The Singapore Grip*. Weidenfeld and Nicholson.

Forster, H. 1958. *Flowering Lotus*. Longman, Green and Co.

Furnivall, J.S. 1963. *Educational Progress in Southeast Asia.* Institute of Pacific Relations, New York.

Ghosh, Amitav. 2001. *The Glass Palace.* Random House.

Grant, Bruce. 1964. *Indonesia.* Melbourne University Press.

Hideo Kishimoto 1962. 'Some Japanese Cultural Traits and Religions', in Charles A. Moore, *Philosophy and Culture East and West.* University of Hawaii Press.

Hill, Alan. 1988. *In Pursuit of Publishing.* John Murray in association with Heinemann Educational Books.

Holroyd, Michael. 2002. *Works on Paper.* Counterpoint, Washington.

Inwood, Stephen. 2005. *City of Cities.* Macmillan.

Khaing, Mi Mi. 1956. *Burmese Family.* Orient Languages, Calcutta.

Knights, Lionel Charles. 1933. *How Many Children Had Lady Macbeth?* The Minority Press, Cambridge.

Kolesnikov-Jessop, Sonia. 2006. 'Indonesian Inspiration'. *Sunday Morning Post* (Hong Kong), February.

Kroeber, A. and Kluckhohn, C. 1952. *Culture.* Cambridge.

Larkin, Emma. 2004. *Secret Histories: Finding George Orwell in a Burmese Teashop.* John Murray.

Latimer, John. 2004. *Burma: The Forgotten War.* John Murray.

Lee Kuan Yew. 1998. *The Singapore Story.* Simon and Schuster under Prentice Hall.

Lewis, G.E.D. 1991. *Out East in the Malay Peninsula.* Penerbit Fajar Bakti Sdn. Bhd.

Lovejoy, Arthur O. 1936.*The Great Chain of Being.* Harvard University Press.

Macarthur, Brian. 2005. *Surviving the Sword.* Abacus.

Marchetti, V. and Marks, John D. 1974. *The Cult of Intelligence.* Alfred Knopf.

Martin, Peter and Martin, Joan. 1970. *Japanese Cooking.* Andre Deutsch Limited.

Matthews, Leslie G. 1983. *Antiques of the Pharmacy.* Pharmaceuticals Limited, Meadow Bank, Hounslow, Middlesex.

Miller, Nancy K. 1991. *Getting Personal.* Routledge.

Moore, Donald. 1957. *The Sacrifice and Other Stories.* Arthur Barker Limited, London.

Moore, Donald. 1999/2000. 'British Colonialism. An Era of Proud Achievement'. in *Freedom Today,* vol. 24, no. 6, December/January.

Morrell, Roy. 1965. *The Will and the Way.* University of Malaya Press, Kuala Lumpur.

Nuttall, A.D. 1983. *A New Mimesis.* Methuen.

O'Hara, Randolph. 2004. *The Homecoming.* Mingun Books, Hong Kong.

Palmier, Leslie H. 1962. *Indonesia and the Dutch.* Oxford University Press.

Paranavitana, Dr D.S. 1956. *Sigiri Graffiti.* Oxford University Press.

Pasaribu, G.B. and Widdowson, H. n.d. *The Open Road to Excellent English.* Djakarta, Penerbit and Toko Buku.

Peek, Ian Denys. 2004. *One Fourteenth of an Elephant: A Memoir of Life and Death on the Burma–Thailand Railway.* Doubleday.

Phillipson, Robert. 1992. *Linguistic Imperialism.* Oxford University Press.

Priestley, J.B. 1934. *English Journey.* William Heinemann in association with Victor Gollancz.

Quiller-Couch, Sir Arthur. 1917. *On a School Of English*. Cambridge.

Robinson, K. 1993. *The Way and the Wilderness*. The Pentland Press Limited.

Scott, Sir George. 1927. *The Burman: His Life and Notions*. Macmillan and Co, Ltd, London.

Sinden, Donald. 1984. *A Touch of the Memoirs*. Hodder and Stoughton.

Sitwell, Osbert. 1958. *Laughter in the Next Room*. Macmillan and Co, Limited.

Slim, Sir William. 1955. *Defeat into Victory*. Cassell & Co.

Thomas, Francis. 1972. *Memoirs of a Migrant*. University Education Press, Singapore.

Tomlin, Frederick. 1950. *The Western Philosophers: An Introduction*. Radius Books/Hutchinson.

Triandis, H. 1977. 'Subjective Culture and Interpersonal Relations Across Cultures', in L. Loeb-Adler (ed.), *Issues in Cross-Cultural Research*, Annals of the New York Academy of Sciences.

Warren, William. 1983. *Jim Thompson: The Legendary American of Thailand*. Jim Thompson Thai Silk Co.

White, A.J.S. 1991. *The Burma of 'AJ'*. BACSA, London.

Wijeysingha, E. 1962. *The Eagle Breeds a Gryphon*. Pioneer Book Centre, Singapore.

Woodman, Dorothy. 1955. *The Republic of Indonesia*. The Cressett Press.

Wrench, Evelyn. 1955. *Geoffrey Dawson and Our Times*. Hutchinson.

Wright, Peter, with Greengrass, Paul. 1987. *Spy Catcher*. Dell Publishing.

Ziegler, Philip. 1985. *Mountbatten*. Alfred K. Knopf Inc.

INDEX

Aung San Suu Kyi (Daughter of Aung San) 174
Awang Ramli Mohammed Deli 132

Ba Maw, Thakin 173
Baker, Alan 234–235, 239
Balfour Education Act 30
Barker, George 235
Barnard ('Barney'), Gunner's Mate, RN 50, 84
Barrault, Jean Louis 95
Barwick, Sir Garfield 211
Beamish, Anthony 124
Becker, Alton 181
Belfrage, Bruce 24
Bell ('Dingle') 60
Bennett, Billy 22
Benvannoch, SS 160
Berlin, Irving 262
Bethell, S.L. 103
Bickley and Male, Dispensing Chemists 9
Bickley, Karen (Daughter) 144, 156, 212–213, 215, 226
Bickley, Simon (Son) 154, 156, 212–213
Bickley, Verner Courtenay xiii, xv, xviii, 6
Biddulph, Isobel 94–95
Binchy, Kate 258
Birkenhead (City of) 9
Black, Stanley 252, 262
Blacker, Carmen 244
Blunden, Edmund 235
Bombay 74–75, 77
Bombay Burma Trading Company 180

Bombay Yacht Club 78
Boothby, Sir Robert 148
Borobudur (Indonesia) 193–194
Bottrall, Ronald 234–235
Bowlly, Al (Vocalist) 25
Bownas, Professor Geoffrey 244
Bradbury, Len 41
Bradman, Donald 107
Braganza, HMS 75–77, 79
Bras Basah Road (Singapore) 121, 151
Breach Candy Club (Bombay) 76
Bresnan, Jack 219
Bridges, Lord 186
British Council, The 161–162, 165–170, 175–176, 178–180, 182, 186–187, 189–190, 202–204, 206, 213–216, 219–220, 227, 230, 234–236, 239–242, 246, 248, 255–256, 258–259, 265, 282, 285
Britten, Benjamin 230
Brooke, Charles Johnson 131
Brooke, Charles Vyner 131
Brooke, Raja James 131
Brown, Capability 104
Brown, John (Publisher) 268
Brown, W.J. (MP) 148
Brownell, John 281, 282
Bu Sosrodihardjo 209
Buhler, Alfred 196
Bujang Sunton 132
Buller, Miss Amy 104
Buller, General Sir Redvers 104